# FINDING VIGANÒ

# FINDING VIGANÒ

## IN SEARCH OF THE MAN WHOSE TESTIMONY SHOOK THE CHURCH AND THE WORLD

ROBERT MOYNIHAN

*in conversation with*

ARCHBISHOP CARLO MARIA VIGANÒ

TAN Books

Gastonia, North Carolina

Cover design by Caroline Green

Cover image: Carlo Maria Vigano, Archbishop during the 8th edition of the 'National March for Life' on May 19, 2018 in Rome, Italy. Photo by Stefano Montesi/Corbis via Getty Images.

Library of Congress Control Number: 2020945692

ISBN: 978-1-5051-1619-9
Kindle ISBN: 978-1-5051-1618-2
ePUB ISBN: 978-1-5051-1620-5

Published in the United States by
TAN Books
PO Box 269
Gastonia, NC 28053
www.TANBooks.com

Printed in the United States of America

*To my father,*
*William Trumbull Moynihan*
*(1926–2020)*
*May eternal light shine upon him.*

*"We have this treasure in earthen vessels."*
—2 Corinthians 4:7

*"The greatest persecution of the Church doesn't
come from enemies on the outside."*
—Pope Benedict XVI

*"'When you see the abomination of desolation standing
in the holy place, let him who reads understand.' Man's
mind is a holy place and a temple of God in which the
demons have laid waste the soul through passionate
thoughts and set up the idol of sin. . . . Some say that these
things will also happen when the Antichrist comes."*
—St. Maximus the Confessor

*"If my people who are called by my name humble
themselves, and pray and seek my face, and turn from
their wicked ways, then will I hear from heaven, and
will forgive their sin and will heal their land."*
—2 Chronicles 7:14

*"You are the fairest of the sons of men;
grace is poured upon your lips."*
—Psalm 45:2

*"He had no form or comeliness that we should look at
him, and no beauty that we should desire him."*
—Isaiah 53:2

# CONTENTS

# PUBLISHER'S PREFACE

Archbishop Carlo Maria Viganò is a man standing in the middle of a storm. His allegations regarding Theodore (former) Cardinal McCarrick, the Roman Curia, and the code of silence permeating the Church have made him the focus of much attention from the media, both Catholic and secular. Many love him; many condemn him.

The archbishop has commented on numerous "hot-button" issues in the Church today. As is often the case in the tangled web of human affairs, it can be a challenge for interested Catholics, laity and clergy alike, to make sense of this difficult time in the Church. TAN's publication of this work is neither a public endorsement nor condemnation of the archbishop. Rather, it is a search for the man himself, his facts, and his opinions.

Shortly after the archbishop's original "Testimony" in August of 2018, we contracted with Robert Moynihan—a man we trust—to shed light on these difficult issues. Moynihan is the longtime publisher of *Inside the Vatican* magazine and one of our generation's most respected journalists covering the Catholic Church. He is widely respected in Rome and throughout the world for his orthodoxy, his love for the Church, and for his fair-mindedness. And, we might add, it is no exaggeration to say that he is one who knows much of the

Vatican's "inside baseball." However, paramount in our estimation of choosing a man for this job was our confident knowledge that Robert Moynihan is truly a son of Holy Mother Church who strives always to think with Her, as do we here at TAN.

Along the path of his distinguished career, Moynihan developed a personal relationship with Archbishop Viganò. This relationship led to his being one of the very few to gain access to the man at an undisclosed location. Through his questioning and analysis of the archbishop and his statements, as well as through the knowledge he brings to this project, Moynihan successfully opens a window into the soul of Viganò so that readers may obtain a more complete picture of the man whose testimony so shocked the Church and whose additional statements and interviews continue to do so.

Upon contracting with Moynihan, the archbishop was not well-known among the Catholic laity, but it was clear that he was, for the foreseeable future, here to stay. He was going to raise more issues; he was going to take on what he believed to be the systematic abuse of Vatican power; he was going to call out those he thought to be apostates in the Church with a vigor to which we are unaccustomed.

We want to assure our readers that the leadership of TAN questioned many times: Does the publication of such an interview help or hinder Holy Mother Church? We did so on our own initiative from the very outset, but also in the ensuing months as some people cautioned us against setting out on this road, given that Viganò has turned into such a lightning rod in Church affairs.

Moynihan, too, has had similar experiences. That said, we concluded the former. We concluded we were taking more of a journalistic approach to this work and that it was a service to the Church for a publisher with TAN's reputation for orthodoxy to engage with this story. If TAN were a newspaper, such considerations would not be an issue. But when one puts the interview into a book, it is often presumed that the publisher endorses every word and utterance. We ask the reader to draw this simple distinction and make up his own mind as to the credibility of the archbishop.

Now, since the signing of this contract with Moynihan, the archbishop has made even more controversial statements that have, frankly, muddied the waters in the sense that the present work does not delve into his statements on Covid, Vatican II, and the like. As a publisher, we have a moving target, and it is difficult to keep up with the news cycle, impossible in fact in this particular case. At any point in the process, from contracting to publication, the archbishop will have said more than is covered in the book.

The present volume serves as a partial biography of the archbishop from childhood to the present day. Furthermore, it is a detailed analysis (by Moynihan) of Viganò's original "Testimony." The interview questions and Viganò's answers help the reader to better understand the archbishop's motivations as well as, in certain ways, the man himself. We feel that this knowledge is essential for Catholics struggling to make sense of these events.

Lastly, the publisher and the author have discussed the possibility of a second volume, referenced in this text, that would explore the archbishop's more recent controversial statements.

In time, Holy Mother Church will have the final word on the archbishop's statements. And TAN Books will faithfully follow all she says, through thick and thin, through financial success or failure, through public praise or scorn.

We pray for the archbishop, his supporters, and his enemies. We pray that the Lord ultimately uses the archbishop to bring about truth and unity within the Church. And lastly, we pray for the good intentions of the Holy Father.

# PREFACE

I WENT in search of Archbishop Carlo Maria Viganò and found him. But what I discovered in finding Viganò was that my journey had not ended but only just begun. It is a journey that continues to this day and promises to continue for a long time yet.

The journey will continue because the true mystery that needs to be unraveled is not the physical mystery of Viganò's whereabouts but the spiritual mystery of what it means to be a father, of what true paternity is, in the world and in the Church.

And so this story of "finding Viganò" is actually a deeper and more difficult story—a story of heavenly ("Our Father, who art in heaven") and earthly fathers ("Dad," "papa"), of present fathers and absent fathers, of a present, visible God and a "hidden," seemingly absent God ("*Deus absconditus,*" my late father always would say to me in times of trouble or turmoil, "our God is a hidden God, but that does not mean he does not exist"), and of what God's hiddenness means to the life of the Church, and that of the world, in our time.

This story deals in the first place with a terrible reality: the sexual abuse of young people.

Inevitably, therefore, this story deals with human sin and its consequences, the desire to deny culpability, to escape punishment, to deny that harm was ever caused or intended.

So this story becomes in part the story both of protecting and of abusing children—of hardened hearts and of broken hearts.

It is thus the story of physical and spiritual fathers (priests, bishops, cardinals, popes) who find ways to guide and protect children, and the story of physical and spiritual fathers who fail to find a way to guide, or protect children, who, instead, abandon children and even abuse children.

In this sense, this story is a story about the virtues of good fathers and the vices of "fallen fathers," false fathers. And so this story also becomes the story of the relationships between various "fathers"—between good fathers and good fathers, between good fathers and bad fathers, between bad fathers and bad fathers.

There is an underlying mystery involving fatherhood deep down at the heart of this story that may be likened to the deep mystery regarding fatherhood we find in the parable told by Jesus of the prodigal son (Lk 15:11–32).

The prodigal son's story begins when he asks for his inheritance, though his father is still alive. So he receives the inheritance before he should and leaves his family to go out into the world. He comes to the great city of Babylon. There he "squandred his property" in "loose living." This recalls Proverbs 29:3: "He who loves wisdom makes his father glad, but one who keeps company with harlots squanders his substance."

Finally, the son is destitute. He falls so low that he becomes an indentured servant tending pigs, and he becomes so hungry that he envies the pigs for the pieces of spoiled food that they are eating. He finally comes to himself and says, "I must return to my father's house," and sets out for his home, thinking he will ask his father to take him in as a mere servant, not as his father's son.

Here is how Jesus describes this inner dialogue: "But when he came to himself he said, 'How many of my father's hired servants have bread enough and to spare, but I perish here with hunger! I will arise and go to my father, and I will say to him, "Father, I have sinned against heaven and before you; I am no longer worthy to be called your son; treat me as one of your hired servants."'" And he arose and came to his father. But while he was yet at a distance, his father saw him and had compassion, and ran and embraced him and kissed him" (Lk 15:17–20).

So the father of the prodigal son—the foolish son, the sinful son, the son who has made the "wrong choices" at every turn—still loves his son (though he does not love what his son has done). This father *is waiting for his son*, and he is *the very first* to see him returning. This father sees his son even when he is *still a long way off*, and this good father comes out to meet his deeply flawed, profligate son "on the way" to accompany him on the last steps of his journey home.

The Eastern Orthodox Church traditionally reads this story on the Sunday of the Prodigal Son, which comes on the Sunday two weeks before the beginning of Great Lent in their liturgical year. One hymn for the occasion reads:

I have recklessly forgotten Your glory, O Father;
And among sinners I have scattered the riches which
    You gave to me.
And now I cry to You as the Prodigal:
I have sinned before You, O merciful Father;
Receive me as a penitent and make me as one of Your
    hired servants.

There are resonances between the parable of the prodigal son and this story of finding Archbishop Viganò.

Many sins have been committed, many tragic offenses given and received. Viganò has made many accusations: against many of his fellow Vatican officials, against Pope Francis, and against himself. And many in the Vatican and around Pope Francis have made accusations against Viganò.

All have acknowledged not doing everything they could have done to protect young people from sexual molestation and abuse. In this sense, all have expressed a certain willingness to repent and change course and, acting as "good fathers," re-establish and reinforce safeguards to protect young people from abuse and make the Church into that "safe home" that the father of the prodigal son created and protected for his son.

But there is one great difference between Jesus's parable and this story: the parable of the prodigal son had an ending. There was a return and a feast. The father celebrated his son's return and rejoiced, even if the elder son, who had remained home all the years of the younger son's absence, expressed his wounded perplexity at the exuberant celebration over his younger brother's return.

This story of "finding Viganò" does not yet have

an ending. In fact, month after month of events have brought new developments, including the arrival of the Coronavirus in early 2020, a letter from Viganò to US President Donald Trump in June 2020, which was read by millions of people, and a series of letters this summer on the Second Vatican Council (1962–1965) and its consequences which prompted a wide debate. Viganò has spoken out on Church matters but also on political matters, in a world that seems increasingly in need of sound and wise leadership rooted in Christian principles. So this book tells only the beginning part of a story that is still "developing."

All we know is that this story echoes in profound ways the parable Christ told. The parable and this story are both tales of fathers and sons, prodigal and not prodigal—but who will play which role in this story still remains unclear.

The only thing clear, seemingly, is that the story of what it means, finally, to be a father is still unfolding. And that is why there will be another book soon after this one: to follow this story along another step of the way.

***

Archbishop Carlo Maria Viganò, seventy-nine, went into hiding in August 2018 after issuing an eleven-page "Testimony" in which he denounced a widespread "cover-up" of sexual abuse crimes by the leadership of the Catholic Church. The archbishop's denunciation reached even to the "reforming Pope," Francis. Viganò famously called on Francis to resign the papacy.

In the days after the testimony's release, it was reported that the Vatican was considering drawing up charges against Viganò to try him for violating the oath he, like all Vatican diplomats, had taken not to reveal "pontifical secrets"—sensitive information gained while serving the Holy See. All Vatican officials swear they will keep such information private. Canon law, however, requires that any such charges must be served on the accused. Partly for this reason, some speculated at the time, Viganò went into hiding so that there would be no known address at which he could be served by any sort of Vatican "indictment."

This was not true. Viganò told me that because he believed everything he had written in his "Testimony" was true and had been written with a right intention—to protect young people from sexual abuse in the Church—he was willing to be questioned publicly about the various facts and allegations he had included in his "Testimony." He told me that he had gone into hiding only because "some friends" had advised him it might be the "prudent thing" to do.

Viganò himself never suggested to me that he was afraid that anything might happen to him. He told me, nevertheless, that he had decided to yield to the urgings of his friends and keep a "low profile," not risking any public appearances.

As of this writing, on one occasion only has he not held to that course: when he attended a public demonstration in Munich, Germany, on January 18, 2020. Viganò joined about one hundred other Catholics to pray and protest against the German Episcopal Conference and its president, Cardinal Marx. The German bishops have decided to embark on a "synodal path" that critics say could create a "new Church" that departs from Catholic teaching on priestly celibacy, contraception, homosexuality, and fornication.[1] Viganò wished to stand with others against such a path.

Is Viganò guilty of revealing pontifical secrets? Pope Francis, on May 7, 2019, changed the law of the Church, abolishing the pontifical secret with regard to sex abuse cases. He issued a decree according to which the pontifical secret binding Church officials to confidentiality "does not apply to accusations" concerning sexual abuse of adults, minors, and vulnerable persons.[2] Therefore, "the person who alleges to have been harmed and the witnesses shall not be bound by any obligation of silence with regard to matters involving the case."[3] This regards any information an official receives in the ordinary course of work for the Church; it does not include information received during the sacrament of confession. Everything said to the priest during the sacrament of confession is still considered covered under the sacramental secret which covers every confession.

---

[1] Maike Hickson, "Viganò comes out of hiding to protest German bishops' 'synodal path' of destruction," *LifeSite* News, January 18, 2020, https://www.lifesitenews.com/news/breaking-Viganò-comes-out-of-hiding-to-protest-german-bishops-synodal-path-of-destruction.

[2] Pope Francis, apostolic letter *Vos estis lux mundi*, May 7, 2019, art. 1, http://www.vatican.va/content/francesco/en/motu_proprio/documents/papa-francesco-motu-proprio-20190507_vos-estis-lux-mundi.html.

[3] Ibid.

Viganò addressed this issue of pontifical secrets in his "Testimony" of September 29, 2018:

> Certainly, some of the facts that I was to reveal were covered by the pontifical secret that I had promised to observe and that I had faithfully observed from the beginning of my service to the Holy See. But the purpose of any secret, including the pontifical secret, is to protect the Church from her enemies, not to cover up and become complicit in crimes committed by some of her members. I was a witness, not by my choice, of shocking facts and, as the *Catechism of the Catholic Church states* (par. 2491),[4] the seal of secrecy is not binding when very grave harm can be avoided only by divulging the truth. Only the seal of confession could have justified my silence.

Viganò revealed his hiding place to me and agreed to sit down with me in a monastery for many days to talk over the situation of the Church today. I agreed to not reveal where he is hiding. And I have kept my promise. Even in conversations with high-ranking Vatican officials, including Secretary of State Pietro Cardinal Parolin, with whom I met for more than an hour at the

---

[4]  The *Catechism of the Catholic Church* states in paragraph 2491: "Professional secrets – for example, those of political office holders, soldiers, physicians, and lawyers – or confidential information given under the seal of secrecy must be kept, save in exceptional cases where keeping the secret is bound to cause very grave harm to the one who confided it, to the one who received it or to a third party, and where the very grave harm can be avoided only by divulging the truth. Even if not confided under the seal of secrecy, private information prejudicial to another is not to be divulged without a grave and proportionate reason."

end of August 2019, I have kept the secret of the archbishop's location. (I told Parolin that I had visited Viganò and that Viganò might be willing to consider meeting privately with Pope Francis if Pope Francis would wish to meet with Viganò.)

But this is more than the story of a physical finding. It is also the story of finding out the secret and center of a man: what he loves, what he lives for, what he dreams about, what moves his soul, what has broken his heart.

As I write this on March 25, 2020, the Feast of the Annunciation, Viganò, whom I set out to find and found, is, arguably, one of the loneliest men in the world. He lives under a regime of strict quarantine, as the coronavirus has led to unprecedented national "lockdowns" throughout the world in an effort to stem the spread of the disease, including in the country where Viganò now is. And even if the quarantine were lifted, his life would remain complicated by rumors and shadows.

Viganò was once a top-ranking Vatican official. Under Pope Benedict (2005–2013), he was a step away from being placed in charge of the administration of all of the Vatican's finances (as prefect of the economic affairs of the Holy See). However, he was whisked away in an abrupt maneuver (as they say in Rome, "*Promoveatur ut amoveatur*," "Let him be promoted that he might be removed"). The maneuver was supported by the then-secretary of state, the controversial cardinal with the grand rooftop Vatican apartment, Tarcisio Bertone. Viganò would be assigned to be the pope's nuncio (Vatican ambassador) to Washington, DC, and after five years, he would retire.

So Viganò would be "removed" as an active force in the Curia where he had worked for decades.

Yet paradoxically, Viganò is now arguably better-known and more influential than he ever was in the Curia. Thousands of Catholics around the world look to him as the one man in the Church's leadership who has been willing to pay the price to "tell the truth" about the sexual abuse cover-ups in the Church and much besides.

At the same time, Viganò has come to be regarded by many of those with whom he worked throughout his life—by monsignors, by bishops, by cardinals, and by Pope Francis himself (it seems clear)—as a modern-day Judas. A loathsome betrayer of his boss and former friends in the hierarchy. Why so? Because in his famous August 22, 2018 "Testimony," Viganò, in an absolutely unprecedented and undiplomatic way, denounced by name dozens of his colleagues for their alleged participation in a "culture of cover-up" with regard to sexual abuse in the Church, and then, most dramatically, he called on "Number 1"—as he often terms him—Pope Francis himself, to step down from the papacy. "An attempted coup," some called it. Evident treachery. A Judas-like betrayal.[5]

Viganò, in his "Testimony," claims he personally told

---

[5]    Michael Sean Winters, "Vigano letter exposes the putsch against Pope Francis," *National Catholic Reporter*, August 26, 2018, https://www.ncronline.org/news/accountability/distinctly -catholic/Viganò-letter-exposes-putsch-against-pope-francis; Massimo Faggioli, "The Viganò Letter, One Year Later," *Commonweal*, August 29, 2019, https://www.commonwealmagazine. org/vigan%C3%B2-letter-one-year-later.

Pope Francis during a forty-minute meeting on June 23, 2013, just three months after Francis was elected pope, that the Vatican Congregation for Bishops had a "large dossier," collected over many years, containing reports that then-Cardinal Theodore McCarrick had sexually molested seminarians and minors over decades.[6]

Francis, Viganò says, did nothing with that explosive information for the next five years. Pope Benedict XVI, Viganò alleges, had done something, issuing at least verbal "restrictions" on McCarrick's activities. But Francis, Viganò contends, reversed direction, *de facto* "lifting" the restrictions, sending McCarrick on missions for him around the world, including to China to help negotiate a September 22, 2018, Vatican-China accord (the text of which is itself still secret eighteen months later). In essence, Viganò charges, Francis turned a blind eye to the allegations against McCarrick, did not take them seriously. Francis, Viganò concludes, should acknowledge this negligence and resign his office to allow a new, more vigilant anti-abuse pope to be elected.

However, many Vatican officials feel to this day that Viganò's allegations and charges were exaggerated, even invented, an act rooted in Viganò's alleged rage and desire for vengeance after Francis did not name him a cardinal and, in a humiliating decision, evicted Viganò from the Vatican apartment he had lived in for many years, and even refused to host him in a Vatican-owned

---

6   This brief EWTN video summarizes the case ultimately made against McCarrick: https://www.youtube.com/watch?v=FifB f4e4C20.

property in the city of Rome, asking him to return to his diocese of origin, Milan, in northern Italy.[7] These officials say Viganò betrayed an innocent Pope Francis, as Judas betrayed Christ, not for thirty pieces of silver, but for a humiliating apartment eviction.

Pope Francis has never responded to Viganò's accusations. "I will not say a word," Francis told journalists on the airplane back from Ireland on August 26, 2018, the day after the charges were made public. And Francis never did say a word until, after almost a year, in a May 28, 2019 interview with respected Mexican journalist Valentina Alazraki of the *Televisa* news station, Alazraki again raised the question, saying, "There are some who keep thinking that it (Viganò's "Testimony") is true and they keep asking themselves, if he (Pope Francis) knew or did not know about McCarrick. In the press there is of course a bit of everything."

Then Francis replied, "I didn't know anything, I had no idea. And when he (Viganò) says he spoke to me that day, that he came . . . and I don't remember if he told me about this, if it's true or not. I have no idea! You know that I didn't know anything about McCarrick, otherwise I would not have remained silent."

This is a bit perplexing, for it seems that, on the one hand, he says, "I don't remember if he told me about this," while on the other, he positively asserts, "You know that I didn't know anything about McCarrick."

---

7    Fabio Marchese Ragona, "Pedofilia, la trappola contro il Papa," *il Giornale*, August 27, 2018, https://www.ilgiornale.it/news/politica/pedofilia-trappola-contro-papa-1568364.html.

Still, in August 2018 when Viganò's "Testimony" first came out, Francis did advise all Vatican journalists to read the text for themselves. "Draw your own conclusions," he said. "I will rely on your professional judgment" as to whether to believe or doubt the content of the "Testimony." "It will do you good (to read and evaluate the "Testimony")," Francis concluded.

Yet few to this day have read Viganò's "Testimony" with the close attention Francis encouraged. To this day, the "Testimony" remains a document reduced to a single issue, the call for Pope Francis to resign: "He asked Pope Francis to resign. He accused the Pope of misconduct, arrogating to himself the role of witness, prosecutor, judge and jury. He went too far." This has been the common opinion both of many journalists who cover the Vatican and of many Vatican officials. Some have said almost these exact words to me. For this reason, in this book, I include the full text of the "Testimony" and offer a close reading of the text—the type of reading Pope Francis encouraged journalists to make—and draw some conclusions about what is needed in order to finally get at the truth of this matter.

Though isolated and alone, from his hiding place, Viganò insists that he is in "good spirits" and "does not feel lonely." So in this, as in so many aspects of this case, we are faced with a striking paradox: a man "of the Church" who has denounced the leadership of the Church, a "consummate insider" who has become the "consummate outsider" (literally, Viganò is "off the grid," as far "outside" of the Vatican as anyone could be). Yet he is in good spirits and content.

Viganò has been in hiding since the end of August 2018, almost two years now. A number of journalists wished to find him and to speak with him. But he chose to reveal his hiding place to me, inviting me to come to talk with him.

He did so in part because he had come to trust me over a decade of journalistic contacts and collaboration which had grown into a friendship. And in part, I think, because Viganò—rightly or wrongly—had come to appreciate the general fairness and balance of my writing. He, along with some twenty thousand others, is a recipient of my "Moynihan Letters" on Vatican and Church affairs, which arrive in his email box every so often, and he told me he felt my writing might help him to research and communicate his message of fighting corruption in the Church.

Once, he said to me, "You are a writer, an historian, an academic. I have spent my life in the service of the Holy See. The many tasks that have been entrusted to me over the years have led me to exercise more my practical and decision-making sense in carrying out various responsibilities of government, leaving me little space to try my hand as a scholar, a writer, a trained historian. As a man of the Church, I have always been animated by an intense love for the Church, my Bride, as well as by a profound sense of justice and truth. My intent has always been to serve the Church, to protect and defend her. Where I am unable to express myself well, I think you may be able to help me."

I decided that perhaps I might be able to help Viganò in his mission to end corruption in the Church, but also perhaps to help him evaluate the possible consequences of various writings and actions, given the difficult, complicated situation of the Church in our strange and dangerous time.

His 2018 "Testimony" had rung true to me because I had had a front row seat for more than thirty-five years at the spectacle of Roman Catholic curial and hierarchical life, marked by a paradoxical range of aspirations and behaviors: on the one hand, an admirable aspiration for the divine, for the holy; on the other hand, a disappointing tendency to cover up inconvenient truths.

Viganò's "Testimony" had rung true to me also because I had seen the haunting charade performed by the founder of the Legionaries of Christ, Father Marcial Maciel Degollado (1920–2008). Maciel was a charismatic leader who prayed and preached in public with impressive eloquence and fervor, but in private, we eventually learned after years of rumor and coverup, he preyed on vulnerable young people, including his own, secret, children, whose souls he crushed, using them for his own sexual pleasure and psychological control.

In fact, the case struck home to me because it literally came into my childhood home. By chance, I was visiting my elderly parents in Connecticut on February 23, 1997, the day the *Hartford Courant* on its front page ran an article with a photo of Maciel entitled "Head of worldwide Catholic order accused of history of abuse" by Gerald Renner and Jason Berry. The article detailed accusations of nine seminarians against then-Father Maciel. All nine had signed affidavits testifying to the truthfulness of their accusations. The paper came to our house. My mother picked it up. She knew I had often written very favorably about the "new movements" in the Church, including the disciplined, energetic Legionaries of Christ. "There is the man and the order you write about with such praise!" my mother said to me, pointing at the picture of Maciel and throwing the newspaper with its terrible headline down in front of me on the kitchen table in our family home. "I wonder if you will put that into your magazine?" Her words still echo in my mind more than twenty years later.

I did publish the report of the accusations in my magazine, *Inside the Vatican*, alongside an official denial of the accusations by the Legionary founder. I paid a price for publishing the accusations. The silence enveloping the allegations in the corridors of Rome was so profound that even the small voice of my little magazine clanged like a false note amid the chorus of praise that usually greeted Maciel as he passed through those vaulted hallways. My mother was pleased and applauded my courage, but some in Rome felt I had "harmed the image of the Church" and should have participated in covering up the alleged crimes of Maciel in order not to "harm the faith" of many ordinary believers. Privately, members of the Legion faulted me for being too naïve, telling me that all nine of the accusers had been paid "$50,000 each"— bribed by "enemies" of the Founder and, it was hastily added, of the Church—to make "false statements."

Later, I was to learn from Viganò that high-ranking cardinals in the Curia, most importantly Secretary of State Angelo Sodano, now ninety-two, had also argued that the accusations were all invented and, therefore, had resisted calls for an official Vatican investigation of the Maciel case.[8]

At one critical meeting on the matter, Sodano and other cardinals after him hewed to this "negationist" line, until finally Nigerian Cardinal Francis Arinze, now eighty-seven, courageously insisted that it would only be right and prudent to conduct a true investigation.

"And at a certain moment," Viganò told me, "Arinze spoke and said, 'What are you saying? Here there are more than forty witnesses regarding this abuse. You're saying that there is nothing?' And Arinze was able to reverse the situation regarding Maciel. If it would not have been for Arinze, Maciel would have been absolved."

So in this, as in so many other ways, Cardinal Arinze was a man of courage and fidelity to the truth.

But it was only in the spring of 2005, when Pope John Paul II was dying and the ensuing conclave imminent, that Cardinal Joseph Ratzinger (days later elected Pope Benedict XVI) finally acted. Ratzinger sent Archbishop Charles Scicluna of Malta to the United States and Mexico to interview as many of the accusers as he could.

Scicluna filed a report which was a devastating indictment of Maciel as a brilliantly mesmerizing but corrupt,

---

8    On Sodano, see Elise Harris, "Cardinal tainted by abuse scandals steps down as dean, pope sets term limit," *Crux*, December 21, 2019, https://cruxnow.com/vatican/2019/12/ cardinal-tainted-by-abuse-scandals-steps-down-as-dean- pope-sets-term-limit/ and Jason Berry, "The last bull: Cardinal Sodano goes out," *National Catholic Reporter*, December 27, 2019, https://www.ncronline.org/news/accountability/ last-bull-cardinal-sodano-goes-out.

manipulative, and both sexually and psychologically abusive man. Maciel, discredited, died in 2008 near Jacksonville, Florida. The order he founded has continued, seeking to find its way amid the moral wreckage left by the founder.

Of course, I also had seen in the Vatican and throughout the Church astonishing goodness and holiness—the warmth, kindness, and courage of so many, including my own parents who found in the Church a source of meaning and beauty in their lives which they have passed on to me. This is the mysterious "hiddenness" of Christ behind the structures of this world. It is like the two disciples walking on the road to Emmaus after the crucifixion who could not recognize the Risen Jesus even though he was walking alongside them.

How could this Church contain such a paradoxical mix of neurotic narcissism and humble charity made incarnate in the daily sacrifice of so many fathers and mothers, priests and nuns, religious and lay? This is the great mystery of the Church: the Church both as the "Body of Christ" and the "Bride of Christ" is truly holy, but the members of the Church are all human beings, and all humans (even saints) are inevitably imperfect, inevitably sinners.

When I first began reporting on the Vatican, I had a conversation with a monsignor in the English Section of the Secretariat of State which framed the problem in a way which startled me, and which I have never forgotten.

"We are wondering who you are and what your intentions are," the monsignor began in a way that I thought was a bit abrupt.

"Who am I?" I replied. "Well, I am a Roman Catholic and a writer. I studied at Harvard and then, under Dr. Jaroslav Pelikan at Yale, the history of the development of Christian doctrine. I wanted to become an historian. Now I am hoping to write the 'first draft of history' as a Vatican journalist. My intent is to write the truth, as far as it is possible. In this I follow Jesus, who told us, 'The truth shall set you free.'"

The monsignor looked at me intently. And then he said something that startled me.

"Well, that is precisely our concern," he said. "You know, there are many truths, and these truths can do more harm than good. For example, what would you do if you came across a truth which would damage the Church if published?"

I had, I realized with surprise, unexpectedly stepped across a threshold—that I was no longer involved in a simple "getting to know you conversation" but rather a conversation which might determine a great deal with regard to my success or failure in covering the Vatican and Church affairs. One of *those* conversations.

"Well," I said, "I would still report the truth. It might seem that the truth could harm the Church, but in the end, that cannot be; the truth will always set us free, as Christ told us."

"But let us consider another aspect," the monsignor said. "Suppose we consider the faith of the people, the simple faith of many believers. Suppose you come across a truth that, if published, might shake that faith, harm that faith. Suppose people would lose their faith because of something you published. Would you be able to accept responsibility for the loss of faith in many souls?"

"Well," I said, "I can understand what you are saying—that much harm can be caused by the effects, unintended, of a news story. So I do think I have to meet readers where they are, to bring them along slowly with me into a knowledge of the truth in such a way that their fundamental faith in God, in Christ, and in the Church would not ever be shaken. But I guess I need to think about this. Maybe the form in which the truth is presented might need to be adjusted. But this would never mean I would compromise the telling of the truth. That would not be right."

The monsignor looked at me, a furrow over his eyes, as if he were trying to decide if I was really serious, if I really did not understand my situation or the required answer.

"Well," he said, "I do applaud you for your idealism and commitment to the truth. But you should always remember one thing: there may come a situation, some story you are covering, where you will discover something so harmful to the Church, and to the faith of the simple faithful, that you must consider whether publishing that truth may not cause incalculable damage, to souls, to the Church. We hope you will keep this in mind and that, as a good Catholic, of course, loyal to the Church, you will make the right choice."

The years have run by. Thirty-five years, in fact, since that conversation. And now we have come to the case of Monsignor Viganò, the "truth-telling" archbishop, the consummate Vatican insider now regarded as a Judas in the halls of the Vatican. And inside of my head, the words of that monsignor still ring.

This story concerns a "culture of cover-up," a "brotherhood of silence," that has for decades grown like a clinging vine around the heart of the Church, even in the Vatican, or perhaps better, especially in the Vatican.

This "culture of silence," cloaked in many fine-sounding phrases of concern for "the faith of the little ones," has become so harmful to our once-glorious and holy Church that the healing light of truth—truth both about the sexual sins of the hierarchy and about the deviations from the saving doctrines of our faith—has become hidden, veiled, obscured. At the heart of the Church, behind a façade of smiles, knowing nods, sonorous blessings, there is increasingly little of that truth once proclaimed from the housetops: "Repent, and believe" in the "Good News" that "Christ is Risen"—yes, he is risen from the dead, as he said.

The Church in these decades has become the desolate habitation of a foul-smelling, rotten spirit of cover-up and "un-truth" which has allowed terrible harm to come to thousands, indeed millions, of innocent souls. Viganò has come forth to denounce this rotten spirit of cover-up. He was right to do so, right to break the silence, right to give hope that the tragic cycle of abuse and cover-up might be broken by the Church leadership, from the Holy Father on down.

But what if Viganò's crusade might tear the Church apart? What if this "truth" might fracture the Catholic Church into factions just at the moment when the Church desperately needs to be united before the threat of a powerful, totalitarian, global attack seeking to impose an a-Christian or anti-Christian "dictatorship of relativism" in all human affairs? To complicate matters further, what if, indeed, forces within the Church herself seem to ally themselves more with those very forces of relativism than with the perennial teaching of Christ? Certainly, this question has been one which has weighed heavily on the mind of Viganò himself and, truth be told, on my own as well.

## ALMOST COMPLETE SILENCE

As I write this in March of 2020, Rome is in almost complete silence, and the entire world seems to be gripped by a panic over the spreading coronavirus. A few days ago, the Vatican announced that all of the celebrations during Holy Week will be held without the presence of any faithful. This has never happened before.

On March 8, the Italian Bishops' Conference announced that all public Masses and liturgical celebrations throughout Italy, including funerals, would be suspended until April 3. On March 12, the pope's vicar general for the city of Rome, Cardinal Angelo De Donatis, for the first time in history, ordered that all churches in Rome be completely closed until April 3, the Friday before Palm Sunday. On March 13, De Donatis revised his decree, saying parishes could remain open, leaving "the ultimate responsibility for entry into places of worship on priests and all the faithful, so as not to expose the population to any danger of contagion."

I spoke by telephone with Viganò on March 14, just

after the revision of the decree. "I'm shocked that *all* the churches were closed," I said. "I would never have imagined such a thing—every church in Italy. It all just seems . . . apocalyptic. Do you think these closed churches fulfill in some way the words of Daniel: 'From the time that the daily sacrifice shall be taken away' (Dn 12:11)?"

"These events are clearly without precedent," the archbishop said. "Never in history have all of Italy's churches been closed. We cannot know, of course, whether we are truly in the 'end times,' but we can say now, as always, that we look forward ever more ardently to the return of Christ. This is increasingly my prayer, '*Maranatha.*' 'Come Lord Jesus.' 'Come quickly.'"

He paused. "I just wrote something about the decision to close the churches," he said. "Did you see it?"

"Yes," I said. "I have the piece in front of me."

"I would be pleased if you would publish it," he said.

In his piece, Viganò writes that the present time is marked by a "darkening of the faith that has struck the heights of the Church." And he considers these recent events to be part of a general pattern in which the world's secular governments are increasingly exercising an authority over the Church that threatens all of the public activity of the Church, and warns with great passion against this sinister development.

"The Church, in order to serve the common good and the State," Viganò writes, "must never give up being Herself, nor fail in her mission to proclaim Christ, our only Lord and Savior. She must beware of obscuring her divine prerogatives of Wisdom and Truth and in no way abdicate the Authority that comes to her from

the Sovereign of the kings of the earth, Our Lord Jesus
Christ.

"The ecclesial events of these hours have manifested
clearly—if there was still any need—the tragic subjection
of the Church to a State that is striving and doing all
it can to destroy the Christian identity of our Italy, by
enslaving it to an ideological, immoral, globalist, Mal-
thusian, abortionist, migrant agenda that is the enemy of
man and of the family. . . .

"Open, throw open wide the doors to Christ! Open,
throw open wide the doors of our churches so that the
faithful may enter in, repent of their sins, participate in
the Holy Sacrifice of the Mass and draw upon the trea-
sury of graces that flow from the pierced Heart of Christ,
our only Redeemer who can save us from sin and death."[9]

## STATE OF EMERGENCY IN THE
## WORLD AND IN THE CHURCH

And yet, the fear of the coronavirus worldwide was continuing to mount. The previous afternoon, on Friday,
March 13, 2020—the seventh anniversary of the election
of Pope Francis as pope—US President Donald Trump
had declared a "national emergency" in the United States
due to the threat of the virus. As of that day, only fifty-
eight deaths had been officially reported in the United
States, and only 2,695 cases of infection. (Viganò was
later to tell me that he had grave doubts about the accuracy of government figures regarding the infections and

---

[9]    Carlo Maria Viganò, March 14, 2020.

deaths caused by the virus: "The numbers do not cor-
respond to the reality," he said. "They are the result of
manipulations carried out to make it appear that there
is a state of pandemic and to strike terror into people.")
Trump had also announced the unprecedented decision to prevent any traveler from Europe from entering
the United States by air for the next thirty days. Such a
restriction has never been imposed before. And in Italy,
the country is not only on complete lockdown against the
virus, with schools, colleges, and sports arenas closing,
but not a single public Mass is being celebrated in the
entire country. Similar lockdowns have been proclaimed
in many other countries. So the situation of the world
today is quite unusual, quite exceptional.

This "situation of exception," this situation when ordinary patterns of life and ordinary laws are not followed,
however, exists not only in the world. It exists also in the
Church. And in a very particular and literal way.

The word "bishop" comes from the Old English *bis-
ceop*, "bishop, high priest (Jewish or pagan)," from the
late Latin *episcopus*, from the Greek *episkopos*, "watcher,
(spiritual) overseer," a title for various government
officials, later taken over in a Church sense, from *epi-*,
"over," and *skopos*, "one who watches, one who looks
after; a guardian, a protector."[10]

Throughout the history of the Church, it has always
been believed that there is only one bishop, one "spiritual
overseer," at a time in any one diocese. This belief holds
very strongly that one man, not a committee of men,

---

[10]   https://www.etymonline.com/word/bishop.

should be "the watcher," "the protector"—the bishop—of a local Church. When there have been splits, schisms, the people have broken away from one head, one bishop, to follow another. The one bishop is the visible sign of the unity of the local Church.

In the same way, the bishop of Rome—the pope—has been the visible sign of the unity of the universal Church.

But for seven years now, there has been, in the eyes of some, a type of "bifurcated" papacy. Not two popes, but a papacy, again according to some, with two men sharing aspects of the papal ministry.

The pope who resigned in 2013, Benedict XVI, is no longer active, but based on his own statements and the statements of his personal secretary, Archbishop Georg Gaenswein, he continues to carry out the "Petrine mission" in a "passive" way, through prayer in the place where he is living, in a small convent in the Vatican Gardens.

This is a very unusual situation, an unprecedented situation. A "situation of exception."

And such an exceptional situation is open to considerable confusion. That confusion, too, will be part of this story.

My feeling is that living in a "period of exception" in the Church, Catholics will inevitably experience a certain confusion, suffer intellectually and spiritually from certain "doubts" (*dubia*, in Latin), until the very stability of our personal faith in Christ and his Church risks being undermined.

This is a serious and dangerous situation, one which requires attention from any "protector" of the Church, whether he be an archbishop with a titular see, like

Viganò, or a bishop of Rome and so successor of Peter, like Francis, or an emeritus bishop of Rome, like Benedict.

This book, then, is an appeal to our bishops, our "protectors," our "guardians," to truly be protectors and guardians, and not to flee in the face of any wolves who may attack the flock. It is an appeal to our bishops to be that which they should be: guardians, protectors. In a word, fathers.

Two examples: We have heard for decades of various "lobbying maneuvers" to influence Church teaching and government, including influencing the 2005 and 2013 conclaves in a "progressive" direction, and we as yet have had no formal or conclusive judgment on these maneuvers from anyone in the Church.

The "San Gallen Mafia" is the nickname of a group of "progressive" theologians, led, arguably, by the late Cardinal Carlo Maria Martini, SJ, archbishop of Milan. The group met annually in January at San Gallen in northern Switzerland from 1996 to 2006.

As the German-born American journalist Maike Hickson wrote in a *LifeSite* news article of March 29, 2019, Cardinal Martini, before he died in 2012, referred to himself as an "ante-pope," one who would be a "precursor and preparer" for a new pope who would bring about "radical . . . change" in a "tired . . . pompous" Church. In the 2012 interview book *Night Conversations with Cardinal Martini*, the Italian cardinal laid out a type of blueprint for how Church teachings on human sexuality, marriage, contraception, sin, the existence of hell, the male-only priesthood, and much else could be revised. One could perhaps be forgiven for wondering if "progressive" is too mild a word, as certain teachings in these areas are immutable and not subject to change as they constitute part of God's law as understood by Catholics since the time of Christ.

And in a new book, *The Church in Changing Times* (*Kirche im Wandel der Zeit*), written by the bishop of San Gallen, Ivo Fürer, another key member (and host) of the St. Gallen "mafia," Fürer confirms that Martini's 2012 book does accurately summarize much of what was discussed over the years by the group. Martini, for instance, wrote about sexual sins that "in the past the Church probably said too much about the Sixth Commandment." (The commandment forbidding adultery specifically but considered to encompass many sins of a sexual nature.)

In a 2015 interview, Argentinean Archbishop Victor Fernández, one of Pope Francis's top advisers, stated that the pope plans to change the Church in ways that cannot be undone by future popes. "The Pope goes slow because he wants to be sure that the changes have a deep impact. The slow pace is necessary to ensure the effectiveness of the changes. He knows there are those hoping that the next pope will turn everything back around. If you go slowly it's more difficult to turn things back. . . . You have to realize that he is aiming at reform that is irreversible," he said.[11]

---

11    Mary Anne Hackett, "Evidence Pope follows blueprint to change Church by dissident cardinal who led St. Gallen 'mafia,'" CatholicCitizens.org, April 3, 2019, https://catholiccitizens. org/views/86098/evidence-pope-follows-blueprint-to-change -church-by-dissident-cardinal-who-led-st-gallen-mafia/.

One wonders, given statements like that, if what the San Gallen "mafia" and others of a similar theological bent had in mind was not so much reform as revolution.

We have in recent years also read in various "magisterial" decisions and statements, ranging from the Abu Dhabi document to *Amoris Laetitia,* passages which have produced great confusion and concern among Church members, even some prominent members of the hierarchy, and we as yet have had no formal or conclusive judgment on these "doubts" from anyone. It is sobering to consider that the famous *dubia* questions of Cardinals Burke, Brandmüller, Caffara, and Meisner remain unanswered all these years later.

It is said that all confusion is "of the devil." It seems, then, that the devil is hard at work in our time, for confusion is widespread.

This book, then, is also an appeal to our "overseers," our "fathers," to rise up to challenge and overcome this confusion by bringing clarity in keeping with the perennial doctrine and pastoral practice of our Church.

Unfortunately, however, even calls to bring clarity and to end confusion can, paradoxically, end up becoming the cause of still further confusion and division, thus dividing and weakening the Church, as the author of the confusion desires. So what is to be done?

As so often in human affairs, or in "family" disputes (as opposed to, for example, in regard to mathematical problems or architectural measurements), there seems to be no solution. The solution seems to transcend our human capacities. The solution, indeed, seems to escape our reason, our logic, demanding that we approach the problem from a higher level, from the level of the spirit, of prayer, from the level of the transcendent, from the level where divine assistance, where a divine inspiration, may help us resolve what humanly speaking seems impossible to resolve.

I asked the archbishop what it might mean that we live in a "period of exception" when two bishops, Benedict and Francis, are said (by Archbishop Georg Gänswein, Benedict's personal secretary) to "share" an expanded Petrine *munus* ("office").

"Bob," Viganò said to me, "it cannot help anyone if you speculate or invent theories or interpretations about the 'two popes.' This situation is an aberration and proceeds from a heresy, since the papacy is of divine institution and cannot be redefined or reconfigured by anyone, not even by a pope. You could rather say that the situation that was created with Benedict's resignation is one of the most devastating confusion. More and more faithful are asking themselves who the real pope is. Many priests celebrate Mass *una cum Benedict* ('One with Benedict,' 'in union with Benedict'). We note with immense pain that from the 'official' Church, no clarification comes. This rampant, spreading confusion is not met by authoritative clarifications. Indeed it seems that Francis wants to promote this confusion."

\*\*\*

Viganò himself, as of this writing, is still well and in good health. He leads a normal life marked by a due reserve and privacy. He celebrates Mass daily in his residence, prays, reads, studies, keeps informed about events in the

Church and in the world, and carries on a discreet correspondence with friends and family members.

His mission, he says, remains a simple one: to seek in every way to ensure that the Church never gives up being herself and never ceases her mission to proclaim Christ, the Lord and Savior of the world.

In June of 2019, I suggested to Viganò that we should sit down and talk at some length about the crisis in the Church and also about his 2018 "Testimony" accusations against Francis. Viganò, after some days of hesitation, contacted me.

"I am willing to meet with you," he said. He told me where he was, and I made the journey to meet him. (Those were the days when one could still travel freely over national borders, take airplane flights, rent cars.) This book is the result.

This book is not an attempt either to praise Archbishop Viganò or to blame him. It is, rather, the account of an attempt to find the man, physically and figuratively. Who is this man who, though a high-ranking Vatican official, an "insider," dared to denounce a pope? Who is this man who dared to denounce as corrupt a clerical culture that he himself was part of for a lifetime? Who is this man who says he has no eloquence, yet writes with an undeniable, deeply moving eloquence? Who is this man who went into hiding and yet has found a way to speak from his hiding place to the entire world?

In the end, the Viganò I found was a man who smiled, a man who laughed, a man who wept. He was a gentle man, a simple man, a humble man, who at age seventy-eight rode a bicycle with bags of groceries on the handlebars, and when the bike skidded in the rain, he took a hard fall and fractured his ankle. He was a helpful man who drove my rented car when I was too tired to drive; he chauffeured me. He was an organized man who took copious notes and made careful plans, yet also a man who could say suddenly, "The time is short now, we must move fast." And then he would move dizzyingly fast.

He was a man of simple tastes, hospitable, a man who prayed the daily holy office (the daily prayers prescribed by the Church to be said by priests) and nourished a profound devotion for the Holy Rosary, of which he prays and celebrates all the Mysteries daily. At the same time, he followed attentively every twist and turn of the news of the Church and world via the internet. He was in some ways an emotional man, a man of profound joys and sorrows, a man who was sometimes nostalgic, sometimes seemingly deeply wounded due to perceived injustices. He was at times a methodical man of the desk and of the dossier, compiling documents and filing summaries of situations for his superiors, and at times a courageous adventurer, as when, almost fifty years ago, he hopped into a car and drove alone all night across the stark desert from Baghdad to Damascus as an official in the Vatican nunciature in Iraq in the 1970s.

He was a man with a marvelous memory for names and dates and circumstances. He lived fully in the present but also fully in his memory, which seemed to have access to crystalline sights from a lifetime ago: the "sea of glass" glacier in the massif of Mont Blanc in the Alps that filled him with exhilaration when he hiked to it as a boy, the dusty and semi-desert region of northern Nigeria where he was a nuncio for several years in the 1990s. A man deeply moved by the sight of the face of his dead father, Adeodato Viganò, still and cold in the first hours after his unexpected death in his early sixties when Viganò was just twenty. A man of principle, of faith, of dignity, of culture, of sorrow over violence and corruption and deceit, a friend.

"What must be done?" I asked Viganò as I left him after days of conversation.

"We have to be clear in our minds, but we cannot continue to hide the facts," Viganò replied. "We must recognize that there is a project of the devil to destroy the Church. The watchwords are a 'new Church' for a 'new humanism.' No more Jesus Christ, no more cross, no more confession and forgiveness of sins. We must fight against this project. Yes, we must fight for the faith. With God's help, with confidence, without pride. The time will come when everything will be out in the open. For now, we must study, and pray, and prepare ourselves spiritually for what is to come.

"I am speaking what I see and telling the truth," he continued. "I cannot any longer stay silent. I am going too fast, yes, but the situation is moving very fast. I know the situation at the top of the Church, leaving the Church defenseless everywhere. I have tried to go further down to understand why we have reached this situation. They have changed the teaching. This is the reason for accelerating. Certainly, they want to go to the conclusion. This *vulnus* ("wound") is already there.

"Pope Francis should be converted by the Holy Spirit.

And then he should turn, as Peter turned, and confirm his brothers, of whom I am only one.

"I am just trying to follow my conscience. I am in daily prayer, prayer to Our Lord, prayer to Our Lady, asking for light, and I am making a step forward where I can.

"They are putting into action what is implicit inside of Vatican II. This possibility has been admitted even by Pope Benedict.

"Everyone has his own responsibility. I am simply trying to do what my conscience tells me I must do now, in this situation, each day. There is no larger plan. There is only praying and asking the Holy Spirit for guidance, step by step, day by day."

This book, then, is the account of how Viganò published his "Testimony," how he went into hiding, how I found him, and how I slowly discovered who he is and what he believes. It is the story of finding the man Viganò behind the myth of the "truth-telling archbishop"—his moral convictions, his prophetic intuitions, but also his weaknesses and failings—and the sharing of those findings.

PART I

# WHO IS CARLO MARIA VIGANÒ?

## CHAPTER 1

# HOW I CAME TO KNOW VIGANÒ

*"Prove me, O LORD, and try me; test*
*my heart and my mind."*
—Psalm 26:2

I HAD come to meet and know Viganò when he was the nuncio to the United States (2011–2016). I was a reporter on Vatican affairs for *Inside the Vatican* magazine, which I had founded in 1993. He agreed to receive me at the nunciature, and once we began to talk, we realized we had much to say to one another. So we began to meet occasionally at the nunciature in Washington, DC, two or three times a year during the five years that Viganò was nuncio—the end of 2011, all of 2012–2015, and the beginning of 2016.

On those occasions, upon my request for a meeting, Viganò would invite me to visit, usually at four o'clock in the afternoon, at the end of a busy working day, and we would talk for an hour, or an hour and a half, or for two hours. He would speak to me about the issues facing the Church in the United States and around the world but also about issues facing the Roman Curia in Rome. He would tell me his opinion on different matters, and he would ask me on occasion also for my opinion.

We discussed Pope Francis's famous remark in the

summer of 2013, returning from his trip to World Youth Day in Rio de Janeiro, Brazil, about a person with homosexual tendencies who repents of homosexual activity and strives to follow the teaching of the Lord, when he said the five most famous words of his pontificate: "Who am I to judge?"

We discussed the Vatican City rooftop apartment of Cardinal Tarcisio Bertone (one of Viganò's great antagonists in the Roman Curia) and the hundreds of thousands of euros Bertone had spent to renovate it (and the seeming corruption implicit in the way he raised those funds, involving the children's hospital of Rome, the Bambino Gesù; the hospital paid for the renovations, and in exchange, Bertone allowed them to visit and make use of his enormous terrace for fund-raising events).

We discussed the dramatic resignation in February 2013 of Emeritus Pope Benedict and why it had occurred and what it meant for the Church and the Roman Curia.

We discussed the "Third Secret" (and the possible "Fourth Secret") connected with the apparitions of the Virgin Mary in Fatima, Portugal, in 1917 and whether the consecration of Russia to the Immaculate Heart of Mary had ever been truly made as Sister Lucia said the Virgin Mary had requested in one of her apparitions to the shepherd children.

We discussed the existence and operation of so-called "gay" and other "lobbies" in the Vatican. The existence of such "lobbies" was confirmed by Pope Francis himself, publicly, in a meeting in Rome in the summer of 2013. On June 6, 2013, the pope received the presiding board of the CLAR (the Latin American and Caribbean

Confederation of Religious Men and Women, *Confederación Latinoamericana y Caribeña de Religiosos y Religiosas*). A transcript of the pope's words was made by those present and given to the Chilean progressive paper *Reflexión y Liberación* (*Reflection and Liberation*) for publication. There seems little doubt that the transcription is reliable. After mentioning the difficulty of being in charge of the Roman Curia and noting that he had created a commission of nine cardinals to support him in this task, the pope reportedly said, "And, yes . . . it is difficult. In the Curia, there are also holy people, really, there *are* holy people. But there also is a stream of corruption, there is that as well, it is true. . . . The 'gay lobby' is mentioned, and it is true, it is there. . . . We need to see what we can do."[12]

Through these many conversations, I came to have a certain familiarity with Viganò's mind and way of viewing the world. As mentioned, Viganò had become a recipient of my "Moynihan Letters." Occasionally, he would even write a little note back after reading a letter.

In mid-2016, Viganò returned to Rome, where he had a Vatican apartment in the old Santa Marta, a house for pilgrims, which in the 1990s, had been turned into a

---

[12]  See first Phil Pullela, "Pope laments 'gay lobby,' corruption in Vatican: report," *Reuters*, June 11, 2013, https://www. reuters.com/article/us-pope-gaylobby/pope-laments-gay-lobby -corruption-in-vatican-report-idUSBRE95B00I20130612; then Rachel Donadio, "Pope Is Quoted Referring to a Vatican 'Gay Lobby,'" *New York Times*, June 12, 2013, https://www. nytimes.com/2013/06/13/world/europe/pope-is-quoted-as -acknowledging-a-vatican-gay-lobby.html.

residence for elderly Curial officials—monsignors, bishops, archbishops, cardinals. The building is just a few steps away from the new Santa Marta, built in the 1990s for the purpose of housing some 120 cardinals during a papal conclave, for which purpose it was used in 2005 when Pope Benedict was elected and in 2013 when Pope Francis was elected.

Viganò, of course, felt "at home" in the Vatican. He had worked for the Holy See all of his adult life. He had spent a number of years "abroad" on assignment in Iraq, Kuwait, Great Britain, Strasburg, Nigeria, and the United States, but he had spent the bulk of his time right in Vatican City, living there and working there. It would not be too much to say that Viganò was the archetypal Vatican official, a man who started at the bottom rung and rose, step by step, to ever higher positions and distinguishing himself at each stage for his work ethic, his attention to detail, and by many accounts, for an inflexible integrity, a character so devoted to the Church and her image in the world that his first thought was always "the good of the Church." But it was to become his fate to discover the "good of the Church" might, in these strange times, require the denunciation of much that is evil and scandalous and which seems to cast a shadow on the reputation of the Church if it is widely known. Therefore, we may say, Viganò, the consummate insider, the institutional man entrusted with the most delicate and difficult and potentially scandalous dossiers, through a strange series of events, became Viganò the outsider, the man in hiding because he knew too much.

I appreciated Viganò for what I judged to be his

honesty and his ability to administer efficiently and fairly a government office, as I thought he had demonstrated in his work at the Vatican City State government. And he had evidently come to appreciate what he thought was the clarity and "Catholicity" of my writing, which is my aim, though I often fall short of it: to express clearly the fruits of my research and thought in a way that is as fully orthodox as I am able to understand.

After Viganò left his post in 2016 and went into retirement, we stayed in touch by email. We met only on one occasion. That meeting was long and memorable. It took place on July 21, 2017 in Rome.

Archbishop Viganò suggested we meet "on the top of the Janiculum Hill" near the great statue dedicated to Giuseppe Garibaldi which looks out over the city.

I went to that place at the appointed hour, met the archbishop—who was wearing a white baseball cap—and we sat down to talk on one of the green benches by the line of statues that marches over the hilltop. We were in full view of any passing cars, but there was no particular reason to feel anyone would note that the two of us were talking at such length. As we spoke, the shadows lengthened and evening came on. An hour passed, two, three . . .

Viganò told me he was worried about many cases of corruption in the Church, but even more so by what he saw as an increasing willingness to abandon traditional Church teaching in a number of areas. Once again he told of his experience of the Church and the Vatican during his more than four decades of service, from 1973 until May 2016, the years of his diplomatic career with the Holy See. It was a story marked by many heroic and noble actions on the part of Church leaders but also by uninformed, incorrect, and corrupt acts. "*La trahison des clercs*" (a "treason, or betrayal, by the clerks, or priests"), indeed.

American scholar Roger Kimball wrote in the *New Criterion* in 1992 about a 1927 book by the French essayist Julien Benda attacking the intellectual corruption of the age entitled *La trahison des clercs* ("The treason of the priests"). The "treason" in question, Kimball writes, was the betrayal by the "clerks" (the learned in society, for centuries almost all of them priests) of their vocation as intellectuals.

"From the time of the pre-Socratics, intellectuals, considered in their role as intellectuals, had been a breed apart," Kimball wrote. "In Benda's terms, they were understood to be 'all those whose activity essentially is not the pursuit of practical aims, all those who seek their joy in the practice of an art or a science or a metaphysical speculation, in short in the possession of non-material advantages.' Thanks to such men, Benda wrote, 'humanity did evil for two thousand years, but honored good. This contradiction was an honor to the human species, and formed the rift whereby civilization slipped into the world.'"[13]

In essence, Kimball's point, and Benda's, is that many of those intellectuals, philosophers, and priests who once

---

[13] Roger Kimball, "The treason of the intellectuals & 'The Undoing of Thought,'" *The New Criterion*, December 1992, https://newcriterion.com/issues/1992/12/the-treason-of-the-intellectuals-ldquothe-undoing-of-thoughtrdquo.

taught that good should be honored now teach that good should no longer be honored and that evil, rather, should be honored. This is the essential tragedy of our age. And this is what Viganò's narrative described.

Viganò told me on that occasion, sitting on a park bench in Rome at the highest point of Rome as the shadows lengthened, almost exactly what he was to put into his now-famous "Testimony" of August 2018, a year later. Essentially, what he told me was that there was an interlocking network at the summit of the Church that covered up cases of sexual abuse and of financial corruption among high-ranking members of the clergy. And though I had felt for many years that a few terrible cases of this type of corruption had occurred (for example, the well-known case of the founder of the Legionaries of Christ already mentioned), I had not imagined that the cases were as numerous as Viganò told me they were. Nor had I imagined that the number of those in the hierarchy who had participated in the cover up of these abuses was so large.

My reaction was that the effort to change such an entrenched Church culture, and thereby to protect young people from abuse by Church prelates, would require heroic firmness of character and strength, as much heroic strength as the Greek hero Hercules had displayed in his fifth labor when he cleansed the filthy Augean stables in a single night by diverting the course of two rivers to pass through the stables and wash them clean.

I am a witness to the fact that Viganò *did not publish his concerns for more than a year*. I bear a certain responsibility for not immediately investigating all the things

Viganò told me, then writing a series of articles on these matters, and in so doing, perhaps, taking away the necessity for Viganò to write his "Testimony."

Viganò wrote and published his "Testimony" in August 2018, thirteen months later. But it contained information that he had been gathering and meditating on for many years.

"What should I do with all of this material?" I asked Viganò. "It is all shocking, but it is also all based only on your word. Do you have evidence to back up what you are saying? How can I publish accusations not corroborated by evidence, by sworn statements, by documents?"

"Don't do anything with it," Viganò said. "Just keep doing your work. Prepare yourself. The time will come when you will have to write. For the moment, just watch, listen, and wait."

"You know," I said, "one way to treat this material would be to make it into one long conversation. Tape-recorded. But we would still need evidence. Documents. But if we want to protect young people from abuse, we should publish this information and help to bring an end to this culture of cover-ups forever."

"I will keep your offer in mind," Viganò said. "When the time is right, I will contact you. But now it is late. Let's get something to eat. You must be hungry."

We dined on wonderful Sicilian dishes in a nearby restaurant, Lumie di Sicilia, managed by a friend, Salvatore, who had just recovered from a heart attack. I had come to know him well over the years because the restaurant is not far from the American Academy in

Rome, where I was a Fellow in Post-Classical Studies in 1985–86.

I did not write anything about the conversation at the time because I felt more work needed to be done checking the facts, confirming precisely what each person he had talked about had said and done. At the time, my intention was to speak to Cardinal McCarrick, Cardinal Bertone, Cardinal Wuerl, Emeritus Pope Benedict, Pope Francis himself, Cardinal Parolin, McCarrick's victims, and to his associates and to either find supporting evidence for Viganò's assertions or disprove the assertions with other evidence. I was unable to carry out even a small part of that agenda for many reasons—my own poor health, many other pressing duties, lack of time and opportunity. But I did become convinced that it would be interesting to sit down again with Viganò with a tape recorder and, if possible, to obtain documents from him supporting his assertions, if he had them. I felt that might be a contribution to protecting young people and healing the Church.

# CHAPTER 2

# VIGANÒ'S EARLY LIFE

*"I will give to the LORD the thanks due to his
righteousness, and I will sing praise to the
name of the LORD, the Most High."*
—Psalm 7:17

WHO IS Carlo Maria Viganò? He is a product of a very
old, very distinguished Italian Catholic culture, a culture marked by its religious worldview. In this religious
worldview, the world is ultimately understood in relation to the sacred, the holy, that indefinable "numinous"
quality that stands over against the "profane" reality of
impersonal space, time, matter, elements, energy. In this
religious view, the world is not ultimately reducible to
atoms and molecules and impersonal energies but is, in
its most profound reality, the product of a holy divinity, a
personal if often hidden God who is in relationship with
men. This religious worldview is persuaded that what is
unseen in the world is more important than what is visible to the eye.

Viganò's personality and character were shaped from
childhood by this old Catholic culture's conviction that
there are things that are sacred, that there is a religious dimension to the world. Formed in this way, he
is not and cannot be a modern "secularist," or "secular

humanist"—someone who regards the world as essentially material, without an invisible but real inner mystery
which is in fact a shining, boundless, overflowing "inner
glory" which religious piety and intellectual conviction
calls "the divine," "the holy," "God."

Viganò was born to Adeodato and Sofia Viganò in
1941, and he was raised, and trained for decades, to
believe and to express in our modern world this old Catholic conviction that at the heart of all things (including at
the heart of man himself, where we are "in the image and
likeness of God") is the holy, the divine. (We are jump-
ing ahead a bit here to our days of conversation after I
found him, but it seems fitting, for here in his own words
we can learn some important things about the boy who
became the man.)

## His Earliest Memory

Viganò's earliest memory reflects this truth. In the very
first moment of his conscious life, as he recalls it now as
an old man, when he was just two years old in war-torn
Milan, Italy, in 1943 (he was born on January 16, 1941),
he recalls a comforting moment of prayer, resting in his
mother's arms in a time of great danger to their physical
lives. It is as if, for Viganò, everything that came after,
his whole personality, grew from that original seed.

"What is your earliest memory?" I asked Viganò. We
were in our second day of conversations after his year in
hiding. I told him I wanted to understand more about
him as a person, not more about the Cardinal McCarrick

case or his well-known allegations against the actions and leadership of Pope Francis.

Viganò was silent for a moment. He suddenly seemed emotionally exhausted. I felt that he was having difficulty shifting gears, mentally, from the present, from his months of hiding, from his public accusations against the Church hierarchy and Pope Francis, for not doing enough to control and punish clerical sexual abuse, to the distant past, to his childhood, to his first memory. His eyes seemed to glisten, as if he might be overcome by his emotions and break into tears. It was as if the past was very far away. Then he began to speak in quiet, measured tones.

"Memories are certainly one of the major gifts that we have received from the Lord, who created us in his image, making us able to have impressed in our minds the most beautiful experiences that we have been living," Viganò said.

"And for me, certainly, my memories help me, in the sense that one of the first memories that I have was to be on the breast of my mother, probably when I was around two years old, bringing me down into the refuge during the bombardment (of Milan), and there was a little image of Our Lady with the light."

I felt I was almost there with him, descending a stairway into the dark: a mother and several small children, a two-year-old boy on her breast, his eyes wide and remembering, the sounds of airplane motors above, the sound of bombs dropping and exploding, a little statue of the Virgin Mary lit up in the dark.

"And so we were starting to pray the Rosary. My father was not there."

"My father was not there." I found that significant. Telling the story of his first memory, being carried by his mother down into a shelter, he recalls that his father was not present.

"I have this very deep, emotional memory of Mary. This marks a presence in my life all along. I remember that we would pray every evening after dinner, all together. I remember my father, just back from his work in Milan, able to pray with us, to sustain those who were already starting to fall asleep, reminding them that it was beautiful to be praying together to our Lady, to our Mother."

Again he recalls the presence of his father as a rushed entrance, "just back from his work." His father's absence during the day, his presence at the evening prayer, keeping the sleepy children awake; these left a deep impression on him.

"So that is my earliest memory: to be on the breast of my mother, looking at the Virgin Mary as the blessing protecting us, during the bombardment during the war."

## HIS CHILDHOOD AND VOCATION

I asked the archbishop to continue to reflect on his childhood. As Wordsworth wrote, "the child is father to the man." To understand a man, it is important to consider the man's childhood.

His parents had nine children, seven boys and two girls. The first, a boy named Emilietto, died only thirteen days after his birth in 1931. The second, a girl, Annamaria, was born in 1932. The third, Leonardo, was born in 1934; he died last year, in 2019. The fourth, Giorgio, was born in 1935; he died in 2004. The fifth, to whom the name Emilio was given again, was born in 1936. The sixth, Lorenzo, who became a priest, was born in 1938. The seventh was Carlo Maria, the archbishop, born in 1941. The eighth, Rosanna, was born in 1944. And the youngest, Alberto, was born in 1947. All nine children were given the same middle name: Maria.

Viganò's father found a house for his wife and children outside of Milan during the bombardment of that city in the war years, the early 1940s. The house was in the small town of Varese and was located just at the bottom of a hill named Sacro Monte on the top of which there is very beautiful shrine dedicated to the crowning of the Virgin Mary as the queen of heaven.

"So my mother was there and my two older brothers, who were not yet in school," Viganò recalled. "My grandmother was also there, but she died when I was just a few months old. Our house was just below the first chapel of this shrine. There were and still are fifteen little chapels, one for each of the fifteen mysteries of the Rosary.

"My father would come out to us sometimes by train when the railways were not bombed. Otherwise, he would even come by bicycle. It was fifty kilometers (about thirty miles) from Milan to Varese, and not completely flat. There were some hills to climb. He would come home on Saturday and Sunday. It was an easier ride for him going back to Milan, slightly downhill. I did it myself."

He continued, "There was nearby a small airplane factory. They never managed to bomb it. For me it was very amusing, when I was two or three years old, to see when fighters swooped down, trying and failing to bomb the factory.

"In the war years, as I remember them, it was snowing quite a lot. So we could put the children on a sled on that hill and slide down.

"In 1944, when I was three and a half years old, my youngest sister was born. I remember her birth in the hospital.

"I was baptized in the Church of St. Victor, *San Vittore*, the main church of Varese. Milan has a parish church with St. Victor's body, as I later came to know when it became our parish.

"As children, after the war, sometimes in the summer we were able to go to the seashore by the Adriatic Sea in Cesenatico, about thirty kilometers south of Ravenna. In July 1946, we went there before the school year started.

"In October 1946, I started primary school in Milan in the Collegio San Carlo. At that time, we were five brothers in that school. I started school at the age of five years and eight months."

The archbishop then remembered two other names: a young priest, Giulio Giacometti, who was the spiritual counselor at Viganò's elementary school, and the pale, brilliant, ethereal, holy cardinal archbishop of Milan, now proclaimed blessed, Alfredo Ildefonso Schuster. These two men influenced the young Viganò from a very early age to decide that he should become a priest.

"In that time, there was a good spiritual assistance.

There was a priest who had been ordained just in June 1946, who had become the spiritual director in the school, Padre Giulio Giacometti. He became my spiritual director. He had a strong relationship with Blessed Cardinal Alfonso Schuster, archbishop of Milan. I received first Communion and Confirmation in the college from Blessed Cardinal Shuster.

"My priestly vocation is dated to my first Communion. I was deeply moved by the Mass, and I attended Mass often—Monday, Wednesday, Friday. The fast then was from midnight before and one hour from water. I took five years of Greek, besides the Latin. What I remember in particular was that at the beginning of every school year, Cardinal Schuster invited all the students to a Mass at 7 a.m. in Milan's Duomo, in one of the major lateral chapels dedicated to Our Lady on the left side. So we were to run there. He had a very tiny voice, but very understandable. In fact, he was a saint. When they exhumed his body, it was intact. He was beatified by John Paul II.

"I later celebrated the funeral Mass of Don Giacometti. He was the pastor of one of the churches built by St. Ambrose, the Holy Apostles of St. Nazaro near the gate of the city which leads toward Rome. Milan is built in a star construction, with the Duomo at the center."

In a sense, Viganò had three fathers: his natural father; the young priest who became his spiritual father, Giacometti; and the austere Cardinal Schuster, who gave him his first Communion and Confirmation, from which time Viganò sensed he had a priestly vocation.

***

I asked Viganò if, as a boy, he had ever heard of cases of clerical sexual abuse.

"The idea of sexual abuse of minors was inconceivable to us," the archbishop replied. "Never was there such a problem in our childhood. When I was at that school, there was never even a mention of such a thing."

Rather, Viganò said, his boyhood was marked by a continuing contact with the Christian tradition of Milan, weaving his daily life into twenty centuries of tradition.

"Our whole life was imbued with the liturgical life of the Church and with the memory of the Church's history in Milan going back to St. Ambrose," he said. "I grew up playing soccer on some ruins of the Basilica of St. Ambrose. Our home was very near to the basilica. I attended Sunday Mass at the Church of St. Victor on the Body, an Ambrosian church with an Ambrosian rite. On Sunday afternoons, we attended catechism class in the St. Victor parish. And we prayed the Rosary and attended the blessing of the Holy Sacrament at the Catholic university attached to St. Ambrose Basilica. The rite of blessing with the showing of the host is different in the Ambrosian rite. In the Roman rite, the priest is silent holding the host. In the Ambrosian rite, the priest sings as he shows the host.

"When I was fourteen or fifteen, I started going by myself to a place very close to the college where there is a hospital that was known as the Hospital of the Brothers of St. John of God.

"When I was fifteen, my father bought a new apartment near the school of the Jesuits, Pope Leo XIII, just across the street. So we could go to school directly across from our home. I studied there for four years, from fifteen to eighteen, with the Jesuits. I remember that the exams to graduate in all my subjects, Latin, Greek, Math, were very demanding and quite oppressive for the students. It was quite a good school, not quite as familial as the Collegio San Carlo. My physics professor was a Jesuit and also the philosophy teacher worked with immigrants.

"Starting when I was fifteen, I was able to travel by bicycle to the edge of the city to visit various poor families. Many were widows who had lost their husbands during the war. We brought them a little cash and some food. We were told that this was true Christian charity—to visit the poor, to visit the sick."

# CHAPTER 3

# HIS FATHER'S DEATH

*"The LORD is near to the brokenhearted,*
*and saves the crushed in spirit."*

—Psalm 34:18

I ASKED Viganò to tell me more about his father, Adeodato (the same name as the illegitimate son of St. Augustine).

"My father was named Adeodato, 'given by God,' because he was born when his father was almost in his sixties.

"My father, born in the last century, in 1898, was the last of six children. He became a successful businessman in the metal-fabrication industry," Viganò said. "He manufactured metal parts for other companies in Italy and all over Europe. He was quite successful and a generous man, giving donations to the Milan seminary and to many other worthy causes.

"My father and mother knew of my vocation when I was very young. But my father wanted me to complete all my studies to allow me to have a career as all my brothers and sisters did, so I promised my father that I would not go to the seminary before finishing university, and I kept my promise.

"My father died on the twenty-fourth of July, 1961.

He was just sixty-three, and I was just twenty years old. He had been at home since May."

Viganò seemed moved emotionally by the memory of his father's death.

"My father, certainly, to say the truth, was central to my life," he continued. "We were raised to tell everything to our mother and father. If we did not, it was a break with our whole life and trust."

Those words struck me. Many of us have close relationships with their parents. But not many of us would say that "if we did not tell everything to our mother and father, it was a break with our whole life and trust."

This is a very unusual bond, I thought, revealing that Viganò was formed from earliest childhood to confide "everything" he was experiencing or dealing with to his parents. This does not mean that the children were constrained to confide everything to our parents. The children confided in them out of a relationship of total trust and love towards their parents.

"My father loved the mountains and he wanted me to experience life in the mountains," he continued, "so every summer as an adolescent I used to go to a hiking camp at the foot of Mt. Blanc for more than a month. It was at altitude, at least 1,500 meters high in a camping area organized by a holy Jesuit father. We had morning Mass, then a meditation. The life of the camp was very demanding—no running water, and a two-day cycle, one day of cleaning, and one day of hiking a very long way. We would sing mountain songs, as the Alpine soldiers used to do. One of the boys was named chief of the camp. The experience of hiking to the glaciers, where there was permanent ice, was indescribably marvelous. We would be hot from hiking, and the cold air would come off of the glacier to cool us."

I was struck by these recollections. Viganò's eyes were lit up with eager nostalgia as he recalled hiking up to the high glaciers of the Alps in summertime. I could almost feel the blast of cold glacial air tumbling down from the white glacier onto the red faces of the young lads as they hiked. A time of innocence, of camaraderie, a time without shadows.

"[Later,] my father's death came unexpectedly. He went to a clinic for a check-up. I think that a medical mistake was made. They had been giving him cortisone for some pain, and suddenly, they stopped giving it, and he got a blood clot in his legs, and it went directly to his lungs. I was in Varese, and we received a terrible call. Father was in critical condition. So we drove to Milan, but we arrived too late. And I saw my father lying there before me, dead. It was terrible for me. He was a very kind father. He died at ten o'clock in the evening."

So these two recollections, Viganò's earliest memory in his mother's arms in the bomb shelter and his memory of his father and his father's untimely death due to a blood clot in his lung, may be considered two moments that frame Viganò's early life—his first conscious moment and the moment when his "youth" ended with his father's untimely, mistake-caused death.

Viganò said his memory of his father's death when he was just twenty was "terrible" for him. (I had not yet lost my own father, so I did not know how terrible the definitive closing of that door of access and advice can be.)

One can imagine the young man entering the hospital room, looking at a clock on the wall to see what time it was. He remembered the exact time: "He died at ten o'clock in the evening." Then, silence. He said nothing more.

Viganò had explained his relationships to his mother and father as relationships of extraordinary intimacy and trust: "We were raised to tell everything to our mother and father. If we did not, it was a break with our whole life and trust." Yet Viganò, after age twenty, could no longer "tell everything" to his father. His father was gone.

# CHAPTER 4

# HOLINESS

*"Holy, Holy, Holy, is the LORD of hosts,
the whole earth is full of his glory."*
—Isaiah 6:3

THE CATHOLIC view of the world—the view that formed Viganò with prayers, rosaries, Masses, confessions, catechism classes, and even boyhood hikes with classmates into the clear high Alps—sees holiness as the ultimate energy of the universe. Or better, the ultimate reality behind all things.

It also tends to connect that energy, that holiness, with the concepts of father and mother (God as Father and St. Mary and the Church as mother). As the human father and mother generate and protect the young person, so the divine reality, the divine being at the source of all being, the holy, generates and protects all who come into being. The holiness of the divine being is an incorruptible force (what can corrupt the holy? nothing), and so the holy is eternal—nothing can harm or destroy it.

All things exist, in this view, because they are supported, nourished, generated by this hidden, holy power. For this reason, this holy power is often called Father, Almighty Father, Father Almighty.

In Catholic belief, this holy power overshadowed a

sinless virgin named Mary, enabling her, though human, to conceive a divine son, Jesus. At Jesus's death, from the cross, he entrusted his mother to the care of the Apostle John and then entrusted John to his mother, Mary, saying to John, "Behold your mother." For this reason, Mary is considered the mother of all Christians and the mother of the Church. (Viganò would later tell me that when he was studying as a seminarian in Rome in the 1960s, he met the Spanish archbishop of Granada who suggested to the Second Vatican Council, and Paul VI, that the council should close with a ceremony declaring that Mary was the *Mater Ecclesiae*, the "Mother of the Church.")

This religious view of reality inevitably creates shrines and sacred spaces, sacred art, sacred music, and sanctuaries; it builds temples—especially builds and protects the dignity of that temple which is the human body itself—where the invisible sacred may become visible in this world and abide.

This religious or sacred view of human life sees all human earthly activities *sub specie aeternitatis*, "under the perspective of eternity."

In this two-thousand-year-old Catholic way of viewing the world, God again walks with man as in the Garden of Eden, since the expulsion from Eden has in part been reversed by the sacrificial work of Jesus Christ.

Thus, each day's actions are intended to be woven into a mysterious fabric dense with significance, dense with meaning.

This fabric is understood to be woven with prayer (conversation with the divine), sacrifice (the offering of the gift of oneself to God), and discernment (the prudential action of the mind in judging what is good and bad, what is better and worse, according to changeless, eternal criteria).

A man who has this worldview prays to a hidden, spiritual God—never an image, or idol, or anything material—in order to draw close to God's Holy Spirit, to hear that Holy Spirit in the deep heart's core, to be in dialogue with the Holy Spirit. This dialogue, this "hearing," this "contemplation of the divine" is the highest act a human person can perform (as Christ told Mary and Martha when he said, "Mary has chosen the better part," as Mary contemplated him while Martha was busy about "many things") for it links the human with the divine.

A man with this worldview sacrifices his own will in order to carry out a holy will that he senses in and through prayer.

And a man with this worldview is committed to a ceaseless process of discernment, a process by which he judges various paths and decides between various possibilities how best to accomplish the holy will of God by bringing his own calm, reasoned judgment to bear on the task or problem at hand. (The Jesuits, of course, following St. Ignatius of Loyola, make this process of discernment into a central principle of their formation and spiritual life.)

The underlying conviction of this old Catholic worldview is that each day is given to men and women to live in such a way as to give honor and glory to God, who, St. John tells us, is the *Logos* ("and the Word was God"); that is, the meaning or reason of all things.

The *Logos* is that divine and fundamental meaning beneath, behind, within, and above all things, which is the invisible, meaning-giving presence of God in this world and in the lives of men. We might say this is what is meant by Christ's saying that "man does not live by bread alone, but by every word." The "word" that man lives by is the word of meaning, the *Logos*. Without that word, men languish and finally perish, spiritually. A meaning-less ("*Logos*-less") life is impossible for men to bear very long. We were meant to live with and in meaning, not bereft of meaning.

What does this divine and fundamental "meaning" (*Logos*) ask of each man, of each woman? In this traditional Catholic spirituality, the "*Logos*" (the meaning, the reason) of our lives—to which we ought to conform our own wills—asks us, so far as it is within our capacity and strength, "to do justice, and to love kindness, and to walk humbly with your God" (Mi 6:8) so that, by so doing, we may give glory to God in this world.

Such was the worldview that was proposed by Viganò's parents and teachers to Viganò, and to so many other Italians of his generation, and to so many other Catholics in many countries over the generations.

Yet human life is troubled by many temptations and challenges, and this religious worldview as well has been troubled by many temptations and challenges throughout the ages, and now in our own time in a special way.

Following the Second World War, once Catholic Italy—a society of saints and pilgrimages, a society with a liturgical Church which sanctified each Sunday as a day of rest and nearly every day in the calendar as a saint's day, a society which with one accord agreed that *la fami-glia*, the family, was the single, final, most important human value—turned slowly, and then with increasing speed, into new modern Italy, a culture marked by sec-ularism, by the removal of the sacred from public life, by ever-increasing wealth and consumerism, and by the glorification of the individual and his or her desires, even at the expense of *la famiglia*. And so Italy, like the rest of our world, changed.

The development of modern science, the arrival of new and plentiful consumer goods—cars, telephones, radios, films, computers, the internet—brought social and cultural changes to Italy. The country where, in the mountain villages, chickens occasionally might still run in the streets, where pasta was made by hand, pushed through wires to make the individual threads, where families would make a Sunday outing to a holy shrine, became a more secular country, one of supermarkets and pasta in cardboard boxes or plastic wrappers and of Sun-day soccer matches in crowded stadiums instead of quiet visits to holy shrines. So the old Catholic Italy has been passing into the sunset now for more than two hundred years.

What I am arguing here is that Viganò, having been shaped to his very core by the old Catholic view of the holiness of God and the duties of men to honor and live in accordance with this holiness, is inevitably a figure in tension with the de-sacralized post-Christian view of this modern world, the view that man's life in this world is without any transcendent meaning.

We live in a world that has attempted to de-mythologize

concepts such as the sacred, the holy, the divine—a world which regards these concepts as crutches for the weak who are unable to face the fact that, as these modern thinkers argue, there is *nothing* intrinsically holy (sacred), there is only the value that a man assigns to something, a value that is unstable, culturally determined and ever-changing, not something stable, eternal, unchanging.

All of this goes a good way to explaining the forming personality matrix lying beneath the mind that, beginning with the "Testimony," has begun to speak out to the Catholic, and increasingly also the non-Catholic, world with ever-greater urgency against the loss of the holy, the loss of God, the loss of a transcendent dimension to human life—even, and especially, when it seems that leading figures in the Church, in the religious orders, and in the Vatican hierarchy have begun to accept and even praise this new "modern" way of viewing the world and human life (a way that in fact isn't all that modern, if one considers, for example, the world of Late Antiquity as portrayed and analyzed by scholars like Charles Norris Cochrane and Peter Brown, or the puzzling world of hermetic Renaissance humanism; *nihil novum sub sole*, "there is nothing new under the sun") (Eccl 1:1).

# CHAPTER 5

# THE FAITHFUL YOUNG PRIEST

*"The LORD has sworn, and will not change his mind, 'You are a priest for ever after the order of Melchisedech.'"*
—Psalm 110:4

VIGANÒ, FOLLOWING in the footsteps of his older brother, Lorenzo Viganò, who was ordained two years before him, was ordained a Catholic priest on March 24, 1968, at the age of twenty-seven. He had already finished degrees in both Civil and Church Law at the Lateran University and a Masters in Theology at the Jesuits Gregorian University in Rome.

He served briefly as a coadjutor priest in Pavia, in northern Italy, together with his brother, Father Lorenzo, and then was sent to Brussels for further study. He would later tell me that those two years in a parish were among "the happiest of my life." He and Lorenzo were two brothers who shared everything: plans, work, visions for their future contributions to the life of the Church. His relations with his brother Lorenzo suddenly was to change after forty-three years in 2008 when Lorenzo suffered a permanent debilitating stroke and other people with differing agendas inserted themselves between the two brother priests. That, Viganò would tell me, was one of the greatest regrets and sorrows of his life.

On July 31, 2019, when we were together, I asked Viganò what memories he had of his first months and years as a priest. What was his first assignment, and how had he experienced his work as a priest? In essence, he told me that those months, in the late 1960s in northern Italy, were a "beautiful time" in his life but also a time when his willingness to defend the faith was already tested, even though he was not yet thirty (he turned thirty in January of 1971).

**Okay. After attending a seminary in Rome, you were ordained a priest at age twenty-seven in 1968, in the diocese of Pavia. So, what was it like to be a coadjutor priest?**

Archbishop Viganò: I was living with my brother Lorenzo, who had already been ordained, in a very small university student college, just in front of the Pavia seminary, but we were not far from the Duomo and also not far from Santa Maria del Carmine, where we were respectively assigned.

So the first Mass at the parish each day was really early morning. At that time there was, in wintertime, a lot of smog. So when we came back from parish work, we used to spend time late in the evenings with the students. So that was pretty intensive work. I remember that in hearing the confessions. I had difficulty sometimes in understanding the dialect of Pavia, which was quite different from the one in Milan. Now nobody will speak it any more. But at that time, they had expressions that were not so easy to understand.

**So you were there for two years.**

Yes.

**But so, did you perform baptisms? Did you have . . .**

Baptisms. Yes. At the beginning, I had the Mass for children at nine o'clock on Sunday. Every morning there was also a Mass starting seven o'clock.

**And how did you feel? Were you happy? Were those happy days?**

Well, very nice. Although it was very . . . The first time at the beginning it was not easy to keep the attention of the children for the Mass. Later, I learned how to do it.

**How do you keep the attention of children?**

Well, I mean, I was just telling stories and making examples, and so . . . I remember there was one, in the afternoon there was, we called it the oratorio, so there was a place where the children may play. It was not a very large place, but sufficient. We also had a hall for projecting films. So, once a small child, very small, came to me. And he asked me, he said—there in Pavia they have a usage that is not in Milan, a priest is just called Don, without giving the name, like "Don Carlo," they just say "Don"—"Don, what do you think?" he said to me. "Should I buy an ice cream or switch on a candle to Our Lady?" We were close to Our Lady statue. So what he said made me laugh. Why did he need to buy anything? No, he was most specific. "Because," he said, "the angel wanted me to switch on a candle, but the devil he said I am to buy an ice cream." This was his problem, deciding who to listen to. I think he was eight years old or something like that. His name is Fabio. He decided to switch on the candle. I kept in touch with him, and later he became a priest, Don Fabio.

**And then, did you have funerals?**

Funerals. Yes. Especially the first winter, it was terrible. Because there was a house for elders. So practically every day there was a funeral. Because it was very cold. Funerals continually.

**So how did you conceive of the comfort that you gave to people? What was the faith? What did it mean to them? To give the sacraments, to give counsel, to celebrate funerals?**

I was explaining the meaning of the *Catechism* to the children. There was a section for the children. There was a group of lay people also who taught the *Catechism*, especially young student girls mainly; they were instructing the children.

**Well, do you think that was a happy time in your life?**

Well, certainly, it was a very nice time. Then, after my ordination, my bishop retired. So there was appointed a new bishop from Sardinia with a very different, narrower mentality. After the new bishop came, there was the time of the campaign for the approval of divorce in Italy. Pavia has one of the first universities in Italy. And . . . who died in Pavia; do you know?

**I don't know. Galileo?**

No. There died in Pavia in the time of St. Benedict the great philosopher Boethius.

**Oh.**

So Boethius was imprisoned in Pavia because there was a castle there. So the first siege of the Lombards was in Pavia. Pavia grew up before Milan.

**Ah. So you were happy in Pavia. Then, at a certain moment, you left being a coadjutor priest. How did that happen?**

Now, that happened . . . Well . . . I should tell you what happened. So my experience in Pavia was marked by this campaign and propaganda and contestation regarding in favor of legalizing divorce. So already the community, in 1970 I think, the law was approved. So I was just back in the parish, Santa Maria del Carmine, in 1969–1970. And a director of one of the big colleges, because in Pavia there are two big colleges for students.

One was founded by the family Borromeo, it's Collegio Borromeo, it's monumental, it's a huge building. Pavia is crossed by the Ticino river. And the other one was Collegio Ghislieri. Also Ghislieri is the name of a pope's family. It's very ancient, I don't know which pope was from the Ghislieri family. Both colleges were founded in the sixteenth century.

So the governing body of the Borromeo College was the board of a foundation, depending on the Borromeo family, on Prince Borromeo, and at the same time on the Archbishop of Milan. And it was agreed that there would always be a priest in charge of the Borromeo College. And it happened, during this time, as this campaign for divorce took place, that Ambrogio Valsecchi was a professor of Moral Theology in the seminary. He was in favor of legalizing divorce.

**Valsecchi . . .**

Valsecchi . . .

**Okay.**

He left the priesthood later on. But I remember everything very clearly: a public meeting in the great hall, called the Aula Magna, very beautiful, all decorated, repainted, at the Borromeo College. The hall was filled with students. A lecture. And I went there. Valsecchi was rector of the Borromeo College, so there were quite a few priests there besides the students. And my brother Lorenzo was also there. My brother Lorenzo was a student of oriental languages at the Pontifical Biblical Institute (like Cardinal Gianfranco Ravasi), so he was much more learned in theology and biblical studies than me.

So at a certain moment at the end there were questions. We hoped that one of the professors of the seminary, or the rector, would make an intervention, try to explain to the students that this Valsecchi was giving his own interpretation of the Gospel, just to justify the possibility of divorce. So none of those in charge of the teaching in the diocese was speaking up. So I looked at my brother and said, "Well, what are you going to do?" He said, "I'm going to make an intervention now." And I told him, "I'll do it." So I stood up. And I said what I felt I had to say.

**Your brother Lorenzo is older?**

Yes, he's older, two years and a half.

**So he was thirty, you were twenty-eight, or something like that. And this was about 1969?**

Yes, should have been in '69. So finally, I stood up. I made an intervention. I tried to destroy what this Valsecchi had said. So at the end of my intervention there was a whistle, all the students against me. They signaled to me, the great majority at least.

**They hissed, whistled . . .**

Yes. So they were in favor [of divorce]. So after that there was another conference at the university. I went there also.

**So you were going to these conferences to speak out?**

Yes. And after that, I protested with the rector of the seminary and said, "Why? Where is the professor of Moral Theology? Why didn't he speak up on the biblical basis of our teaching?"

After that campaign ended, life returned to normal. In my parish, we were two priests. There was a pastor, a very nice man, who used to preach very well, and he was making pilgrimages to Lourdes with Unitalsi, with the sick people. He was very close to the new bishop and he saw that the bishop was also very affectionate to me. The other priest was older than me, of course. He started a Mass with guitars; I was not pleased with that.

Anyway, before the end of summer, the bishop told me that he was sending me for further study to specialize in catechetics. So the bishop sent me to Brussels for a year.

**Which place?**

Brussels, Belgium. The Lumen Vitae Institute. It is for pastoral studies, to train to be a chaplain for the students at university. And I went there.

**That's where you learned French. You learned French there.**

No, I learned French at school. Before going there, the French language was very familiar to me. Sometimes I was dreaming in French.

(In the early seventies, Vigano would find himself in Rome, where the trajectory of his service to God as a Vatican diplomat would be determined.)

# CHAPTER 6

# CHOSEN FOR ROME

*"The LORD is my chosen portion and
my cup; you hold my lot."*
—Psalm 16:5

IN ROME, Viganò was soon noticed and selected to enter the diplomatic academy of the Holy See. In 1973, at the age of thirty-two, he was posted to his first overseas assignment: the nunciature in Iraq. Viganò was to give the next forty-three years of his life to the Vatican's diplomatic service until his retirement at the age of seventy-five in 2016, now four years ago. He is, as I write in early 2020, seventy-nine years old.

Viganò's first assignment abroad was as a junior diplomat under a much more experienced older nuncio, Archbishop Jean Rupp, in Baghdad (1973–76). His second assignment was in Great Britain (1976–78). Those were the final years of Pope Paul VI (1963–1978).

Viganò would be recalled to Rome in the tumultuous final weeks of Paul's pontificate, thereby becoming a witness, at the age of thirty-seven, to two conclaves: the one which elected John Paul I at the end of August 1978 and the one that elected John Paul II in October 1978 after John Paul I's sudden death on September 28, 1978, after just thirty-three days as pope. Viganò was to tell me that the very last act of John Paul I's pontificate was to draft a letter to Fr. Pedro Arrupe, the superior general of the Jesuits, asking Arrupe to clarify whether his top assistant and possible successor, Fr. Vincent O'Keefe, an American, had really given an interview to a Dutch magazine in which he had said that the time was very near when the Jesuit order would make some revolutionary changes in its religious life. "If the interview is inaccurate, O'Keefe should make that clear. If it is accurate, he should resign," John Paul I's letter said. "I had that letter in my hands," Viganò said. "I sent it on to the Jesuit Curia. The next day, John Paul I was dead."

Having arrived in Rome, at the nerve center of the global Church, Viganò was quite content. He stayed for eleven years, from 1978 to 1989, working at the Vatican Secretariat of State. This was the dramatic first decade of the pontificate of John Paul II, when the Soviet Union began to tremble due to the demonstrations of Solidarnosc in Poland, when an assassin tried to kill John Paul on May 13, 1981, and when a young girl named Emanuela Orlandi, age fifteen, who lived with her family inside the Vatican, was abducted by unknown kidnappers on June 22, 1983. Individuals claiming to be her captors telephoned the Vatican to try to arrange a deal with Cardinal Secretary of State Agostino Casaroli for her release. It was Viganò who answered the phone when a man known as the "Americano" called and asked to speak with Casaroli. "I do not think he was an American," Viganò told me. "His accent was rather . . . Maltese." In the end, no deal was ever arranged, and Emanuela has never been seen again, evidently a casualty of the Cold

War, or of some other peculiar intrigue which has never been explained.

These years of work in Rome gave Viganò a profound experience of the Vatican, making him undoubtedly an "insider" with regard to the government of the universal Church. He worked alongside men like Cardinals Agostino Casaroli, Angelo Sodano, Eduardo Martinez Somalo, Giovanni Battista Re, Justin Rigali, later archbishop of Philadelphia, Italian Cardinal Achille Silvestrini, who understood the political currents of Italy and other nations like no other Vatican diplomat, and Argentine Cardinal Leonardo Sandri, who now heads the Congregation for Oriental Churches but who was then a substitute of the secretariat of state desk officer, like Viganò, during those important years of the 1980s. According to Vigano, though Silvestrini considered himself to be exceedingly canny, he was profoundly conditioned by his friendships with Italians of the Left, Romano Prodi and others like him, and was a member of the St. Gallen mafia. I note all this to give an indication of the depth and breadth of Viganò's curial associations: as a young man, he knew almost everyone who today is at the leadership level of the Church.

During the period from 1989 to 1998, Viganò left Rome. He was appointed Permanent Observer of the Holy See to the Council of Europe in Strasbourg, the capital of Alsace in northeastern France, on April 4, 1989. This appointment occurred just as the Berlin Wall was about to fall. That historic fall ended the half-century division of Europe into Western Europe and the Soviet East bloc. So, during his three years in Strasbourg, as the "new united Europe" was being formed, Viganò gained considerable exposure to the world of international diplomacy.

## CONSECRATION AS A BISHOP

On April 3, 1992, Pope John Paul II named him a bishop. He was now fifty-one. He was granted the Titular See of Ulpiana and made the apostolic pro-nuncio to Nigeria. (Many bishops and archbishops in the diplomatic service who hold administrative posts and are never bishops in an active diocese are given "titular" bishoprics. These are episcopal sees that once flourished but for one reason or another became inactive. The cities are still listed as titular, "having the title of," episcopal sees, but they do not function in any way; many are cities from the time of the Roman Empire which were destroyed during the age of the barbarian invasions, or during the centuries of Islamic expansion. Ulpiana is an ancient Roman city in Kosovo that is now an archaeological site. It has been a titular see since 1933.)

Viganò was consecrated by Pope John Paul II himself, with Polish Cardinal Franciszek Macharski and Italian Cardinal Angelo Sodano serving as co-consecrators, on April 26, 1992.

Viganò then was moved the following year from Strasbourg to become nuncio in the most populous country in Africa, Nigeria. He spent the next six years there (1992–1998).

Then, at the wish of Pope John Paul II, Viganò was summoned back to Rome, taking a quite important post:

delegate for pontifical representations in the Vatican's central governing office, the Secretariat of State. He was now fifty-seven years old, at the height of his powers. And for the next twelve years, until age sixty-eight, he was the very capable and hard-working personnel chief for the entire Roman Curia as well as for all Vatican diplomats.

For this reason, it does not seem improper to maintain that no one living today could know more firsthand details of the activity of the Vatican's far-flung global diplomatic service in the first years of the twenty-first century than Viganò. This is an important point because it supports the contention that what Viganò has to say about the Vatican may be as informed as what anyone in the world may have to say on the subject.

## TO THE GOVERNORATE

After twelve years in this role, Pope Benedict XVI named Viganò the secretary general of the Vatican City Governorate on July 16, 2009. This was essentially a move from the wide world of Vatican diplomacy to the more administrative work of running the Vatican City State, which manages things like the Vatican Museums, the Vatican police force, the Vatican Communications (Post Office, Internet), the Technical Department for Construction and Maintenance of buildings inside the Vatican City and the four Major Basilicas in Rome, the Vatican pharmacy and grocery store, all of the people employed in the Vatican offices to handle the Vatican's cleaning, upkeep, and bookkeeping, and the administration of the Pontifical Villas in Castel Gandolfo and the Vatican Observatory.

The striking fact is that Viganò immediately rolled up his sleeves and took on this new task with extraordinary diligence. As secretary general, Viganò centralized the Vatican City State's accounting procedures and began to keep a watchful eye on all cost overruns. He succeeded: he turned a deficit for the Vatican City State of US $10.5 million into a surplus of $44 million during his first year. A certain mystery surrounds what happened next. As a strong supporter of the sovereignty of the Vatican, Viganò suggested to his superiors in 2010 that the Vatican City State should drop out of a Euro currency agreement that included a Vatican commitment to comply with new European banking regulations. Still, in 2011, the Vatican under Pope Benedict chose to adhere to the Euro agreement and accept the new scrutiny of its financial activity that Europe's banking regulations required. During 2010 and into 2011, Viganò continued to carry out his strict control of cost overruns in Vatican contracts for things like the annual purchase of the Christmas tree and creation of a Nativity scene in St. Peter's Square; he managed to find a way to save about half of the expense, worth several hundred thousand euros.

Then, suddenly, Viganò was, to put it bluntly, out. He was removed from his administrative post and assigned to become the new papal nuncio to the United States.

In the United States, Viganò succeeded the extraordinarily effective Italian Archbishop Pietro Sambi. Sambi, whom I knew fairly well, was supposed to return to Rome and become a cardinal in the Roman Curia, but he died under somewhat mysterious circumstances in July of 2011. He went into the hospital for what was expected to be a minor lung surgery, and he never came out again. His family, I was reliably informed, was taken completely by surprise. Family members had no inkling that Sambi might pass away during the hospital visit. Moreover, officials in the archdiocese of Washington were also taken by surprise and indicated that they were perplexed and disturbed by what had occurred. For my part, I felt that Sambi could have become a real leader in the Roman Curia and possibly even have been elected pope after Pope Benedict XVI, since he had a gregarious, attractive, strong personality, with enormous experience, having served in Israel, giving him knowledge of the Middle East, and in Washington, giving him knowledge of the United States. I do recall that once I said to Sambi, "What can be done about this problem in our Church?" And he replied, "The way you pose the question itself is wrong: you must recognize that this Church is not 'our' Church but 'his' Church. Christ said, 'This is my Church.' It is *his* Church, not *ours.*"

Sambi's death opened up a spot for a man as experienced as Viganò—the post of nuncio to the United States—so that he could be promoted out of Rome without the promotion seeming like a demotion. As the Romans say, "Let him be promoted that he may be removed" ("*Promoveatur ut amoveatur*"). A better translation might be: "Let him be promoted to get rid of him, to get him out of the way." In any case, Viganò would leave Rome in late 2011 and not return for five years.

When he did return, in the spring of 2016, he would be seventy-five years old and retired, his active career as a Vatican diplomat complete.

# CHAPTER 7

# "VATILEAKS" AND TRANSFER TO THE UNITED STATES

*"I call upon the L*ORD*, who is worthy to be praised, and I am saved from my enemies."*
—Psalm 18:3

DURING THE tumultuous pontificate of Pope Benedict XVI (April 19, 2005 to February 28, 2013), Viganò had become a lightning rod for factional struggles at the highest levels of the Roman Curia. These struggles pitted a reform-minded Viganò against his powerful superior, the Cardinal Secretary of State Tarcisio Bertone from Piemonte in northern Italy. Bertone, for various reasons, some known only to him, wished to block Viganò as Pope Benedict's choice to become either the head of the Vatican City State government (to become, as it were, the governor of the Vatican City State) or the head of the Prefecture for the Economic Affairs of the Holy See (the chief oversight post for all of the Vatican's financial affairs). Either post would have made Viganò one of the top four or five men in the Vatican's hierarchy and would, by all accounts, have diminished corruption at the higher levels of the Roman Curia

But that did not happen. Viganò lost the battle. Bertone preferred that Viganò be "promoted" out of the

Vatican to the post of nuncio (ambassador) of the Vatican to the United States—a prestigious post to be sure, but not the summit of the Vatican government which either the governorship or the Prefecture of the Economy would have been.

How did this transfer happen? There remains a certain mystery in this regard. During 2010, anonymous emails began to circulate among cardinals and Vatican embassies alleging nepotism by Viganò in the career of his nephew, Msgr. Carlo Maria Polvani, who also worked within the Vatican Secretariat of State. Evidently, Viganò had an enemy in the Curia who was attempting (or enemies who were attempting) to blacken his reputation. A commentary in the Italian newspaper *Il Giornale*, also anonymous, suggested Viganò was a danger because he was allegedly intent on controlling all of the Vatican's security services.

These events in 2010 and into 2011, when Viganò was becoming ever more involved with the Vatican's finances, were apparently the first time in Viganò's career that he received less than stellar reviews for his work. During these months, certain media, especially in Italy, began to carry stories attacking Viganò, printing calumnious, unsubstantiated allegations critical of his work. It was alleged that he had created an atmosphere of "conflict" and "tension" among the staff and employees in the Vatican City State government. But was this really true? And if true, was it so because he was a true reformer, the type of individual who makes less honest people uncomfortable?

From 2011 on, I knew that if I ever had a chance to

talk at length with Viganò, I would wish to question him on these events. And when I met with him in 2019, I had the opportunity to do so at some length.

In January 2012, after Viganò had already departed Rome for the United States, an Italian television program called *Gli intoccabili* (*The Untouchables*) was broadcast. The program revealed several confidential letters taken directly from the desk of Pope Benedict. This is what came to be known as the "Vatileaks" affair. Viganò would later tell me, "The Vatileaks affair was about me." Later, it would be revealed that the thief of the documents was the pope's own trusted butler, Paolo Gabriele, who would be tried and convicted of these illegal acts by a Vatican court. It was said that Pope Benedict was completely taken by surprise to learn that he had been betrayed in this way. But it was also said that Gabriele stole the letters and gave them to journalists to publish because he felt Benedict was being "kept in the dark" about certain problems in the Roman Curia and only could be made aware of these problems by such a dramatic act as stealing the correspondence and revealing the situation to the general public.

Among the letters were ones written by Viganò on March 27, 2011, to Pope Benedict and on May 8, 2011, to Benedict's secretary of state, Cardinal Tarcisio Bertone. In his letter to Benedict, Viganò said there was, regrettably, considerable corruption occurring in aspects of the Vatican's finances and that the pressure to remove him was because he was the one man attempting to stop the corruption. He said he had begun to build up a culture of honesty and that Vatican employees had come to trust that he would be there to continue this reform but that many would feel frightened and betrayed if he were sent away and could no longer be a point of reference in the efforts to clean up the corruption. Viganò asked Pope Benedict in his letter not to transfer him to be nuncio in America but to keep him at his side in Rome in the same office of secretary general to continue the anticorruption work he had begun. But the appeal failed. Benedict chose to send Viganò to Washington.

On February 4, 2012, Cardinal Lajolo, head of the Governorate, along with three of his colleagues, issued a statement saying:

> The unauthorized publication of two letters of Archbishop Carlo Maria Viganò, the first addressed to the Holy Father on March 27, 2011, the second to the Cardinal Secretary of State on May 8 (2011), for the Governorate of Vatican City is a source of great bitterness. . . . The allegations contained in them cannot but lead to the impression that the Governorate of Vatican City, instead of being an instrument of responsible government, is an unreliable entity, at the mercy of dark forces. After careful examination of the contents of the two letters, the President of the Governorate sees it as its duty to publicly declare that those assertions are the result of erroneous assessments, or fears based on unsubstantiated evidence, even openly contradicted by the main characters invoked as witnesses.

So Lajolo denied there were "dark forces" that had, in the end, ousted Viganò, but to this day, there has never been a full-scale, impartial investigation of the facts.

Let the reader judge.

## To the United States

On August 13, 2011, Bertone informed Viganò that Pope Benedict was appointing him nuncio to the United States. Viganò, disappointed and feeling he was letting down many who had trusted him, wondered if Pope Benedict had really made the decision himself. Benedict had earlier in 2011, in a private meeting, told him, Viganò later would tell me, that he would become not head of the Governorate but prefect of the Economic Affairs of the Holy See—a top post indeed, with oversight over all of the Vatican's finances (essentially the job that Cardinal George Pell would receive under Pope Francis, though at the time with a different name). Viganò concluded that Cardinal Bertone, the secretary of state, had arranged to have him transferred to Washington despite his objections.

The Vatican officially published Viganò's Washington appointment on October 19, 2011. Viganò officially said that he welcomed the appointment and that he thought being apostolic nuncio to the United States is an "important, vast and delicate" task. He said he was grateful to Pope Benedict for entrusting him with the mission and felt called to renew his "trust in the Lord, who asks me to set out again." Being an apostolic nuncio in America, he said, is "a call to know this people, this country, and come to love them."

CHAPTER 8

# THE KIM DAVIS MEETING: SEPTEMBER 24, 2015

*"But you, take courage! Do not let you hands be weak, for your work shall be rewarded."*
—2 Chronicles 15:7

WITHIN HIS first few months in the United States, Viganò began to be seen as a conservative nuncio. Bishops William Lori, Samuel Aquila, and Salvatore Cordileone, all three active defenders of traditional Catholic teaching, were appointed to archdioceses in Baltimore, Denver, and San Francisco, respectively.[14] When Viganò left his post in May of 2016, the conservative Catholic writer George Weigel would call him "the best nuncio we've had thus far." He added, "The archbishop understood that there was no honorable retreat from what some deplored as 'culture wars.' He knew who had declared war on whom; that the Church had not been the aggressor in this struggle; and that the battle had to be engaged, with the tools of reason and persuasion."

One such front in those culture wars concerned the question of gay marriage, and one incident in particular

---

[14] The nuncio plays a key role in nominating bishops for vacant sees in the nation to which he is assigned.

served as a sort of foreshadowing of things to come between Viganò and Francis, as well as other Church officials.

On September 24, 2015, during his papal visit to the United States, Pope Francis met for several minutes with Kim Davis, the Kentucky clerk who refused to issue marriage licenses to same-sex couples, and her husband in the Vatican nunciature on Massachusetts Avenue in Washington, DC.

On October 2, Father Thomas Rosica, a Canadian priest serving as a Vatican spokesman for the English-speaking press, said Viganò was responsible for extending the invitation to Davis, suggesting that Pope Francis had never been informed that she would be invited to meet him.

Vatican spokesman Father Federico Lombardi depicted the meeting as just a second or two, one among many brief introductions rather than an audience. This was not true: the meeting occurred in a separate room and lasted several minutes. During those days, many American commentators, basing themselves on the Vatican's confusing and contradictory statements, publicly accused Davis of having invented the entire "meeting with the pope" in order to gain fame. This was never the case; it was unfair and uncourteous to someone who was invited to meet the pope and felt honored and grateful to do so.

Father Lombardi and Father Rosica subsequently confirmed that on September 23, the evening prior to Francis's meeting with Davis, Viganò had indeed spoken "with the Pope and his collaborators and received a consensus" regarding the meeting.

Cardinal Donald Wuerl of Washington told a reporter that both he and Archbishop Joseph Kurtz, then-president of the US Conference of Catholic Bishops, had advised Archbishop Viganò against arranging the meeting.

Had the pope himself been misinformed by his advisors? Or was he himself untruthful when, in remarks about the meeting three years later, he spoke in a seemingly disparaging way about Davis, who entered the meeting in good faith, having been invited by others?

"I didn't know who that woman was, and he snuck her in to say hello to me—and of course they made a whole publicity out of it," Pope Francis later said, according to Juan Carlo Cruz of Santiago, Chile, a survivor of sexual abuse who met with Pope Francis in 2018. Cruz said Pope Francis told him that he was "horrified" and that he then "fired that nuncio."[15]

Viganò replied by releasing a letter to *LifeSiteNews*, stating that "the Pope knew very well who Davis was, and he and his close collaborators had provided the private audience." And he included the text of a memo which he gave to Pope Francis in Italian on September 23, and showed on the evening of September 23 to members of the pope's entourage, explaining briefly who Kim Davis was. Both texts are below.

---

[15]  Cindy Wooden, "Vigano, Vatican spokesmen dispute facts of pope meeting Kim Davis," *National Catholic Reporter*, September 3, 2018, https://www.ncronline.org/news/vatican/Viganò-vatican-spokesmen-dispute-facts-pope-meeting-kim-davis.

***

Here below is the official English text of Archbishop Carlo Maria Viganò's statement on Pope Francis's private meeting with Kim Davis and what really happened.

### POPE FRANCIS MET PRIVATELY WITH KIM DAVIS: HERE IS WHAT REALLY HAPPENED

by His Excellency Carlo Maria Viganò
Titular Archbishop of di Ulpiana
Apostolic Nuncio

On August 28, 2018, the *New York Times* reported part of a conversation that Juan Carlos Cruz, the most well-known Chilean sexual abuse victim of Father Karadima and Bishop Barros, allegedly had with Pope Francis. Inexplicably, in his conversation with Cruz, the Pope is said to have spoken about his meeting with Kim Davis during his visit to Washington on September 24, 2015, and to have said that he knew nothing about the case before the meeting.

Faced with the Pope's reported statement, I feel obliged to recount the events as they really unfolded.

At the end of the dinner, at the Nunciature in Washington, on the evening of September 23, 2015, I told the Pope that I needed him to grant me a half hour, because I wished to bring to his attention, and possible approval, a delicate and easily achievable initiative; that is, to meet personally and in a completely confidential way, out of the media spotlight, with Kim Davis, a clerk in Rowan County, Kentucky, the first American citizen condemned and imprisoned for one week for having exercised her right to conscientious objection.

At the beginning of our meeting, on the evening of September 23, I gave the Pope a one-page memo summarizing the Davis case. The Pope immediately appeared in favor of such an initiative, but added that the meeting would have political implications, and said, "I don't understand these things, so it would be good for you to hear Cardinal Parolin's opinion."

It was already 9:30 in the evening, so I went in person with two of the counselors of the Nunciature (an Italian and a Lithuanian) to the hotel not far away, where the Pope's entourage was being hosted. Since I had called ahead to give advance notice of my arrival, His Excellency Archbishop Angelo Becciu (Substitute of the Secretary of State) and His Excellency Archbishop Paul Gallagher (Secretary for Relations with States, and Head of the Political Section of the Secretariat of State) were waiting for me in the hotel lobby. They immediately notified me that Cardinal Parolin had already retired to his room, and they did not consider it appropriate to disturb him, since they could easily make him aware of our meeting the following morning.

We then met in a small lounge of the hotel. As I said, there were five of us. I gave them the same memo that I had given to the Pope, setting forth its content and explaining the reason for my visit, which had been requested by the Pope. After considering the case, Archbishop Becciu was immediately in favor of the Pope receiving Davis privately before he left Washington for New York.

Archbishop Gallagher, while showing support for the idea given the importance of defending the right to conscientious objection, said that it was appropriate to verify from the point of view of common law whether there were any reasons that would render the meeting inadvisable; namely, whether the legal proceedings brought against Davis were concluded or were still open. I therefore had him speak by telephone with the canonist for the Nunciature, who before becoming a priest had been a judge in the American military courts and a professor of canon law. After the conversation with the canonist to clarify matters—he said there were no procedural obstacles—Bishop Gallagher gave an unconditionally favorable opinion that the Pope should receive Davis.

The following morning, after the Mass that the Pope concelebrated with us in the Nunciature, I informed the Pope of the positive opinion of his two principal collaborators, who had then told Cardinal Parolin about our meeting. The Pope then gave his consent, and I organized to have Davis come to the Nunciature without anyone noticing, by having her sit in a separate room. Everything was made much easier by the fact that Davis was already in Washington, where she was invited to receive a Cost of Discipleship Award from the Family Research Council.

Before the meeting took place, I alerted the photographer from *L'Osservatore Romano* that he should not release the photographs of the meeting without the permission of his superiors. He of course observed the orders, but took many photographs, which have never been published, and are currently kept in the photographic archive of *L'Osservatore Romano*. I also had Davis promise me in advance that she would not give any news to the media until after the Pope's return to Rome, at the end of his pastoral visit to the USA. Davis faithfully kept her promise.

Early in the afternoon of September 24, before leaving for New York City, the Pope entered as planned into the sitting room where Davis and her husband were waiting for him. He embraced her affectionately, thanked her for her courage, and invited her to persevere. Davis was very moved and started crying. She was then taken back to her hotel in a car driven by a pontifical gendarme, accompanied by an American Monsignor and staff member of the Nunciature.

Once the Pope returned to Rome from Philadelphia after the World Meeting with the Families, the news of his meeting with Davis broke out in the media. An avalanche of phone calls, faxes and emails arrived at the Nunciature in Washington and the Vatican Press Office, many with insults and protests, but also many in favor of the Pope's meeting with Davis. In an article of September 30, 2015, the *New York Times* reported that "Vatican officials initially would not confirm that the meeting occurred, finally doing so on Wednesday afternoon, while refusing to discuss any details."

The Vatican Press Office then issued a statement—without their superiors in the Secretariat of State ever consulting me—stating that the Pope had never received Davis in a private audience, and that at most he may have greeted her among many other people before departing for New York.

Father Rosica and Father Lombardi increased the lies, and were quoted as follows in the October 2, 2015 edition of the *New York Times*: "But the Rev. Thomas Rosica, a Vatican spokesman, said on Friday that the office of Archbishop Viganò had extended the invitation to Ms. Davis and that the Pope was probably not briefed about her case. And the Rev. Federico Lombardi, the chief Vatican spokesman, depicted the meeting as one meet-and-greet among many." This is the transparency of the Holy See under Pope Francis!

The next morning, at about 6:00 a.m. in Washington—I remember it well because I had just entered the chapel at the Nunciature—I received a frantic telephone call from Cardinal Parolin, who told me, "You must come immediately to Rome because the Pope is furious with you!" I left as soon as possible and was received by the Pope at the Domus Sanctae Marthae, around 7 o'clock in the evening on October 9, at the conclusion of one of the afternoon sessions of the Second Synod on the Family.

The Pope received me for almost an hour, and was very affectionate and paternal. He immediately apologized to me for troubling me with coming to Rome, and he lavished continuous praise on me for the way I had organized his visit to the USA, and for the incredible reception he received in America. He never expected such a welcome.

To my great surprise, during this long meeting, the Pope did not mention even once the audience with Davis!

As soon as my audience with the Pope was over, I immediately phoned Cardinal Parolin, and said to him,

"The Pope was so good with me. Not a word of reproach, only praise for the success of his visit to the USA." At which point Cardinal Parolin replied, "It's not possible, because with me he was furious about you."

This is a summary of the events.

As mentioned at the beginning, on August 28, 2018, the *New York Times* reported an interview with Juan Carlos Cruz, in which Cruz reported that during his meeting with the Pope, in April 2018, the Pope told him about the Davis case. According to Cruz, the Pope said: "I did not know who the woman was and he [Msgr. Viganò] snuck her in to say hello to me—and of course they made a whole publicity out of it. And I was horrified and I fired that Nuncio."

One of them is lying: either Cruz or the Pope? What is certain is that the Pope knew very well who Davis was, and he and his close collaborators had approved the private audience. Journalists can always check, by asking the prelates Becciu, Gallagher and Parolin, as well as the Pope himself.

It is clear, however, that Pope Francis wanted to conceal the private audience with the first American citizen condemned and imprisoned for conscientious objection.

+ Carlo Maria Viganò
Titular Archbishop di Ulpiana
Apostolic Nuncio
August 30, 2018
Feast of Saint Jeanne Jugan and Blessed Alfredo Ildefonso Schuster

\*\*\*

And here is the text of the memo Viganò prepared for
the pope and his advisors and gave to them on the evening of September 23, 2015.

9. Mrs. KIM DAVIS. As noted, the United States
Supreme Court recently decided that "marriage"
between persons of the same sex are a right by law, in
all of the States of the U.S.A, radically changing the
concept of marriage, as well as its very definition. Mrs.
Kim Davis, who was elected an Official of her County,
in Kentucky, has refused to sign marriage licenses for
same-sex couples, stating that her conscience does not
permit her to become a participant in this new way of
understanding marriage. Mrs. Davis, who belongs to
a charismatic Christian church, several years ago had
a personal conversion and wants to remain faithful to
her conscience, following "the Law of God rather than
the law of man." She has been careful not to impose her
religious beliefs on others, while they have sought to
impose on her these new "beliefs" about marriage. For
this she was unjustly arrested and put in prison. Hers
is the first case in which an American citizen has been
imprisoned for reasons of freedom of conscience and
religious liberty even though these rights are guaranteed
by the First Amendment of the Constitution of the
United States of America. Mrs. Davis is a humble person
who has not sought publicity for her case, but she has
become an exemplary witness to freedom of conscience
and religion for the entire country. News of the meeting

of Mrs. Davis with the Holy Father has remained secret until now.[16]

***

In January of 2016, Archbishop Viganò submitted his resignation, as he was turning seventy-five years old. On April 12, 2016, Pope Francis accepted Viganò's resignation and named Archbishop Christophe Pierre to succeed him as nuncio to the United States.

Viganò's long, forty-three-year career as a Vatican diplomat was over. He had given substantial charitable contributions to a convent in Burundi and a seminary in Nigeria and might have been expected to continue such charitable work. There was certainly no indication that he would suddenly explode on the Church scene as perhaps the single most insistent and controversial critic in the entire Church of high-level sexual abuse cover up and of the apparent betrayal of traditional Church teaching from the very top levels of the Vatican hierarchy.

---

[16]  The last line, "news of the meeting . . . has remained secret until now," means, it would seem, that Vigano has seen to it that the meeting with Kim Davis he has organized for the next day is not yet known publicly in any way; her name is not on other lists of people with whom the pope will meet; in other words, the preparations for the Kim Davis meeting were done outside of ordinary channels.

# PART II

# ELEVEN PAGES THAT SHOOK THE CHURCH ... AND THE WORLD

# CHAPTER 9

# A BRIEF SYNOPSIS

*"Let them be ashamed who are wantonly treacherous."*
—Psalm 25:3

On August 25, 2018, about two and a half years after Viganò resigned and went into retirement, he released his "Testimony," an eleven-page letter in which he claimed that many officials in the Vatican had received warnings over the years about the abusive behavior of then-Cardinal Theodore McCarrick.

In the key revelation in this text, Viganò claimed that he had conveyed this information directly to Pope Francis himself in a June 23, 2013, private conversation and that Francis had nevertheless taken no action to reign in or discipline McCarrick in any way.

According to Viganò's "Testimony," in the year 2000, Archbishop Gabriel Montalvo (nuncio to the United States from December 7, 1998 to December 17, 2005, and therefore Archbishop Sambi's immediate predecessor) had informed the Vatican of McCarrick's "gravely immoral behavior with seminarians and priests."

Subsequently, Viganò alleges, Sambi (nuncio from December 17, 2005 to July 27, 2011) informed the Vatican again of these problems before Viganò himself, working in the Vatican office overseeing all nunciatures, wrote his own memo regarding McCarrick in 2006.

Viganò says that in 2008, he wrote a second memo that included material from American clerical sexual abuse expert Richard Sipe.

Viganò says this led Pope Benedict XVI in 2009 or 2010 to place severe restrictions on McCarrick's movements and public ministry, not allowing him to venture beyond the seminary grounds where he was living and not permitting him to say Mass in public.

Nevertheless, according to Viganò, Pope Francis removed these sanctions and made McCarrick, Viganò alleges, "his trusted counselor." Even though Francis "knew from at least June 23, 2013 that McCarrick was a serial predator," Viganò sums up, though "he [Francis] knew that he [McCarrick] was a corrupt man, he covered for him to the bitter end."

In his "Testimony," Viganò called on Francis and all others who covered up McCarrick's conduct to resign. Viganò said, in paragraph 74, "In this extremely dramatic moment for the universal church, he [Pope Francis] must acknowledge his mistakes and, in keeping with the proclaimed principle of zero tolerance, Pope Francis must be the first to set a good example to cardinals and bishops who covered up McCarrick's abuses and resign along with all of them. . . . We must tear down the conspiracy of silence with which bishops and priests have protected themselves."

# CHAPTER 10

# VIGANÒ'S INTEGRITY

*"The LORD opens the eyes of the blind. The LORD lifts up those who are bowed down; the LORD loves the righteous."*
—Psalm 146:8

IN THE summer of 2011, Viganò had been "promoted" to the nunciature post, and he had reacted by appealing to Pope Benedict to keep him at his side in Rome to help him run the Vatican. In retrospect, one wonders if this was one of the decisions that later made it inevitable that Benedict would seek to resign. If Viganò had been retained in Rome, would Benedict have been more able to support the strains and pressures of the papacy and remain at his post? We do not know.

In any case, the letters Viganò wrote to Pope Benedict to appeal his "promotion" to the USA were copied from Pope Benedict's correspondence and published in the Italian press. In essence, Viganò warned Benedict that all of his many months of efforts to streamline and reform many aspects of the finances of the Vatican City State would be rendered useless if he were removed midstream and sent to America.

Benedict called Viganò to his side for a conversation. (Viganò told me about this meeting during our days of conversations.) The meeting took place on April 4,

2011. The sequence of events, according to Viganò, are as follows.

Viganò told me that Cardinal Tarcisio Bertone, the Secretary of State, summoned him to a meeting at the end of March 2011.

Viganò recalled, "Bertone told me, speaking in monosyllables, that I could no longer continue in my post at the Governorate, because, he said, I had 'created tensions.' Bertone supported in my presence the slanders published in *Il Giornale*—namely, that I had created tensions in the Vatican. I replied, 'It is evident that someone is not happy! Of course someone is not happy! Because if in the management of the Vatican Gardens alone I was able to save 800,000 euros, with which savings I was able to rebuild the entire heating system of the Vatican City State, it is clear that that sum of 800,000 euros would have ended up in someone else's pockets.'

"In reply, Bertone again mentioned, making it his own and supporting it, the slanderous criticism that appeared in *Il Giornale*, according to which I was not up to my task and that at most I would be able to be a parish priest. I then gave Bertone a draft of the preliminary balance sheet of the Vatican State in which it appeared that, from a previous deficit of 14 million euros, we would now be showing a 36 million euro *advance* (thanks to the work I did!). However, Bertone remained firm in his view that I could no longer continue at my post.

"Following this conversation, I wrote my first letter, later published by Vatileaks, addressed to Bertone, but which I sent to Pope Benedict, leaving him to decide what follow-up to give to my letter.

"Following this, Pope Benedict summoned me to an audience on April 4. He began our conversation by telling me, without referring to the letter, that he believed that the position in which I could render the best service to the Holy See was as President of the Prefecture for the Economic Affairs of the Holy See, in place of Cardinal Velasio de Paolis. The Prefecture was erected on August 15, 1967, to oversee all the offices of the Holy See that manage finances, regardless of their degree of autonomy. (*Nota bene*, that position offered to me by Benedict normally involved being made a cardinal.)

"I replied to the pope, thanking him for the esteem and trust he showed me, but I asked him to wait six months or a year, so as to allow me to complete my 'cleaning work' in the Governorate.

"I said to Benedict that I believed that my work at the Governorate could have significant impact and bring many positive results, and that I would like to be able to carry it out, making use of the collaboration of a team of people who believe with me that it is possible to end many corrupt practices that have developed in the Vatican over time. If I leave this position, my staff of collaborators will also be dispersed.

"Benedict replied by noting that recently, the powers of the Prefecture for Economic Affairs had been strengthened, going beyond the oversight of the budgets of the various Vatican departments, to include also the possibility of inspection.

"I replied, 'Perhaps it would be even better to postpone my appointment in the place of Cardinal De Paolis, also because of the new assignment you have entrusted to Cardinal De Paolis to oversee the reform of the Legionaries of Christ, a task he will have greater authority to carry out effectively if he remains as head of the Prefecture.'

"To which Benedict, closing the audience, reiterated that he remained convinced that the place where I could best serve the Holy See was as President of the Prefecture of Economic Affairs. He told me that he would reflect and pray, and that he would inform me of his decision.

"Later in 2011, the pope appointed a three-member commission of cardinals, chaired by Julian Herranz, with Burke and Lajolo, to investigate the situation in the Governorate. But Bertone intervened. He met with Herranz and convinced him not to follow up on the pope's instructions to institute this commission.

"The subsequent events are as follows: (1) Bertone convinced Herranz not to proceed with the task entrusted to him by the pope, telling him the investigation could be best carried out by the Disciplinary Commission of the Governorate already in existence; (2) Bertone unilaterally appointed a new Disciplinary Commission of the Governorate, something not within his competence, as it violated the constitutive rules of the Governorate. And Bertone had the indecency to say that this commission was to be used to settle a dispute with Nicolini. What dispute was there? I acted in my role as a superior in the Governorate, as was my duty. I would have been remiss in my duty had I not denounced this situation. That Disciplinary Commission was created on June 27, 2011, as Bertone informed me in a letter. It completed its work in just over two weeks, on July 16, 2011, delivering its decisions to Bertone on that date. The Disciplinary Commission created by Bertone took the decision that Monsignor Nicolini should be dismissed. But Bertone kept secret and swept under the table the decision of his own commission, and it was not executed. It was never even made known. All this in agreement with Lajolo, president of the Governorate. But even before the commission started its work, on July 1, Bertone informed me via letter that Pope Benedict had already 'reconfirmed' my appointment as Nuncio in the United States, a decision taken because Benedict had been duped, influenced, and put under pressure, or perhaps bypassed.

"A month later, on August 14, 2011, Pope Benedict wrote me the following letter, which has never before been published."

To my Venerable Brother
Carlo Maria Viganò
Titular Archbishop of Ulpiana
Secretary General of the Governorate
of the Vatican City State

I would like to thank you cordially for your recent letter, for your renewed sentiments of affection and fidelity and for the reflections that you wished to confide to me, written in a sincere spirit of faith, regarding your present situation and regarding your mission.

I understand the difficulties that you experience in regard to the attitude and behavior of a few of the leaders of the above-named Governorate, and I wish to assure you that you will be informed in a timely way regarding the result of the work of the Commission established for this purpose.

I would like, moreover, to communicate to you that I have reflected and prayed in regard to your condition after the most recent events. The sad news of the death of His Excellency Msgr. Pietro Sambi has confirmed me in the conviction that your providential position in this moment would be the Nunciature in the United States of America. On the other hand, I am certain that your knowledge of this great country will help you to take into your hands the difficult challenge of this work, that in many senses seems likely to play a decisive role for the future of the universal Church. My prayer and my encouragement will accompany you along your way.

While I entrust your dear person and your ecclesial service to the maternal protection of the Virgin Mary, who in these days we contemplate Assumed into Heaven in glory beside her Son Jesus, I send you from my heart my Apsotolic Blessing.

From Castel Gandolfo, 14 August 2011
+ Benedict XVI, Pontifex Maximus

Viganò concluded this lenghty narrative by noting, "Only with the events of recent years have I slowly come to understand something that I could not understand at the time: that my appointment to the United States would place me in a position to do important work that might be decisive for the universal Church."

Cardinal Bertone, it appears, had told Benedict that Viganò was causing "friction" in the Curia and among Vatican employees.

I am not in a position to judge whether such alleged "friction" was an invention or due to Viganò's crusading anti-corruption agenda, in which case it would be to his credit, not his blame. In any case, Benedict decided to send Viganò away.

Viganò left Rome in the fall of 2011. He was not to

return permanently to Italy until 2016. During those five years, Benedict resigned and Pope Francis was elected.

In the summer of 2011, at the annual open-air party at the residence of the American ambassador to the Holy See held on the Fourth of July, by coincidence, I met an old friend, an English-speaking woman. I had known her fifteen years earlier and had lost touch with her. I had thought she had left Rome. But as we talked, she told me that she had left, then returned to Rome and had been hired in a Vatican office connected with the upkeep of the Vatican Gardens and St. Peter's Basilica. "Ah!" I said. "So have you been following these controversies concerning Archbishop Viganò and his management of the Vatican City State."

"Yes," she said. "I have had occasion to work closely with Archbishop Viganò on several occasions."

"And how do you judge the man?" I asked. She was silent for a moment.

"Look," she said, "I don't know any other way to tell you this except to speak in superlatives. I have dealt with many Vatican officials, and truly of all of them, the most direct, forthright, honest, reliable, and trustworthy is Archbishop Viganò. He is a man of the utmost integrity. If he says something is true, you can be sure it is true."

She had no special reason to speak to me in those terms. So I took them as the honest evaluation of one non-biased person. I did not assume she knew everything about the archbishop's decisions, or his character, or his manner of dealing with colleagues and subordinates. I took it for what it was: one person's testimony. And I filed it away in my mind for future reference.

# CHAPTER 11

# THE CONTEXT IN WHICH THE "TESTIMONY" APPEARED

*"Be angry, but sin not."*

—Psalm 4:4

"As A priest and bishop of the holy Church, spouse of Christ, I am called like every baptized person to bear witness to the truth. By the gift of the Spirit who sustains me with joy on the path that I am called to travel, I intend to do so until the end of my days."[17]

In the summer of 2018, Italian archbishop Carlo Maria Viganò, then seventy-seven years old and two years into a well-deserved retirement after a lifetime of generally acknowledged exemplary service to the Vatican in its globe-spanning diplomatic service, released to a number of Catholic websites an eleven-page text he called his "Testimony." The text was dated August 22, 2018, the Feast of the Queenship of the Blessed Virgin Mary, but its first public appearance was August 25 of that year in the late afternoon.

Viganò's "Testimony" dealt principally with allegations of sexual abuse made against one of the most prominent cardinals in the Catholic Church, Theodore

---

[17] Archbishop Viganò in his "Testimony" of August 25, 2018.

"Uncle Ted" McCarrick, now ninety (he was born on July 7, 1930).

McCarrick had been archbishop of Washington, DC, the nation's capital, so he was clearly one of the most influential Catholics in America. The allegations that he had sexually molested many young men over many years had been whispered for decades but had only drawn widespread notice in June of 2018 when, for the first time, the Archdiocese of New York said it had concluded the allegations against McCarrick were "credible."

The McCarrick case exploded on June 20 of that year. The Archdiocese of New York had that day announced publicly that accusations of sexual abuse against a minor had been judged as "credible" and that McCarrick would lose his status as a cardinal. (Note: It has never been made clear why the accusations against McCarrick were finally judged "credible" in June of 2018, and never before. What was the dramatic change that suddenly made the allegations more "credible" in June of 2018 than ever before? This would be a good subject for further investigation.) A few weeks later, Rome removed McCarrick from the college of cardinals. Then, on August 10, 2018, the Pennsylvania state's attorney announced that a multi-year grand jury investigation had gathered allegations against three hundred priests of sexual abuse against more than one thousand minors.

This, it seemed, was particularly striking evidence of that "filth" which Pope Benedict XVI had denounced in the spring of 2005 just before he was elected pope on April 19. Speaking on Good Friday, at the open air Stations of the Cross held next to Rome's Colosseum,

Benedict reflected on the meaning of the three times Christ fell while carrying his cross on the first Good Friday. Then-Cardinal Joseph Ratzinger said:

> Recent history shows how a Christianity which has grown weary of faith has abandoned the Lord: the great ideologies, and the banal existence of those who no longer believing in anything, who simply drift through life, have built a new and worse paganism, which in its attempt to do away with God once and for all, have ended up doing away with man. Christ's third fall reminds us of the fall of man in general, and the falling of many Christians away from Christ and into a godless secularism. Should we not also think of how much Christ suffers in his own Church? How often is the holy sacrament of his Presence abused, how often must he enter empty and evil hearts! How often do we celebrate only ourselves, without even realizing that he is there! How often is his Word twisted and misused! What little faith is present behind so many theories, so many empty words! How much filth there is in the Church, and even among those who, in the priesthood, ought to belong entirely to him!

A lack of hierarchical discipline, a willingness to overlook sexual passions directed toward innocent young people, the vast majority of them post-pubescent males, a culture of "cover-up" in order not to harm the "image" of the Church had all combined to make the Church appear "filthy."

So, in America, an outraged public opinion, in and out of the Catholic Church, cried out for some sort of explanation: How could this have happened? How could a man have risen to the pinnacle of power in the Catholic

Church, in America and in Rome, despite decades of sexual molestation and abuse against young men? Who had known about his activity, and when had they known it, and why had no one taken any sort of disciplinary action against him earlier? And had this same type of laxity in confronting the perpetrators of sexual abuse played a role in the hundreds of cases in Pennsylvania? In short, was anyone in the Catholic Church actively and effectively seeking to prevent the epidemic of sexual abuse of young people by Catholic priests, bishops, and in the case of McCarrick, a cardinal?

This was the context in which Viganò's "Testimony" appeared. Many Catholics were relieved to read what he said: finally, many thought, someone has "pulled back the curtain" and explained to us in a simple way that we can understand what has gone wrong with our Church— that there has been a well-connected "old boys' network" in the hierarchy that has covered up abuse, and tolerated abusers, for decades.

Viganò spoke at the end of August 2018. He put together all of what he had been carrying in his heart for many months, many years, and he drafted his "Testimony." He went to two Italian journalists, Aldo Maria Valli and Marco Tosatti, showed them the draft text he had prepared, and received suggestions. Viganò then sent the text out to several press agencies: to John-Henry Westen and Diane Montagna at *LifeSiteNews*, to Edward Pentin at the *National Catholic Register*, to Prof. Roberto de Mattei at *Corrispondenza Romana*, and, last of all, also to me.

In his "Testimony," Archbishop Viganò did something

quite extraordinary, without precedent: as a lifelong servant of the Holy See, sworn to obedience to the head of the Church, the pope, he not only denounced leading bishops, cardinals, and Vatican officials, but he went further; he denounced Pope Francis as in some way negligent in regard to Cardinal McCarrick, based on his own personal conversations with the pope, and Viganò called upon Francis to resign. Viganò writes, "Bob, if you remember, a short time before, Bergoglio had invited the Chilean bishops to resign for having been involved in cover-ups of abuse. I therefore took the pope at his word, asking him to be consistent and to set a good example. Do you understand? Often this statement of mine has been interpreted as a reckless and brazen act. Not at all. Having clearly covered for McCarrick, it was only right that he first did what he asked the Chilean bishops to do."

Viganò's "Testimony" exploded onto the landscape of the Catholic Church with the effect of a neutron bomb, casting aspersions on the characters of many Church prelates while affirming that what he wished was a reform of the Church that would finally, efficiently and effectively, protect young people from abuse by priests. Viganò wanted the Church to remain standing; he wanted many of the personnel running the Church to change. It was in this sense that his "Testimony" was like a neutron bomb, which irradiates and destroys people but does not destroy cities.

By attacking the reputations of dozens of high-ranking Catholic prelates as accessories to what Viganò alleged was a widespread cover-up of clerical sexual abuse which extended all the way to the desk of Pope Francis himself, Viganò left a "scorched earth" for himself inside the Vatican—dozens of officials who felt he had linked them to McCarrick, or to abuse cover-ups, or to sexual abuse of young people, without prior warning, without accompanying evidence. The entire higher leadership of the Church wondered if Viganò might issue new accusations, allege new crimes, because the entire leadership had been close collaborators in running the Church. Only Viganò had spoken out in such a public way, naming names. Maybe he would name still more names, Vatican prelates thought—as they told me.

And for this reason, alleging that Pope Francis knew of McCarrick's behavior but did nothing to punish him or restrict his activities, Viganò ended his "Testimony" with an unprecedented call for Pope Francis to resign his office for the equivalent of dereliction of duty and allow another man to take his place as pope.

In this one step, Viganò placed himself at the center of a series of theological, canonical, doctrinal, political, economic, cultural, and, one might argue, supernatural forces seeking to defend or to destroy the Roman Catholic Church.

CHAPTER 12

# THE COMPLETE TEXT WITH COMMENTARY AND ANALYSIS

*"We must have the courage to tear down the culture of secrecy and publicly confess the truths we have kept hidden."*
—Archbisop Viganò, "Testimony," August 22, 2018

WHEN VIGANÒ'S "Testimony" was released on the evening of August 25, 2018, *New York Times* religion reporter Ross Douthat tweeted: "This document is quite possibly a truly historic bombshell in the life of the Roman Catholic Church." He continued:

> Written by the former papal nuncio to the U.S., it does exactly what many have called for, and offers testimony concerning who in the hierarchy knew what, and when, about the crimes of Cardinal McCarrick. The testimony implicates a host of high-ranking churchmen. And the pope. In fact, both popes. But Benedict appears as a figure (weakly, insufficiently) attempting to act on testimony concerning McCarrick's crimes, while Francis is portrayed as intent on restoring the pederast cardinal to activity and influence despite his awareness of those crimes. This is either an extraordinary and vicious slander or an act of revelation that should be the undoing of just about every figure mentioned in its pages. It has an apocalyptic feel either way.

The "Testimony," with its "apocalyptic feel," was immediately a profoundly controversial document, read in very different ways by readers with differing backgrounds and agendas. For this reason, a careful reading of the text seems essential for any sensible evaluation of its contents and importance. Below is a commentary on the "Testimony" paragraph by paragraph via comments between each of the document's eighty paragraphs.

In a preliminary way, I have made a list of all of the persons named in this eleven-page text, counting sixty-six of them. The "Testimony" unfolds in seven major parts or movements: **1) The McCarrick Case:** the background of the McCarrick case, from paragraph 1 to paragraph 19. **2) The Roman Curia:** the various positions of leaders of the Roman Curia, from paragraph 20 to 31. **3) To the USA**: the various prelates in the USA who played some role in these events, from paragraph 32 to 39. **4) Pope Francis:** the section where Viganò tells of his conversations with Pope Francis, from paragraph 40 to 46. **5) Back to the USA:** where Viganò speaks of events in the United States after he spoke with Pope Francis, including episcopal appointments, from paragraph 47 to 59. **6) Latin America:** where Viganò speaks about cases of sexual abuse or corruption in Honduras, Venezuela, and Chile, from paragraph 60 through 65. **7) Summary:** where he concludes his "Testimony" with prayers, paragraph 68 to 80.

Viganò put down his version of events, providing for us all in the process a framework to orient ourselves in this mysterious, opaque world of the Roman Curia. The conclusion I draw from reading the "Testimony" is that it might provide a good start for some sort of objective commission of investigation to go down every "rabbit hole" in the text and determine if there may be, in the end, a rabbit hiding in the hole, or nothing at all.

In other words, this "Testimony" is a cry of alarm from someone who lived for decades in an environment which he came to conclude was not very serious about a "one strike and you're out" attitude toward sexual molestation of young people, most often young men, by prelates of varying degrees of importance in the hierarchy.

Viganò offers four proposals in this text. His first proposal is in **paragraph 37,** where he says, "**Bishop Paul Bootkoski**, emeritus of Metuchen, and **Archbishop John Myers**, emeritus of Newark, covered up the abuses committed by McCarrick in their respective dioceses and compensated two of his victims. They cannot deny it and they must be interrogated in order to reveal every circumstance and all responsibility regarding this matter." So he is asking for the interrogation of two bishops connected to McCarrick.

His second proposal is given in **paragraph 58:** "Pope Francis has repeatedly asked for total transparency in the Church and for bishops and faithful to act with *parrhesia.* The faithful throughout the world also demand this of him in an exemplary manner. He must honestly state when he first learned about the crimes committed by McCarrick, who abused his authority with seminarians and priests." So Viganò's second proposal is that Pope Francis state "when he first learned about the crimes committed by McCarrick."

His third proposal is in **paragraph 68:** "A time of

conversion and penance must be proclaimed. The virtue of chastity must be recovered in the clergy and in
seminaries. Corruption in the misuse of the Church's
resources and of the offerings of the faithful must be
fought against. The seriousness of homosexual behavior
must be denounced. The homosexual networks present
in the Church must be eradicated." This final phrase was
Viganò's declaration of war and is what caused Viganò
to be attacked so strongly as a wild, unreliable man. He
had called for the removal of what are evidently some of
the most influential networks in the Church. For that,
he was *persona non grata* wherever those networks are
entrenched, networks which will fight any effort to lessen
or eliminate their presence and their influence over the
Church.

His fourth proposal concerns Pope Francis and a
number of other cardinals and bishops. It comes toward
the end of the "Testimony" in **paragraph 74**: "In this
extremely dramatic moment for the universal Church,
he must acknowledge his mistakes and, in keeping with
the proclaimed principle of zero tolerance, **Pope Francis must be the first to set a good example for cardinals
and bishops who covered up McCarrick's abuses and
resign along with all of them**."

This phrase "along with all of them" came to characterize in some way this testimony. One cardinal told me
privately, "Viganò is right about many things, but the
way he went about it frightened us all. It was as if he had
picked up a machine gun and was spraying bullets right
and left. None of us knew whether we might be the next
to be brought into his sights and fired upon."

Here below is the text, annotated throughout, which struck fear into the hearts of almost every member of the Roman Curia. For this reason alone, it is an historic document and worth our attention.

The "Testimony" is almost like a script for a film. The cast of characters includes sixty-six people named by Viganò, and he tells us that he composed or read a half dozen documents which could be used to prove or disprove the truthfulness of his "Testimony." All of the underlining, italicizing, and bold-facing in the text are in Viganò's original text.

***

## Testimony

*by His Excellency Carlo Maria Viganò,*
*Titular Archbishop of Ulpiana and Apostolic Nuncio*
August 22, 2018

**Paragraph 1.** In this tragic moment for the Church in various parts of the world—the United States, Chile, Honduras, Australia, *etc.*—bishops have a very grave responsibility. I am thinking in particular of the United States of America, where I was sent as Apostolic Nuncio by Pope Benedict XVI on October 19, 2011, the memorial feast of the First North American Martyrs. The Bishops of the United States are called, and I with them, to follow the example of these first martyrs who brought the Gospel to the lands of America, to be credible witnesses of the immeasurable love of Christ, the Way, the Truth and the Life.

In this first paragraph of his "Testimony," Viganò begins by speaking sternly of this "tragic moment" for the Church globally, and of the "very grave" responsibility of the Church's bishops throughout the world. Why is the moment "tragic"? We do not immediately know, but we assume it has to do with the Church's sexual abuse crisis. This will turn out to be the case in the first sentence of the second paragraph. Viganò immediately tells us that his concern is focused on the United States of America, where he was the papal nuncio for almost five years, more than in any other country. Viganò mentions the date of October 19, Feast of the First North American Martyrs, the date he was sent to America. We understand that this date and this feast are important for the archbishop. He then mentions two names: (1) **Pope Benedict XVI**, because it was Benedict who "sent" Viganò to America in 2011, and (2) **Christ**, because the American bishops are called, as he himself is, to be "credible witnesses" to Christ's "immeasurable love." This first paragraph thus begins with a note of concern and sadness for the tragedy of sexual abuse and ends on a "Christo-centric" note: Christ is the way, the truth, and the life for all people.

> **Paragraph 2.** Bishops and priests, abusing their authority, have committed horrendous crimes to the detriment of their faithful, minors, innocent victims, and young men eager to offer their lives to the Church, or by their silence have not prevented that such crimes continue to be perpetrated.

Viganò, in this second paragraph, makes his purpose very clear: it is the reality of "horrendous crimes" that Viganò wishes to confront, and it is "silence" that has been the reason these crimes have not been prevented. We understand that Viganò will be breaking with this pattern of "silence" in order to "prevent" more of these "horrendous crimes." We sense already that he is going to "speak out" himself in order to no longer participate in this culture of "silence," which is, *de facto*, a culture of "cover-up." So we understand already that Viganò intends to "break ranks" with his brother bishops, and we sense that he may have to pay a high price for doing so because only by a widespread consensus to not "rock the boat" could such a situation have emerged. Therefore, Viganò will be taking on a large number of members of the hierarchy, not just one or two, because the problem is not limited to one or two abusers but rather concerns a general culture of cover-up. And he will make this point very clearly in the next paragraph.

**Paragraph 3.** To restore the beauty of holiness to the face of the Bride of Christ, which is terribly disfigured by so many abominable crimes, and if we truly want to free the Church from the fetid swamp into which she has fallen, we must have the courage to tear down the culture of secrecy and publicly confess the truths we have kept hidden. We must tear down the conspiracy of silence with which bishops and priests have protected themselves at the expense of their faithful, a conspiracy of silence that in the eyes of the world risks making the Church look like a sect, a conspiracy of silence not so dissimilar from the one that prevails in the mafia. "Whatever you have said in the dark... shall be proclaimed from the housetops" (Lk. 12:3).

In this third paragraph, Viganò pulls no punches, raising his standard and declaring his purpose without any equivocation: he intends to help launch a process that will "tear down the culture of secrecy" in the Church. He calls on the Church to "publicly confess the truths we have kept hidden." He calls again for the Church to "tear down the conspiracy of silence," a conspiracy of silence that "risks making the Church look like a sect," a conspiracy of silence not unlike "the one that prevails in the mafia." Yet it is interesting that each time he speaks of "we" as the ones who have been silent, who have kept truths hidden. In a certain sense, he is including himself as part of this problem. We understand that he wishes to break with the "old boy network" which caused the face of the Bride of Christ to be "terribly disfigured by so many abominable crimes." In an act of humility, it is also, in a sense, a sign of his own repentance for any participation he may have had in this culture of cover-up.

> **Paragraph 4.** I had always believed and hoped that the hierarchy of the Church could find within itself the spiritual resources and strength to tell the whole truth, to amend and to renew itself. That is why, even though I had repeatedly been asked to do so, I always avoided making statements to the media, even when it would have been my right to do so, in order to defend myself against the calumnies published about me, even by high-ranking prelates of the Roman Curia. But now that the corruption has reached the very top of the Church's hierarchy, my conscience dictates that I reveal those truths regarding the heart-breaking case of the Archbishop Emeritus of Washington, D.C., Theodore McCarrick, which I came to know in the course of the

duties entrusted to me by St. John Paul II, as Delegate for Pontifical Representations, from 1998 to 2009, and by Pope Benedict XVI, as Apostolic Nuncio to the United States of America, from October 19, 2011 until end of May 2016.

In this fourth paragraph, Viganò mentions two new names, the third and fourth names in the "Testimony": (3) **Cardinal Theodore McCarrick** and (4) **St. Pope John Paul II**, while mentioning Pope Benendict for a second time. This paragraph focuses on two issues: (1) the reason why Viganò has not spoken out earlier—"I had always believed and hoped that the hierarchy of the Church could find within itself the spiritual resources and strength to tell the whole truth, to amend and to renew itself"—and (2) the assertion that he had acquired personal knowledge of the facts of the McCarrick case during many years as a high-ranking official in the Vatican. So we know now that Viganò is going to focus on the McCarrick case, and we assume we will learn the things that Viganò learned over many years but never spoke of publicly before. So this is Viganò's "truth-telling" moment. But already we may begin to have in the back of our minds the question: Why, really, is it necessary for things to come to this sort of "truth-telling" moment? Why is this information not being released by a Vatican commission under the authority of the pope himself, in keeping with ordinary procedure and practice? And already we may begin to weigh the beginnings of an answer between two possibilities: (1) Viganò has some personal ax to grind and so he is dispensing with all ordinary procedures or (2) for some reason, the ordinary processes have proven not to work, they have led to a dead end, they have been "short-circuited," making it impossible for the truth to come out. We do not yet see a clear answer to the important question: what was so deficient in the Vatican's institutional structure that the truth about McCarrick could not be made public for several decades, while young men continued to be abused? Viganò will give his own answer to that question in the course of the rest of his "Testimony."

> **Paragraph 5.** As Delegate for Pontifical Representations in the Secretariat of State, my responsibilities were not limited to the Apostolic Nunciatures, but also included the staff of the Roman Curia (hires, promotions, informational processes on candidates to the episcopate, *etc.*) and the examination of delicate cases, including those regarding cardinals and bishops, that were entrusted to the Delegate by the Cardinal Secretary of State or by the Substitute ("Deputy")[18] of the Secretariat of State.

Viganò, in this paragraph 5, gives his credentials for being taken seriously. He says he was precisely the man whose

---

18 Note: As Vaticanist Andrea Gagliarducci writes, "The position of the '*Sostituto*' is important for the functioning of the Secretariat of State and the entire Roman Curia. According to *Pastor bonus*, the apostolic constitution that defines the tasks and competencies of Curial offices, the '*sostituto*' is at the helm of the first section of the Secretariat of State, the section on 'general affairs.' In practice, the '*sostituto*' works as a coordinator, and as a link between the Pope and the Secretary of State, becoming in many cases the person closest to the Pope." https://www.catholic-newsagency.com/news/waiting-for-a-new-deputy-at-the-vatican-secretariat-of-state-71569.

job it was in the Vatican to have a general oversight over all the Vatican's diplomats throughout the world, and a particular oversight over "delicate cases, regarding cardinals and bishops" throughout the world. In other words, he read all the dossiers and summarized their contents for his superiors, who were "the Cardinal Secretary of State or the Substitute of the Secretariat of State." That is, he was "in the know." He knew the dossiers.

> **Paragraph 6.** To dispel suspicions insinuated in several recent articles, I will immediately say that the Apostolic Nuncios in the United States, Gabriel Montalvo and Pietro Sambi, both prematurely deceased, did not fail to inform the Holy See immediately, as soon as they learned of Archbishop McCarrick's gravely immoral behavior with seminarians and priests. Indeed, according to what Nuncio Pietro Sambi wrote, Father Boniface Ramsey, O.P.'s letter, dated November 22, 2000, was written at the request of the late Nuncio Montalvo. In the letter, Father Ramsey, who had been a professor at the diocesan seminary in Newark from the end of the '80s until 1996, affirms that there was a recurring rumor in the seminary that the Archbishop "shared his bed with seminarians," inviting five at a time to spend the weekend with him at his beach house. And he added that he knew a certain number of seminarians, some of whom were later ordained priests for the Archdiocese of Newark, who had been invited to this beach house and had shared a bed with the Archbishop.

In this sixth paragraph, we are getting quickly into the details of the McCarrick case—from Viganò's perspective. He names three new names, the fifth, sixth, and seventh names in the "Testimony": (5) **Archbishop**

**Gabriel Montalvo**, nuncio to the United States from 1998 to 2005, (6) **Archbishop Pietro Sambi,** nuncio to the United States from 2005 until his death in 2011, and (7) **Father Boniface Ramsey, O.P.**, a professor in the diocesan seminary of Newark, New Jersey, from the late 1980s until 1996, who is said to have written a letter at the end of the year 2000, on November 22, expressing his concern over the "rumor" that the archbishop "shared his bed with seminarians" at his beach house.[19]

This is the first actual document that Viganò refers to: the "**Father Ramsey letter**" of November 22, 2000. So we may name this "**Document 1**" (without for the moment assessing whether the document actually exists or not). Viganò tells us that this letter was written "at the request of the late Nuncio Montalvo." We conclude that Father Ramsey had in some way communicated to Nuncio Montalvo his concern about McCarrick's behavior, evidently not in writing, perhaps in a conversation, and that Montalvo had decided to seek to document the report by inviting Father Ramsey to put it all in writing, in a letter.

Viganò affirms that it was Nuncio Sambi who reported that this letter was requested of Ramsey by Montalvo: "Indeed, according to what Nuncio Pietro Sambi wrote, Father Boniface Ramsey, O.P.'s letter, dated November 22, 2000, was written at the request of the late Nuncio Montalvo." So this indicates the existence of a second document, which we may call "**Document 2: the Nuncio**

---

19  See Ramsey in this video: https://www.youtube.com/watch?v =y8MRimOkagY.

**Sambi Letter about the Father Ramsey Letter**." Viganò had evidently read this letter personally—or at least he leads us to believe that he had read this letter—because he quotes from it, putting one phrase inside of quotation marks, saying that Father Ramsey "affirms that there was a recurring rumor in the seminary that the Archbishop 'shared his bed with seminarians.'"

We would ordinarily conclude that there exists a letter in the nunciature in Washington, DC, signed by Father Ramsey which contains this quoted phrase and a second letter signed by Nuncio Sambi describing how this letter of Ramsey came to be written at the request of Montalvo. However, we are still at this point on the level of an unproven allegation. Even should the Ramsey letter exist, and be published, it is still not firsthand evidence of misconduct on the part of McCarrick. It is evidence that there was a rumor about that conduct—and one would think that this would certainly have been a matter of concern to Vatican officials. But it is not evidence about that conduct itself from an eyewitness—from someone seduced or abused by McCarrick.

> **Paragraph 7.** The office that I held at the time was not informed of any measure taken by the Holy See after those charges were brought by Nuncio Montalvo at the end of 2000, when Cardinal Angelo Sodano was Secretary of State.

In this seventh paragraph, Viganò tells us that he himself was kept in the dark about any Vatican decision with regard to the "rumors" about McCarrick's conduct. Here we can only wonder: was any further investigation ordered? Were any seminarians invited to give their own testimony about their relations with McCarrick? Was McCarrick ever called in to be questioned about these "rumors"? We do not know and Viganò does not know. But we are about to get another piece of seemingly damning evidence.

**Paragraph 8.** Likewise, Nuncio Sambi transmitted to the Cardinal Secretary of State, Tarcisio Bertone, an Indictment Memorandum against McCarrick by the priest Gregory Littleton of the diocese of Charlotte, who was reduced to the lay state for a violation of minors, together with two documents from the same Littleton, in which he recounted his tragic story of sexual abuse by the then-Archbishop of Newark and several other priests and seminarians. The Nuncio added that Littleton had already forwarded his Memorandum to about twenty people, including civil and ecclesiastical judicial authorities, police and lawyers, in June 2006, and that it was therefore very likely that the news would soon be made public. He therefore called for a prompt intervention by the Holy See.

In this eighth paragraph, Viganò brings in the names of an eighth and a ninth person: (8) **Cardinal Tarcisio Bertone**, the Vatican Secretary of State from one year into Pope Benedict's pontificate (June 22, 2006) until the end of Pope Benedict's pontificate seven years later, and (9) **Gregory Littleton**, a priest of the diocese of Charlotte, North Carolina, who was, Viganò tells us, "reduced to the lay state for a violation of minors."[20] Viganò tells us

---

[20] Reliable sources in North Carolina inform us that Littleton has been stripped of his priestly faculties but not, in fact, reduced to the lay state. Ed.

that Nuncio Sambi sent to Bertone three documents, which we may number **Documents 3**, **4**, and **5**. These documents were evidently forwarded to Rome shortly after June 2006 because Viganò says that Sambi notes that Littleton "had already forwarded his Memorandum to about twenty people, including civil and ecclesiastical judicial authorities, police and lawyers, in June 2006." So Sambi, writing sometime after June 2006, tells Rome that it was "very likely that the news would soon be made public."

**Document 3** is "an Indictment Memorandum against McCarrick" signed by Littleton (so Littleton, in this document, is accusing McCarrick of sexually abusing him); **Documents 4** and **5** are two documents attached to Littleton's indictment which recount "his [Littleton's] tragic story of sexual abuse by the then-Archbishop of Newark and several other priests and seminarians."

Clearly by this paragraph of the "Testimony," we are sensing the "ripple effect" of the McCarrick case—whatever the truth of the allegations against him. The case seems to be involving more and more people. We are beginning to get a sense of how the sexual abuse crisis was truly a moral cancer in the Church, spreading and metastisizing from abuser to abuser, victim to victim.

The Horowitz Law firm of Fort Lauderdale, Florida, on February 26, 2019 posted information about Littleton stating that he had "shared information about almost 20 other victims of Archbishop McCarrick and himself."

The *Catholic News Herald* of Charlotte, North Carolina, reported on August 28, 2018, that "Littleton's story . . . began in 1987 when Archbishop McCarrick, then head of the Archdiocese of Newark, N.J., allegedly abused an unnamed Metuchen seminarian while in New York City. In 1994, Littleton wrote an account of abuse at the hands of Archbishop McCarrick and claimed that it led to his inappropriate touching of two boys."

So, eight paragraphs into his "Testimony," Viganò is telling us the Vatican was being informed, by word of mouth (rumor) and then by written documents, about a widening web of sexual abuse cases, allegedly connected to McCarrick, from the late 1990s into the early 2000s. And yet no action of any type was taken against McCarrick.

> **Paragraph 9.** In writing up a memo on these documents that were entrusted to me, as Delegate for Pontifical Representations, on December 6, 2006, I wrote to my superiors, Cardinal Tarcisio Bertone and the Substitute Leonardo Sandri, that the facts attributed to McCarrick by Littleton were of such gravity and vileness as to provoke bewilderment, a sense of disgust, deep sorrow and bitterness in the reader, and that they constituted the crimes of seducing, requesting depraved acts of seminarians and priests, repeatedly and simultaneously with several people, derision of a young seminarian who tried to resist the Archbishop's seductions in the presence of two other priests, absolution of the accomplices in these depraved acts, sacrilegious celebration of the Eucharist with the same priests after committing such acts.

In paragraph 9, we have *the first action* on the part of Viganò alluded to in the "Testimony": he writes a memo on December 6, 2006. This would be **Document 6,** and it ought to exist in the Vatican archives. We also are introduced to a **tenth** person, "the Substitute **Leonardo Sandri**," now a cardinal in the Roman Curia. In my conversations with him, Viganò would tell me that he and Sandri became "good friends" during their years of working together in the Curia. Viganò reveals here that he felt "the facts attributed to McCarrick by Littleton were of such gravity and vileness as to provoke bewilderment, a sense of disgust, deep sorrow and bitterness." So Viganò was taking Littleton's allegations quite seriously. And in the next paragraph, Viganò claims that he asked *already in 2006* that disciplinary action be taken against McCarrick.

> **Paragraph 10.** In my memo, which I delivered on that same December 6, 2006 to my direct superior, the Substitute Leonardo Sandri, I proposed the following considerations and course of action to my superiors:
> - Given that it seemed a new scandal of particular gravity, as it regarded a cardinal, was going to be added to the many scandals for the Church in the United States,
> - and that, since this matter had to do with a cardinal, and according to can. 1405 § 1, No. 2, "*ipsius Romani Pontificis dumtaxat ius est iudicandi*" ["it is solely the right of the Roman pontiff himself to judge"];
> - I proposed that an exemplary measure be taken against the Cardinal that could have a medicinal function, to prevent future abuses against innocent victims and alleviate the very serious scandal for the faithful, who despite everything continued to love and believe in the Church.

Viganò gives us in paragraph 10 the synthesis of a memo, Document 6, that he says he wrote on the McCarrick case, based on the Littleton allegations, on December 6, 2006, just about one and a half years into the pontificate of Pope Benedict. Note that there seems still in 2006 to be *no clear procedure already laid out by the Holy See for dealing with such allegations.* Viganò is, as it were, "on his own," seemingly without the aid of a "road map," a set procedure which he can appeal to. His memo is, in this sense, "*ad hoc.*" He proposes that "an exemplary measure" be taken "against the Cardinal," but he does not tell us what this measure might be. He says this measure would have "a medicinal function" and would "prevent future abuses against innocent victims." Would it be that McCarrick retire to a life of isolation and prayer? We do not know. Viganò is suggesting that the measure will "prevent future abuses," and a retirement in isolation would seem to be one way to accomplish that. But there seems no direct suggestion here of any sort of canonical trial and no hint that McCarrick might need to be removed from the College of Cardinals, much less be laicized, which is eventually what happened to McCarrick after the case became public in the summer of 2018. So Viganò's 2006 "memo," if it were to be produced, could perhaps be viewed in two ways. One way of looking at it would seemingly not show a tough, uncompromising Viganò but rather a Viganò who is doing the best he can to work within a system which, if the truth be told, still implicitly embraces the path of "cover up" and "handle discreetly." The other, however, would hold that Viganò was a diplomat, and "reading between the lines" of the memo, one would see there a diplomat calling for vigorous action in admittedly non-specific terms. It is true that the nature of the punishment, if any, was not ultimately up to Viganò in any case.

> **Paragraph 11.** I added that it would be salutary if, for once, ecclesiastical authority would intervene before the civil authorities and, if possible, before the scandal had broken out in the press. This could have restored some dignity to a Church so sorely tried and humiliated by so many abominable acts on the part of some pastors. If this were done, the civil authority would no longer have to judge a cardinal, but a pastor with whom the Church had already taken appropriate measures to prevent the cardinal from abusing his authority and continuing to destroy innocent victims.

In this paragraph 11, Viganò gives us further insight into his 2006 memo on the McCarrick case. Again, perhaps one can read this paragraph and the referenced memo in two possible ways. One way of reading would hold that what is striking is that Viganò again here is writing still from within the context of protecting the Church from the harm of scandal rather than from the context of immediately acting to protect sexual abuse victims and to punish their abusers. Viganò does say this is his goal. He wishes the Church in this case will act quickly, before the secular authorities become involved. Yes, this action will have the effect of making further abuse impossible, but the reason to act now is to "intervene . . . before the scandal had broken out in the press," which would "restore some dignity" to the Church. The protection of the Church's image seems to compete neck and neck with the desire to protect potential abuse victims as the motivation for action in this case. This seems to suggest that Viganò was still very much a "team player" within the hierarchical structure of the Church—something that he will no longer be after the publication of this "Testimony" twelve years later.

An alternative reading would see his text as implying the application of severe sanctions. And rather than seeing him as advocating a cover-up as in a "get out ahead of civil authorities for damage control" purposes, this view would see Viganò claiming that the Church should deal harshly with McCarrick and then let the civil authorities do what they will. He is not trying to avoid having the scandal break out in the press; rather, he is saying something akin to "Don't wait for that; we have the facts. Do the right thing for once and deal with this man. At least then, when it does break out in the press, the Church will have done the right thing." He told me during our conversations that this latter reading exactly corresponds to his intent.

> **Paragraph 12.** All the memos, letters and other documentation mentioned here are available at the Secretariat of State of the Holy See or at the Apostolic Nunciature in Washington, D.C. My memo of December 6, 2006 was kept by my superiors, and was never returned to me with any actual decision by the superiors on this matter.

In paragraph 12, Viganò stresses one key point: that the evidence he is presenting may be seen and evaluated both in Rome in the Secretariat of State and in Washington in the Holy See's nunciature to the United States. Is this true? Viganò would tell me in our conversations that he almost managed to obtain a copy of one or more of these documents from the nunciature but that an official there got frightened and did not copy the document and send it to Viganò. From Rome, the Vatican has been promising a "full report" on the McCarrick case ever since Viganò's "Testimony" was released in August of 2018. Cardinal Pietro Parolin told me personally in a meeting in August 2019 in his offices in the Apostolic Palace that the report on the McCarrick case would appear "soon," leading me to believe it would be in the period September-November 2019. It has not yet appeared as of the time this book is going to press in the late summer of 2020. Here is the point: Viganò claims the memos and letters he is referring to exist and that they say what he says they say; he does not seem to fear he will be contradicted or proven wrong. Of course, it is hard to prove a negative. The Vatican could say that these letters and memos are not found in their archives, but that would not prove that they never existed; they could have been misfiled or somehow lost or destroyed. But the fact that the Vatican has never stated categorically that such memos and letters do not exist, that Viganò invented this entire story, suggests that they do exist, as Viganò claims they do.

> **Paragraph 13.** Subsequently, around April 21–23, 2008, the *Statement for Pope Benedict XVI about the pattern of sexual abuse crisis in the United States*, by Richard Sipe, was published on the internet, at richardsipe.com. On April 24, it was passed on by the Prefect of the Congregation for the Doctrine of the Faith, Cardinal William Levada,

to the Cardinal Secretary of State Tarcisio Bertone. It was delivered to me one month later, on May 24, 2008.

In paragraph 13, Viganò brings in two new names, (11) **Richard Sipe** and (12) **Cardinal William Levada**, and a text published by Sipe on the internet in April 2008, seen by Cardinal Levada, then sent by Levada to the secretary of state, Tarcisio Bertone. Viganò concludes by saying this "Sipe Statement" came to his own desk (evidently for inclusion in a "McCarrick Dossier") on May 24, 2008. This "Sipe Statement" we may number **Document 7** in Viganò's "Testimony," dating to April or May 2008. If Viganò is telling the truth, this document ought to be in the Vatican archives. If it is, this would also mean that the Vatican leadership knew of the allegations contained in Sipe's writing already in 2008. For this reason, it seems important to spend a moment to understand more about Sipe.

Who was Richard Sipe, and what was his "Statement"? Sipe's full name was Aquinas Walter Richard Sipe. He was born in the state of Minnesota on December 11, 1932 and died on August 8, 2018 at the age of eighty-five—just after Cardinal McCarrick's history of abuse was made public and just before Viganò released his "Testimony." Sipe was an American Benedictine monk for eighteen years, from 1952–1970, at St. John's Abbey, Collegeville, Minnesota, and he was ordained a priest in 1959. He left the priesthood in 1970 and married a woman he had fallen in love with, a former nun, Dr. Marianne Benkert Sipe. They had one son. Sipe became a psychotherapist and the author of six books about Catholicism, clerical sexual abuse in the Catholic Church, and clerical celibacy. "During Sipe's lifetime, critics dismissed his findings as the projections of a bitter man, alienated from his faith and former colleagues," Peter Rowe, journalist for the *San Diego Union-Tribune*, wrote on January 2, 2019. His widow told Rowe, "Richard got pounded. He was called an angry, discredited ex-priest who just wants to destroy the church." Rowe added, "No longer. Throughout 2018, especially after his death August 8 at the age of 85, he's been cited by clerics and laity, liberals and conservatives." Thus, it seems fair to say that, despite his critics, Sipe was generally regarded as one of the world's leading experts in the problem of clerical sexual abuse. This explains why Cardinal Levada thought it fitting to forward his "open letter" to Pope Benedict via Cardinal Bertone. Here is an edited version of Sipe's "Statement," focusing on what he says about McCarrick.

### *Statement for Pope Benedict XVI About the Pattern of the Sexual Abuse Crisis In the United States*

By Richard Sipe, April 2008

Your Holiness, I, Richard Sipe, approach you reluctantly to speak about the problem of sexual abuse by priests and bishops in the United States, but I am encouraged and prompted by the directive of Vatican II, *Lumen Gentium*, Chapter IV, No. 37. "By reason of knowledge, competence . . . the laity are empowered—indeed sometimes obliged—to manifest their opinion on those things that pertain to the good of the Church." And also moved by your heartfelt demonstration of concern for victims on your recent visit to the United States I bring to your attention a dimension of the crisis not yet addressed. . . .

This sexual aberration is not generated from the bottom up—that is only from unsuitable candidates—but from the top down—that is from the sexual behaviors of superiors, even bishops and cardinals.

The problem facing us in the American church is systemic. I will present Your Holiness with only a few examples:

Bishop Thomas Lyons, now deceased, who was an Auxiliary in the Archdiocese of Washington D.C., groomed, seduced, and sexually abused a boy from the time he was seven years old until he was seventeen. When that boy grew into manhood he in turn abused his own child and young relatives. When I asked him about his actions he said to me, "I thought it was natural. Father (Lyons) told me a priest showed him this when he was growing up." A pattern was perpetuated for at least four generations. . . .

While I was Adjunct Professor at a Pontifical Seminary, St. Mary's Baltimore (1972-1984) a number of seminarians came to me with concerns about the behavior of Theodore E. McCarrick then bishop of Metuchen New Jersey. It has been widely known for several decades that Bishop/Archbishop now Cardinal Theodore E. McCarrick took seminarians and young priests to a shore home in New Jersey, sites in New York, and other places and slept with some of them. He established a coterie of young seminarians and priests that he encouraged to call him "Uncle Ted." I have his correspondence where he referred to these men as being "cousins" with each other. . . .

And even at this point the complete story cannot be published because priest reporters are afraid of reprisals.

I know the names of at least four priests who have had sexual encounters with Cardinal McCarrick. I have documents and letters that record the first hand testimony and eye witness accounts of McCarrick, then archbishop of Newark, New Jersey actually having sex with a priest, and at other times subjecting a priest to unwanted sexual advances.

Your Holiness, you must seek out and listen to the stories, as I have from many priests about their seduction by highly placed clerics, and the dire consequences in their lives that does [not] end in their victimization alone.

Such behavior fosters confusion and makes celibacy problematic for seminarians and priests. This abuse paves the way for them to pass the tradition on—to have sex with each other and even with minors.

The pattern and practice of priests in positions of responsibility for the training of men for the priesthood—rectors, confessors, spiritual directors, novice masters, and other clergy—who have sexual relations with seminarians and other priests is rampant in the Catholic Church in the United States. I have reviewed hundreds of documents that record just such behavior and interviewed scores of priests who have suffered from this activity. Priests, sexually active in the above manner have frequently been appointed by the Vatican to be ordained bishops or even created cardinals. I approach Your Holiness with due reverence, but with the same intensity that motivated Peter Damian to lay out before your predecessor, Pope Leo IX, a description of the condition of the clergy during his time. The problems he spoke of are similar and as great now in the United States as they were then in Rome. If Your Holiness requests I will submit to you personally documentation of that about which I have spoken.

Your Holiness, I submit this to you with urgent concern for our Church, especially for the young and our clergy.[21]

---

21    The full text is available here: http://www.awrsipe.com/Docs_ and_Controversy/Statement-to-Pope.html.

\*\*\*

**Paragraph 14.** The following day, I delivered a new memo to the new Substitute, Fernando Filoni, which included my previous one of December 6, 2006. In it, I summarized Richard Sipe's document, which ended with this respectful and heartfelt appeal to Pope Benedict XVI: *"I approach Your Holiness with due reverence, but with the same intensity that motivated Peter Damian to lay out before your predecessor, Pope Leo IX, a description of the condition of the clergy during his time. The problems he spoke of are similar and as great now in the United States as they were then in Rome. If Your Holiness requests, I will personally submit to you documentation of that about which I have spoken."*

In paragraph 14, we learn that Viganò on May 25, 2008, drafted a new, second memo on the McCarrick case, following his December 6, 2006 memo on the Littleton allegations on the Sipe document, summarizing the "Sipe Statement." We may number Viganò's May 25 memo as **Document 8.** If Viganò is telling the truth, this memo should be in the Vatican archives. We also have three new names in this paragraph: (13) **Archbishop Fernando Filoni**, Viganò's new superior in the Vatican, and two names cited by Sipe in his letter to Pope Benedict in a passage Viganò quotes: (14) **Pope Leo IX**, the great reforming pope of the mid eleventh century (pope from February 12, 1049 to April 19, 1054, he opposed simony and enforced clerical celibacy), and (15) **St. Peter Damian** (1007-1072), the great reforming Benedictine monk and cardinal in Leo IX's circle who denounced the sexual immorality and homosexuality of the clergy of his time. Dante placed Damian in one of the highest circles of paradise as a great predecessor of St. Francis of Assisi, and Damian was declared a Doctor of the Church in 1828.

Therefore, Viganò was, via these two memos from 2006 and 2008, actually at the institutional crossroads of the Church's efforts to document concerns about McCarrick. In other words, Viganò was directly involved in the "McCarrick affair" from 2006 on, twelve years before he published this "Testimony." When concerns were raised, the concerns came to Viganò's desk, and it was his duty to summarize the concerns in memos. In the version of events sketched by Viganò, these concerns were being expressed by Montalvo, by Sambi, by Littleton, and by Sipe, and Viganò was passing on these concerns to his superiors, yet nothing was seemingly being done. No word came back to him from above.

> **Paragraph 15.** I ended my memo by repeating to my superiors that I thought it was necessary to intervene as soon as possible by removing the cardinal's hat from Cardinal McCarrick and that he should be subjected to the sanctions established by the *Code of Canon Law*, which also provide for reduction to the lay state.

In paragraph 15, Viganò tells us something new about the content of his May 25, 2008 memo regarding McCarrick: he says action should be taken "as soon as possible" to "remove the cardinal's hat" and, possibly, to reduce him to the lay state; that is, dismiss him from the priesthood. If his recollection is accurate, then this would support the more favorable reading of Viganò's actions; that is, that he had pushed for vigorous action against McCarrick.

> **Paragraph 16.** <u>This second memo of mine was also never returned to the Personnel Office, and I was greatly dismayed at my superiors for the inconceivable absence of any measure against the Cardinal, and for the continuing lack of any communication with me since my first memo in December 2006.</u>

In paragraph 16, Viganò expresses his frustration and his "dismay." No action against McCarrick was taken, he tells us, and no explanation for this lack of action is given. The natural question any reader has at this point is: Why not? Why is McCarrick so influential, so powerful, that no one seems willing or able to act against him in any way? As we reflect on this question, we recall that McCarrick had a special post in the Church: he had been the archbishop of Washington, DC, the capital city of the most powerful country in the world, from 2001 to 2006, and had been closely connected with many leading politicians and had been considered politically powerful himself. But would Pope Benedict have turned a blind eye to McCarrick's misconduct for this reason? Or had Benedict never received the memos of Viganò summarizing the Littleton allegations and the "Sipe Statement"? We do not know.

> **Paragraph 17.** But finally I learned with certainty, through Cardinal Giovanni Battista Re, then-Prefect of the Congregation for Bishops, that Richard Sipe's courageous and meritorious Statement had had the desired result. **Pope Benedict had imposed on Cardinal McCarrick sanctions similar to those now imposed**

**on him by Pope Francis: the Cardinal was to leave the seminary where he was living, he was forbidden to celebrate [Mass] in public, to participate in public meetings, to give lectures, to travel, with the obligation of dedicating himself to a life of prayer and penance.**

In paragraph 17, our question is answered. Benedict, Viganò tells us, *was* informed of McCarrick's misconduct, and he claims Benedict, not intimidated by McCarrick's power and influence, did take action. Viganò tells us that Benedict "imposed sanctions" on McCarrick. He claims that these sanctions were: to change where he was living, to cease celebrating Mass in public, participating in public meetings, giving lectures, and traveling in order to dedicate his life to prayer and penance. Viganò says that he learned of these "sanctions" from person 16, **Cardinal Giovanni Battista Re**, Prefect of the Congregation for Bishops. Now, this claim of Viganò, that "sanctions" were imposed by Benedict on McCarrick, will become one of the most contested points in this entire affair. Why is it so contested? First, because there is evidently no document, no text, no written declaration, where Benedict says to McCarrick, "I am sanctioning you in this and this and this way." Viganò acknowledges that there is no such text. He says he learned about the sanctions *only in a conversation with Cardinal Re*. So what we are dealing with here is, once again, an action—if there was an action at all—which is secret in order not to cause public scandal. Second, because McCarrick never did cease his speaking, and traveling, and participating in public meetings. So we are left, it would seem, with a choice between three possibilities: either (1) there were no such sanctions and Viganò is lying, or (2) there were such sanctions but they were not really sanctions, only "suggestions," in which case Viganò is exaggerating Benedict's action with regard to McCarrick, or (3) there were sanctions but McCarrick never obeyed them and no one ever insisted that he obey them, which suggests the impotence of Benedict to impose his will in governing the Church. But which is the truth? We do not know. One thing seems very clear: Cardinal Re knows whether or not Viganò is telling the truth about whether he told Viganò that Benedict had imposed sanctions. It would seem that a key "action point" would be *to talk to Cardinal Re* and ask him to confirm or deny Viganò's story.

> **Paragraph 18.** I do not know when Pope Benedict took these measures against McCarrick, whether in 2009 or 2010, because in the meantime I had been transferred to the Governorate of Vatican City State, just as I do not know who was responsible for this incredible delay. I certainly do not believe it was Pope Benedict, who as Cardinal had repeatedly denounced the corruption present in the Church, and in the first months of his pontificate had already taken a firm stand against the admission into seminary of young men with deep homosexual tendencies. I believe it was due to the Pope's first collaborator at the time, Cardinal Tarcisio Bertone, who notoriously favored promoting homosexuals into positions of responsibility, and was accustomed to managing the information he thought appropriate to convey to the Pope.

Paragraph 18 marks a departure, a shift, in the "Testimony." In the first 17 paragraphs, Viganò has been talking about documents and events that he knows about firsthand due to his work in the Vatican. Here, in paragraph 18, Viganò begins to speculate in order to try to explain the peculiar lack of transparency in the entire McCarrick situation. He twice tells us "I do not know" (first, when Benedict took these measures and, second, who was responsible for the "incredible delay"), and then he gives his opinion: "I do not believe" that it was Pope Benedict, he says. Therefore, he concludes that someone else was responsible. Here Viganò offers his first completely unsupported allegation: he says "I believe" (not "I know") that the delay in taking firm action in the McCarrick case was *due to the Pope's first collaborator* at that time: Cardinal Bertone.

Viganò gives two reasons for his belief that Bertone may have delayed bringing McCarrick's actions to Benedict's attention: (1) because of Bertone's alleged sympathy, even favoritism, for homosexual prelates (Bertone, Viganò claims, "notoriously favored promoting homosexuals into positions of responsibility") and (2) because Bertone, Viganò claims, "was accustomed to managing the information he thought appropriate to convey to the Pope."

These allegations about how Bertone viewed homosexuals and how he handled the task of giving information to or withholding information from Pope Benedict are not supported by any documentary evidence. However, as a longtime Vatican insider, I can attest to the fact that there have been whispers, and more than whispers, about Bertone that tend to support Viganò's claim. Nevertheless, this paragraph is the beginning of an opening

Viganò leaves in his "Testimony" that his critics will exploit.

> **Paragraph 19.** In any case, **what is certain is that Pope Benedict imposed the above canonical sanctions on McCarrick and that they were communicated to him by the Apostolic Nuncio to the United States, Pietro Sambi**. Monsignor Jean-François Lantheaume, then first Counsellor of the Nunciature in Washington and Chargé d'Affaires *a.i.* after the unexpected death of Nuncio Sambi in Baltimore, told me when I arrived in Washington—and he is ready to testify to it—about a stormy conversation, lasting over an hour, that Nuncio Sambi had with Cardinal McCarrick whom he had summoned to the Nunciature. Monsignor Lantheaume told me that "the Nuncio's voice could be heard all the way out in the corridor."

Paragraph 19 sketches one of the most dramatic scenes in the "Testimony": the alleged "shouting match" between Cardinal McCarrick and Archbishop Sambi, Viganò's predecessor as nuncio, when Sambi attempted to communicate Benedict's sanctions on McCarrick to McCarrick. Did such a shouting match really occur as Viganò describes? The answer seems to be yes because Viganò introduces an eyewitness who has gone on the record saying that the story is true. This witness is person 17 **Monsignor Jean-François Lantheaume**, "then first Counsellor of the Nunciature in Washington and Chargé d'Affaires *ad interum* after the unexpected death of Nuncio Sambi in Baltimore." Lantheaume had been in charge of the Vatican nunciature in Washington during the time between Sambi's (unexpected) death at the end of July 2011 and Viganò's arrival in Washington at the end of October 2011, three months later. Lantheaume, thus, has a certain institutional credibility as a witness. And on Monday, August 27, 2018, two days after the publication of Viganò's "Testimony" on Saturday, August 25, Lantheaume was asked by a reporter to comment on Viganò's description of the encounter between Sambi and McCarrick. Lantheaume corroborated Viganò's story. Viganò "tells the whole truth," Lantheaume said. "I am a witness." And in an exchange posted on his Facebook page, Lantheaume wrote, "The bishops are neither unscathed nor untouchable. They are just as sinful as others!!! Let's say it once and for all."

So, if Sambi did meet McCarrick in the Washington nunciature, and if at that meeting Sambi did inform McCarrick of some restrictive measures that Pope Benedict had decided to impose on him due to his sexually abusive conduct with seminarians (perhaps not using the word "sanctions" but indicating that McCarrick would need to change his living arrangements and limit his public activity), and if Sambi instructed McCarrick to obey the sanctions, and if McCarrick resisted so that Sambi reacted with loud, angry shouts (overheard by Lantheaume, who was just down the hall and confirms that he did hear the shouts, yes, but also that, in his words quoted above, he asserts that Viganò "told the whole truth" which would endorse not just that there were shouts but that Viganò's account of what the shouts concerned was accurate), then it seems reasonable to conclude that, yes, Benedict decided to impose "disciplinary measures" (perhaps not "sanctions"—Viganò in the next paragraph will call them "dispositions") on McCarrick which McCarrick was reluctant to comply with. Again, we do not know for certain exactly what Sambi said; Viganò does not cite a word of the conversation. Nor do we know what McCarrick said. But we do know that Lantheaume was present and that Lantheaume knew Sambi well, and Lantheaume has confirmed that the meeting had to do with communicating to McCarrick that Benedict had decided to impose "the above canonical sanctions on McCarrick." There does not seem any good reason to doubt the accuracy of this account.

> **Paragraph 20.** Pope Benedict's same dispositions were then also communicated to me by the new Prefect of the Congregation for Bishops, Cardinal Marc Ouellet, in November 2011, in a conversation before my departure for Washington, and were included among the instructions of the same Congregation to the new Nuncio.

In paragraph 20, we meet another new character: (18) **Canadian Cardinal Marc Ouellet**. Viganò claims that Ouellet told him about "Pope Benedict's same dispositions" against McCarrick in a conversation in Rome on the eve of Viganò's departure to start his service as papal nuncio in America in November of 2011. Once again, there is nothing in writing. It is merely the recollection of a conversation. Viganò is *en route* to America to be the pope's representative in America for the next five years (2011 to 2016), and on the eve of his departure, he says, Ouellet told him in a conversation that Pope Benedict had imposed on McCarrick, the most powerful of the

American cardinals, "dispositions" in response to the reports of McCarrick's years of alleged sexual misconduct. We will see that Ouellet and Viganò exchanged open letters touching on this point in October 2018, a few weeks after Viganò's "Testimony" was released. And we will see that in his letter, Ouellet, while sharply criticizing Viganò for his attitude toward Pope Francis, does not deny that such a conversation as Viganò describes here occurred. This suggests strongly that the conversation with Ouellet that Viganò describes did, in fact, occur.

> **Paragraph 21.** In turn, I repeated them to Cardinal McCarrick at my first meeting with him at the Nunciature. The Cardinal, muttering in a barely comprehensible way, admitted that he had perhaps made the mistake of sleeping in the same bed with some seminarians at his beach house, but he said this as if it had no importance.

In paragraph 21, Viganò recounts the story of his first meeting with McCarrick in America. We do not note the date. We will have to assume it is in the first months of Viganò's stay in Washington, where McCarrick is living and is the retired archbishop, either at the end of 2011 or at the beginning of 2012. The American President is Barack Obama, and Pope Benedict is still pope; he will not resign until February of 2013. No words are in quotes, so the account is not particularly detailed, but we do catch intriguing glimpses of the two men. In Viganò's telling, McCarrick "mutters in a barely comprehensible way" (so he is not shouting, or angry, but muttering, almost quiet). McCarrick admits, Viganò says, that "perhaps" he "made a mistake" by "sleeping in the same bed with some seminarians at his (New Jersey shore) beach house." So clearly, (if we are to give any credibility to this recounting of the meeting) Viganò raised with McCarrick the matter of the various allegations of sexual misconduct which Viganò had himself read about over the previous several years in the Littleton, Ramsey, and Sipe documents and which he had summarized and made his own recommendations about in his memos to his superiors. So McCarrick (in Viganò's telling) confirms certain aspects of the allegations—that he did share a bed with seminarians. But, Viganò tells us, "he [McCarrick] said this as if it had no importance." This is Viganò's way of characterizing McCarrick as a man whose conscience is no longer sensitive to the moral wrongness or sinfulness of certain actions or behaviors—like sleeping, while a bishop, in the same bed with the seminarians of his diocese.

> **Paragraph 22.** The faithful insistently wonder how it was possible for him to be appointed to Washington, and as Cardinal, and they have every right to know who knew, and who covered up his grave misdeeds. It is therefore my duty to reveal what I know about this, beginning with the Roman Curia.

In paragraph 22, though it is very short, Viganò shifts course. This is a transition paragraph in the "Testimony." Viganò is from this point on no longer talking about McCarrick himself but rather about *those who supported and covered up for him*. Viganò asks how it was possible for McCarrick to rise in the Church. And he answers: through the support of many other prelates. Viganò will now spend considerable time and energy building a case that McCarrick rose to the very highest posts in the Church because many archbishops, cardinals, and even popes supported him. He will name dozens of names. And one of the last names will be that of Pope Francis himself.

> **Paragraph 23.** Cardinal Angelo Sodano was Secretary of State until September 2006: all information was communicated to him. In November 2000, Nuncio Montalvo sent him his report, passing on to him the aforementioned letter from Father Boniface Ramsey in which he denounced the serious abuses committed by McCarrick.

Paragraph 23 introduces character 19, **Cardinal Angelo Sodano**. Cardinal Sodano was Vatican secretary of state, making him the number two man in the Vatican after the pope, from June 29, 1991 to June 22, 2006. For those fifteen years, every important decision passed, in part, through his hands. And Viganò now makes Sodano the first one to be blamed for the non-action on McCarrick. Sodano knew about McCarrick's misdeeds already in the year 2000, due to the letter from Father Ramsey forwarded to Sodano by nuncio Montalvo, Viganò says. This forwarded report ought to be in the Vatican archives. Still, no action was taken against McCarrick, who in 2001 was actually promoted to become archbishop of Washington.

> **Paragraph 24.** It is known that Sodano tried to cover up

the Father Maciel scandal to the end. He even removed
the Nuncio in Mexico City, [Archbishop] Justo Mullor,
who refused to be an accomplice in his scheme to cover
Maciel, and in his place appointed Sandri, then-Nuncio
to Venezuela, who was willing to collaborate in the
cover-up. Sodano even went so far as to issue a statement
to the Vatican press office in which a falsehood was
affirmed, that is, that Pope Benedict had decided that
the Maciel case should be considered closed. Benedict
reacted, despite Sodano's strenuous defense, and Maciel
was found guilty and irrevocably condemned.

Paragraph 24 introduces new characters 20, **Father
Marcial Maciel**, the Mexican founder of the Legionaries of Christ, and 21, **Archbishop Justo Mullor**, a
career Vatican diplomat like Viganò. Viganò contends
that Sodano "tried to cover up the Father Maciel scandal
to the end." He tells us that Mullor refused to participate in the coverup and so was removed as the nuncio to
Mexico. And he refers to a famous incident among those
who follow Vatican affairs. In 2004, the then-Cardinal
Joseph Ratzinger sent Msgr. Charles Scicluna, a native
of Malta who was an official of the Congregation for
the Doctrine of the Faith (CDF) in Rome, to Mexico
to investigate the Legion. After Scicluna returned from
one of his trips in April, 2005, just after the conclave
that elected Cardinal Ratzinger as Pope Benedict XVI,
a communiqué was sent to the Legion from Cardinal
Sodano's office saying "there is no canonical procedure
in course nor is one foreseen for the future with regard
to Father Maciel." The communiqué was given without
consulting the CDF. The Legion took that statement

and put a spin on it to say Father Maciel had been exon-
erated. But the case was still very much open and would
soon lead to Maciel's condemnation as a sexually abusive
priest who had also fathered several children by different
women and abused them too.

In 2006, Cardinal Sodano helped minimize harm
caused to the Legion's name and structure. Although the
Vatican ordered Maciel to refrain from all public min-
istries and to adopt a "life of prayer and penitence," the
Vatican statement continued to praise the Legion and
*Regnum Christi* (the Legion's lay movement), though the
Legion was still directly attacking, not supporting, the
victims. The Vatican statement allowed the Legionaries
to publish their own communiqué saying that Maciel
had accepted the Vatican's decision "with faith, complete serenity and tranquillity of conscience, knowing
that it is a new cross that God, the Father of Mercy, has
allowed him to suffer." American author and investigative journalist Jason Berry said that he had it "on good
authority" that "Sodano's fingerprints were all over that
[Vatican] statement."

> **Paragraph 25.** Was McCarrick's appointment to
> Washington and as Cardinal the work of Sodano, when
> John Paul II was already very ill? We are not given to
> know. However, it is legitimate to think so, but I do not
> think he was the only one responsible for this. McCarrick
> frequently went to Rome and made friends everywhere,
> at all levels of the Curia. If Sodano had protected Maciel,
> as seems certain, there is no reason why he wouldn't have
> done so for McCarrick, who according to many had the
> financial means to influence decisions. His nomination

to Washington was opposed by then-Prefect of the Congregation for Bishops, Cardinal Giovanni Battista Re. At the Nunciature in Washington there is a note, written in his hand, in which Cardinal Re dissociates himself from the appointment and states that McCarrick was 14th on the list for Washington.

In this paragraph 25, Viganò tells us he thinks Sodano helped and supported McCarrick's rise in the Church, but that he thinks Sodano was not alone. He thinks this, he says, because "McCarrick frequently went to Rome and made friends everywhere, at all levels of the Curia." And he gives a special detail: "McCarrick, according to many, had the financial means to influence decisions." In this regard, I am able to provide one anecdote. In 2008 in Washington, I spoke with Archbishop Sambi and asked if he knew of any Catholics who might wish to support the work of a small Catholic magazine—my own. Sambi said, "Ask McCarrick. He knows where the pockets are." So Viganò is correct, I think, in saying that "according to many" (Sambi included) McCarrick "had the financial means to influence decisions." Exactly how McCarrick came to possess or administer large sums of money, and whether there were any political or ideological "strings" attached to these funds, would seemingly be an important topic for further research.

We should note here that Viganò mentions another document, which we may call **Document 9**: a note from Cardinal Re, prefect of the Congregation for Bishops in Rome, in which Re "dissociates himself" from the appointment of McCarrick to the the archbishop of Washington "and states that McCarrick was 14th

on the list for Washington." Viganò says the note is in
the archive of the nunciature in Washington. But now
almost two years after Viganò's "Testimony," the Vatican has still not published its promised report on all
aspects of the McCarrick affair, including this one, his
appointment as the archbishop of Washington, though
the man in Rome charged with evaluating the candidates
for that post, Cardinal Re, had, according to Viganò,
placed McCarrick in the fourteenth position for that
post. Who then overruled Re and chose McCarrick? We
do not know. Sodano had the authority to do so.

> **Paragraph 26.** Nuncio Sambi's report, with all the
> attachments, was sent to **Cardinal Tarcisio Bertone**,
> as Secretary of State. My two above-mentioned memos
> of December 6, 2006 and May 25, 2008, were also
> presumably handed over to him by the Substitute. As
> already mentioned, the Cardinal had no difficulty in
> insistently presenting for the episcopate candidates
> known to be active homosexuals—I cite only the well-
> known case of Vincenzo de Mauro, who was appointed
> Archbishop-Bishop of Vigevano and later removed
> because he was undermining his seminarians—and in
> filtering and manipulating the information he conveyed
> to Pope Benedict.

In paragraph 26, Viganò, in his effort to shed light on
who backed McCarrick in his ecclesiastical career, turns
his attention from Cardinal Sodano back to Cardinal
Bertone. Again, Sodano was secretary of state from 1991
to 2006, so he was in power during the years McCarrick was rising step by step to the highest position in
the Church in the United States. Bertone was Sodano's

successor as secretary of state from 2006 (under the new Pope Benedict) until 2013 (when Pope Francis chose Pietro Parolin to replace Bertone; Parolin remains secretary of state to this day). Viganò essentially repeats his two allegations about Bertone: (1) that Bertone "had no difficulty in insistently presenting for the episcopate candidates known to be active homosexuals" (here he cites one case well-known in Italy of a bishop, (22) **Vincenzo de Mauro,** who was appointed bishop of Vigevano and later removed "because he was undermining his seminarians") and (2) that Bertone "filtered" and "manipulated" the information he conveyed to Pope Benedict.

The argument Viganò is making is that the "dossier" implicating McCarrick has been growing and now contains material—the Ramsey letter, the Littleton material, the Sipe letter, and Viganò's two memos from 2006 and 2008—which would have, had it been brought to the attention of Pope Benedict, led to action from Benedict.

What Viganò is saying is that Bertone (Viganò believes) held back the McCarrick dossier from Benedict for some time, evidently from 2006 until 2009, did not present the dossier to Benedict or tell him about it verbally, and this would explain why Benedict did not take any earlier action against McCarrick until 2009 or 2010. Of course, at some point, as Ouellet, Re, and Lantheaume all told Viganò, Benedict did act and issue his "dispositions." Viganò says this seems to have been either in 2009 or 2010, but in any case before mid-2011 because Sambi was telling McCarrick about these "dispositions" shortly before his own death in July of 2011.

**Paragraph 27.** **Cardinal Pietro Parolin**, the current Secretary of State, was also complicit in covering up the misdeeds of McCarrick who had, after the election of Pope Francis, boasted openly of his travels and missions to various continents. In April 2014, the *Washington Times* had a front page report on McCarrick's trip to the Central African Republic, and on behalf of the State Department no less. As Nuncio to Washington, I wrote to Cardinal Parolin asking him if the sanctions imposed on McCarrick by Pope Benedict were still valid. Ça va sans dire ["It goes without saying"] that my letter never received any reply!

In paragraph 27, Viganò charges that the Vatican secretary of state, (23) **Pietro Parolin**, "was also complicit in covering up the misdeeds of McCarrick." So now we have three Vatican secretaries of state in a row, Sodano, Bertone, and Parolin, all allegedly "complicit in covering up the misdeeds of McCarrick."

Viganò refers here to another document, which we might call **Document 10**, a note Viganò wrote to Parolin asking "if the sanctions imposed on McCarrick by Pope Benedict were still valid." Viganò says Parolin never answered him.

The picture Viganò is painting is one where Pope Benedict did act but three powerful cardinals in the number two slot at the Vatican, as secretaries of state, all saw to it that McCarrick continued to travel, speak in public, and in general function as he always had, despite all of the evidence against him over the years. We do not know this to be the case; Viganò presents no smoking gun to prove that these cardinals acted to protect McCarrick.

But his argument takes account of and jibes with many of the facts as we know them. The way to shed more light on the matter would be to summon Sodano, Bertone, and Parolin to some sort of forum or tribunal or investigative panel and ask each of them when they knew what about McCarrick and why disciplinary actions against him were not taken sooner.

> **Paragraph 28.** The same can be said for **Cardinal William Levada**, former Prefect of the Congregation for the Doctrine of the Faith, for **Cardinals Marc Ouellet**, Prefect of the Congregation for Bishops, **Lorenzo Baldisseri**, former Secretary of the same Congregation for Bishops, and **Archbishop Ilson de Jesus Montanari**, current Secretary of the same Congregation. They were all aware by reason of their office of the sanctions imposed by Pope Benedict on McCarrick.

In paragraph 28, Viganò casts his net still further, claiming that four other high-ranking Vatican officials—(12) **Levada**, (18) **Ouellet**, (24) **Baldisseri**, and (25) **Montanari**—"were all aware by reason of their office of the sanctions imposed by Pope Benedict on McCarrick." Each of these men could be asked to testify what they knew when about McCarrick. Levada will not be able to be questioned: he died on September 26, 2019 at the age of eighty-three.

> **Paragraph 29. Cardinals Leonardo Sandri, Fernando Filoni** and **Angelo Becciu**, as Substitutes of the Secretariat of State, knew in every detail the situation regarding Cardinal McCarrick.

In paragraph 29, Viganò tells us that (10) **Sandri**, (13) **Filoni**, and (26) **Becciu** "knew in every detail the situation regarding Cardinal McCarrick." These men could all be questioned on the matter.

> **Paragraph 30.** Nor could **Cardinals Giovanni Lajolo** and **Dominique Mamberti** have failed to know. As Secretaries for Relations with States, they participated several times a week in collegial meetings with the Secretary of State.

In paragraph 30, Viganò indicts two other cardinals, saying they "could not have failed to know" about McCarrick because of their positions: (27) **Lajolo** and (28) **Mamberti**. Both men are still alive and could be questioned.

> **Paragraph 31.** As far as the Roman Curia is concerned, for the moment I will stop here, even if the names of other prelates in the Vatican are well known, even some very close to Pope Francis, such as **Cardinal Francesco Coccopalmerio** and **Archbishop Vincenzo Paglia**, who belong to the homosexual current in favor of subverting Catholic doctrine on homosexuality, a current already denounced in 1986 by Cardinal Joseph Ratzinger, then-Prefect of the Congregation for the Doctrine of the Faith, in the *Letter to the Bishops of the Catholic Church on the Pastoral Care of Homosexual Persons*. **Cardinals Edwin Frederick O'Brien** and **Renato Raffaele Martino** also belong to the same current, albeit with a different ideology. Others belonging to this current even reside at the *Domus Sanctae Marthae*.

In paragraph 31, Viganò begins by saying "as far as the Roman Curia is concerned, I will stop here," but then he continues and indicts (29) **Coccopalmerio**, (30) **Paglia**,

(31) **O'Brien**, and (32) **Martino** not for withholding information about McCarrick but for "belong(ing) to the homosexual current in favor of subverting Catholic doctrine on homosexuality."

What is happening in this paragraph is that Viganò is leaving behind the particular question of McCarrick and beginning to explore a wider question: the existence and extent of the so-called "gay lobby" (or lobbies?) in the Vatican.

> **Paragraph 32.** Now to the United States. Obviously, the first to have been informed of the measures taken by Pope Benedict was McCarrick's successor in Washington See, **Cardinal Donald Wuerl**, whose situation is now completely compromised by the recent revelations regarding his behavior as Bishop of Pittsburgh.

In paragraph 32, Viganò finally does leave behind the Roman Curia and shifts his attention to the United States. Up to now he has been attempting to shed light on how McCarrick rose in the hierarchy, who in Rome assisted or "covered up" for him, and why it took so long for someone in Rome to act on his case. Now he will attempt to explain McCarrick's network of friendship and support in America. And the first and most important figure in this regard is the man who succeeded McCarrick as the cardinal archbishop of Washington, (33) **Donald Wuerl**. Viganò notes that Wuerl has been accused of mishandling cases of clerical sexual abuse in his prior diocese in Pittsburgh. It is also interesting to note here that there has not yet been any mention in this "Testimony" of Pope Francis. The mention is coming, but Viganò's initial goal was to show what information the Vatican had received about McCarrick and then only afterward to speak about what was done with the information received.

> **Paragraph 33.** It is absolutely unthinkable that Nuncio Sambi, who was an extremely responsible person, loyal, direct and explicit in his way of being (a true son of Romagna) did not speak to him about it. In any case, I myself brought up the subject with Cardinal Wuerl on several occasions, and I certainly didn't need to go into detail because it was immediately clear to me that he was fully aware of it. I also remember in particular the fact that I had to draw his attention to it, because I realized that in an archdiocesan publication, on the back cover in color, there was an announcement inviting young men who thought they had a vocation to the priesthood to a meeting with Cardinal McCarrick. I immediately phoned Cardinal Wuerl, who expressed his surprise to me, telling me that he knew nothing about that announcement and that he would cancel it. If, as he now continues to state, he knew nothing of the abuses committed by McCarrick and the measures taken by Pope Benedict, how can his answer be explained?

In paragraph 33, Viganò continues to develop his indictment of Wuerl, adducing Wuerl's willingness to cancel an ad in an archdiocesan publication "inviting young men who thought they had a vocation to the priesthood to a meeting with Cardinal McCarrick" after Viganò drew the ad to Wuerl's attention. Viganò says Wuerl knew of Pope Benedict's request that McCarrick lead a life of "prayer and penance" and not remain in the limelight, meeting with young people, and so forth. Wuerl, however, has stated that he "knew nothing of the abuses committed by McCarrick and the measures taken by Pope Benedict." If Viganò is right, Wuerl is not telling the truth. But is Viganò right? We do not know for certain. However, one wonders why Wuerl would so quickly say that he knew nothing about the ad and move to cancel it if he knew nothing about McCarrick?

> **Paragraph 34.** His recent statements that he knew nothing about it, even though at first he cunningly referred to compensation for the two victims, are absolutely laughable. The Cardinal lies shamelessly and prevails upon his Chancellor, Monsignor Antonicelli, to lie as well.

In paragraph 34, Viganò continues his indictment of Wuerl and of Wuerl's secretary, (34) **Monsignor Charles Antonicelli**. Viganò mentions that Wuerl "at first cunningly referred to compensation for the two victims," meaning Wuerl did know that McCarrick had been accused of sexual abuse and is lying when he says he never knew anything obout such allegations. Viganò says that Wuerl has persuaded his vicar for canonical services to lie about this matter as well.

> **Paragraph 35.** Cardinal Wuerl also clearly lied on another occasion. Following a morally unacceptable event authorized by the academic authorities of *Georgetown University*, I brought it to the attention of its President, Dr. John DeGioia, sending him two subsequent letters. Before forwarding them to the addressee, so as to handle things properly, I personally gave a copy of them to the Cardinal with an accompanying letter I had written. The Cardinal told me that he knew nothing

about it. However, he failed to acknowledge receipt of my two letters, contrary to what he customarily did. I subsequently learned that the event at Georgetown had taken place for seven years. But the Cardinal knew nothing about it!

In paragraph 35, Viganò, still speaking about Wuerl, refers to a specific incident involving Georgetown University and its president, (35) **Dr. John DeGioa**. Viganò says Georgetown was allowing the performance of a morally unacceptable program and that he wrote to the president to express his concern. He says he personally gave copies of the letters to Wuerl before sending them so that Wuerl would be informed. "The Cardinal told me that he knew nothing about it," Viganò writes. But the event had been occurring annually for seven years. Viganò, therefore, judges that it is not possible that the cardinal did not know anything about it and concludes that he was lying when he said he knew nothing about it. But this as well is not probative evidence, only a conclusion based on the apparent likelihood that the cardinal did know about the performance. Admittedly, however, it is difficult to believe that the cardinal of Washington, DC, was unaware that *The Vagina Monologues* was being performed at one of the pre-eminent Catholic universities in the country, which happened to be in his archdiocese. It caused a national controversy in both the Catholic and the secular press.

> **Paragraph 36.** Cardinal Wuerl, well aware of the continuous abuses committed by Cardinal McCarrick and the sanctions imposed on him by Pope Benedict, transgressing the Pope's order, also allowed him to

reside at a seminary in Washington D.C. In doing so, he put other seminarians at risk.

In paragraph 36, Viganò continues to assert that Wuerl was "well aware" of the "continuous abuses committed by Cardinal McCarrick" and "the sanctions imposed on him by Pope Benedict." Viganò tells us Wuerl continued to allow McCarrick to reside at a seminary in Washington, "transgressing the Pope's order." If Viganò is right, what he is describing is the mechanism by which Church leaders "cover" for one another, even against the wishes of their own pope.

**Paragraph 37. Bishop Paul Bootkoski**, emeritus of Metuchen, and **Archbishop John Myers**, emeritus of Newark, covered up the abuses committed by McCarrick in their respective dioceses and compensated two of his victims. They cannot deny it and they must be interrogated in order to reveal every circumstance and all responsibility regarding this matter.

In paragraph 37, Viganò indicts two other American bishops who had served in dioceses after McCarrick, inheriting problems connected with his activity, for allegedly "covering up" for McCarrick: (36) **Bishop Paul Bootkowski** and (37) **Archbishop John Myers**. Viganò says they "compensated two of his [McCarrick's] victims." He concludes, "They must be interrogated . . . regarding this matter." That seems to be a good idea, and Viganò is the one who has been calling for it: let everyone be questioned until the truth is revealed fully.

**Paragraph 38. Cardinal Kevin Farrell**, who was recently interviewed by the media, also said that he didn't have the

slightest idea about the abuses committed by McCarrick.
Given his tenure in Washington, Dallas and now Rome,
I think no one can honestly believe him. I don't know if
he was ever asked if he knew about Maciel's crimes. If
he were to deny this, would anybody believe him given
that he occupied positions of responsibility as a member
of the Legionaries of Christ?

In paragraph 38, Viganò suggests that (38) **Cardinal
Kevin Farrell**, who lived for several years in the same
house with McCarrick in Washington, cannot be
believed when he says that he did not have "the slightest idea" about "the abuses committed by McCarrick."
Again, Viganò is sketching a picture of a hierarchy that
is compact around McCarrick, aware of what he has
done and enabling or covering up for him. But this picture is a deduction based on perceived probabilities: if
Farrell lived with McCarrick for several years, he must
have known about his activities. But there is no evidence presented that he did know. Disinterested readers
may, perhaps, be forgiven for being skeptical, however,
of such claims of ignorance, especially when, as I can
attest, rumors of the sort have surrounded McCarrick
for decades.

> **Paragraph 39.** Regarding **Cardinal Sean O'Malley**,
> I would simply say that his latest statements on the
> McCarrick case are disconcerting, and have totally
> obscured his transparency and credibility.

In paragraph 39, Viganò charges that (39) **Cardinal Sean
O'Malley** of Boston, by denying knowledge of McCarrick's predatory sexual behavior, has "totally obscured his

transparency and credibility." There is no concrete proof brought forward to settle the matter. And now, for many paragraphs, Viganò turns to the most controversial part of his "Testimony": his recollections of his meetings with Pope Francis.

> **Paragraph 40.** My conscience requires me also to reveal facts that I have experienced personally, concerning Pope Francis, that have a dramatic significance, which as Bishop, sharing the collegial responsibility of all the bishops for the universal Church, do not allow me to remain silent, and that I state here, ready to reaffirm them under oath by calling on God as my witness.

This is the first mention of (40) **Pope Francis** in the "Testimony." One conclusion: Viganò was interested in giving the institutional context for the career-long cover-up of McCarrick's misconduct with seminarians. That was what was weighing on his mind: how the institution had not acted to control or restrain McCarrick. He spends thirty-nine paragraphs detailing what happened from his own knowledge. And only then does he bring in Pope Francis, at the very end of the story.

In other words, this "Testimony" is an institutional indictment more than an indictment of Pope Francis alone. It asks for an institutional reform before it asks Pope Francis to accept what Viganò believes is his own responsibility in the matter. But the main thrust of the "Testimony" is not to condemn Pope Francis or ask for his resignation. The main thrust is to condemn an institutional sclerosis that made it impossible, year after year, to take effective action on a case that required action. Francis was only the final chapter in that long novel, almost an epilogue in a story which had shown for fifteen years that the Roman Catholic Church was profoundly incapable of taking action against the misconduct of the leading members of the hierarchy. It would be wrong to characterize the "Testimony" as "that passionate text where Viganò calls on Francis to resign." It would be right to characterize the "Testimony" as "that detailed reconstruction by Viganò where he explains how, in the case of McCarrick, the institutional incapacity of the Church to discipline a high-ranking prelate for misconduct is made crystal clear for the first time—for which Viganò should be thanked."

The fact that most commentators dismiss this "Testimony" as a radically flawed "attack on Francis" simply reveals that the commenter has not read the "Testimony" with care—or, if the text has been read with care, it has been misunderstood. This is not Viganò the "bitter right-winger" against Francis the "merciful reformer" as is so often said. Rather, it is Viganò the lonely, solitary "truth-teller" against an entire ecclesial system, which he himself had been part of, which had failed to do anything about McCarrick except continually promote him to ever higher honors for some twenty years in a row.

**Paragraph 41.** In the last months of his pontificate, Pope Benedict XVI had convened a meeting of all the apostolic nuncios in Rome, as Paul VI and St. John Paul II had done on several occasions. The date set for the audience with the Pope was Friday, June 21, 2013. Pope Francis kept this commitment made by his predecessor.

Of course I also came to Rome from Washington. It was my first meeting with the new Pope elected only three months prior, after the resignation of Pope Benedict.

We are being prepared for the fateful meeting between Pope Francis and Viganò. Viganò here makes mention of (41) **Pope St. Paul VI**.

> **Paragraph 42.** On the morning of Thursday, June 20, 2013, I went to the *Domus Sanctae Marthae*, to join my colleagues who were staying there. As soon as I entered the hall I met Cardinal McCarrick, who wore the red-trimmed cassock. I greeted him respectfully as I had always done. He immediately said to me, in a tone somewhere between ambiguous and triumphant: "**The Pope received me yesterday, tomorrow I am going to China.**"

And we find that McCarrick, of all people, has just been in to see Pope Francis, a day before Viganò met with Francis in the audience with all of the other Nuncios. The two meet in the main entrance hall of the Domus Sanctae Marthae, where the pope lives. It is an entrance area like in any ordinary hotel in the world, with a reception desk, elevators, and a dining room all off to the one side, with a chapel at the far end. The only difference from most hotels is that a Swiss Guard is usually on duty, standing just outside the main doors. And two plainclothes Vatican gendarmes are standing or sitting just near the main reception desk to keep an eye on things, just in case.

> **Paragraph 43.** At the time I knew nothing of his long friendship with Cardinal Bergoglio and of the important

part he had played in his recent election, as McCarrick himself would later reveal in a lecture at Villanova University and in an interview with the *National Catholic Reporter*. Nor had I ever thought of the fact that he had participated in the preliminary meetings of the recent conclave, and of the role he had been able to have as a cardinal elector in the 2005 conclave. Therefore I did not immediately grasp the meaning of the encrypted message that McCarrick had communicated to me, but that would become clear to me in the days immediately following.

In this paragraph, Viganò gives us a condensed version of many events and themes. He begins by saying he had "no idea" of two things: (1) the long friendship between Cardinal Bergoglio (Pope Francis) and McCarrick and (2) the "important part" that McCarrick played in the election of Pope Francis in the conclave of 2013. He then tells us that "McCarrick himself" would reveal both things—the long friendship between himself and Francis and his role in the 2013 conclave—in two places: a lecture at Villanova University and an interview in the *National Catholic Reporter*. So we understand that in 2013 in June, Viganò did not know some things about McCarrick and Francis that he has come to know as of the time of writing this "Testimony" in 2018, five years later. Then in the next sentence, Viganò tells that he also had "never thought" of the fact that McCarrick had been a "player" at both the 2013 and the 2005 conclaves—that he had participated in the preliminary discussions for many days in 2013, though not eligible to vote as he was already past age eighty, and had been at the pre-conclave meetings and a voter in the conclave itself in 2005, when Pope Benedict XVI had been elected. All of this, we are to understand, is important to understand what McCarrick was saying, in a tone "somewhat between ambiguous and triumphant," when he told Viganò, "The Pope received me yesterday, tomorrow I am going to China."

In other words, McCarrick is signaling to Viganò that he is closely connected to the new Pope, that the new Pope is speaking with him, and that that speaking may have something to do with important Church affairs, specifically, with the Church in China. But Viganò is telling us that he could not understand at the time that McCarrick had also played a key role during two conclaves, in 2005 and 2013, in supporting and gathering support for the election of Cardinal Bergoglio to the papal throne.

> **Paragraph 44.** The next day the audience with Pope Francis took place. After his address, which was partly read and partly delivered off the cuff, the Pope wished to greet all the nuncios one by one. In single file, I remember that I was among the last. When it was my turn, I just had time to say to him, "I am the Nuncio to the United States." He immediately assailed me with a tone of reproach, using these words: **"The Bishops in the United States must not be ideologized! They must be shepherds!"** Of course I was not in a position to ask for explanations about the meaning of his words and the aggressive way in which he had upbraided me. I had in my hand a book in Portuguese that Cardinal O'Malley had sent me for the Pope a few days earlier, telling me *"so he could go over his Portuguese before going to Rio for World Youth Day."* I handed it to him immediately, and

so freed myself from that extremely disconcerting and embarrassing situation.

In paragraph 44, we have a kind of "pre-meeting" between the pope and Viganò. This is not yet the conversation that would be held two days later. This is the very brief meeting, together with all of the other nuncios, where the pope gives an address and all the nuncios come up one by one just to say hello and perhaps to say one thing, not more. And we are privy here to that moment when Viganò came up, tells the pope that he is the nuncio to the United States, and the pope replies, "The Bishops in the United States must not be ideologized! They must be shepherds!"

Clearly the pope had his own understanding of the point he was making, but what was that understanding? What did the pope mean by "the bishops of the United States must not be ideologized"? In a certain way, this is one of the central points of this book and this present crisis in the history of the Church. It is interesting and important, then, that Viganò and the pope return to this question in their next meeting, which Viganò writes about three paragraphs below.

> **Paragraph 45.** At the end of the audience the Pope announced: "**Those of you who are still in Rome next Sunday are invited to concelebrate with me at the** *Domus Sanctae Marthae*." I naturally thought of staying on to clarify as soon as possible what the Pope intended to tell me.

So the pope invited all the nuncios to concelebrate Mass with him at Sunday Mass, and Viganò was among those concelebrants.

> **Paragraph 46.** On Sunday June 23, before the concelebration with the Pope, I asked Monsignor Ricca, who as the person in charge of the house helped us put on the vestments, if he could ask the Pope if he could receive me sometime in the following week. How could I have returned to Washington without having clarified what the Pope wanted of me? At the end of Mass, while the Pope was greeting the few lay people present, Monsignor Fabian Pedacchio, his Argentine secretary, came to me and said: *"The Pope told me to ask if you are free now!"* Naturally, I replied that I was at the Pope's disposal and that I thanked him for receiving me immediately. The Pope took me to the first floor in his apartment and said: **"We have 40 minutes before the Angelus."**

Before the Mass, Viganò spoke with (42) **Monsignor Ricca,** asking if he might have a few minutes with the pope during the following days. This shows the importance of Ricca as a go-between. By the end of the Mass, Ricca had evidently mentioned Viganò's request to (43) **Father Fabian Pedacchio,** the pope's personal secretary, and a meeting had been arranged on the spot, right after Mass. It would be a long meeting: forty minutes.

> **Paragraph 47.** I began the conversation, asking the Pope what he intended to say to me with the words he had addressed to me when I greeted him the previous Friday. And the Pope, in a very different, friendly, almost affectionate tone, said to me: **"Yes, the Bishops in the United States must not be ideologized, they must not**

> **be right-wing like the Archbishop of Philadelphia** (the
> Pope did not give me the name of the Archbishop), **they
> must be shepherds; and they must not be left-wing"**—
> and he added, raising both arms—**"and when I say
> 'left-wing,' I mean homosexual."** Of course, the logic
> of the correlation between being left-wing and being
> homosexual escaped me, but I added nothing else.

The meeting opened in an absolutely normal, ordinary
way. Viganò returns to that very important remark that
the pope had made two days before about the bishops
in the United States. Viganò had not had a chance to
ask for any details. Since it was Viganò's job as nuncio
to evaluate the possible episcopal appointments, this
was a matter that would naturally be of central importance to him. And so he began with this. He asked Pope
Francis "what he intended to say to me with the words
he had addressed to me the previous Friday." Francis
answers. He offers a bit of explanation. And he speaks
"in a friendly, almost affectionate, tone." Saying that
"the bishops in the United States must not be ideologized," Francis begins, meant that "they must not be
right-wing." One first might think that this is a special
use of the term "ideologized": that the pope thinks *only*
the "right-wing" is ideologized and not the "left-wing."
Logically, the polarities are "pastoral" and "ideologized."
But then one realizes that the pope does also insist that
the bishop should not be "left-wing" either. As Viganò
recalls it, the pope says: "they must not be left-wing . . .
and when I say 'left-wing,' I mean homosexual." This is
a startling statement. It does suggest that the pope sees
the cultural-political battle of our time, the "ideological"

battle of our time, not as a battle between classes over the distribution of wealth and the ownership of the means of production, as in the long struggle between Capitalism and Communism, nor as a battle over the role of race and ethnicity in human affairs, as during the struggle between the ideal of the "Volk" of the German National Socialists and their allies over against the ideal of a pluralist, multi-racial society of the Western democracies, but a battle over two divergent conceptions of morality, family life, and gender identity; one traditional, one "fluid" and open to previously stigmatized relationships and family models. The concept seems to be as follows. The pope wishes to have "shepherds" and bishops, bishops interested in the spiritual lives of their people, in their souls, their consciences, their sins and repentances, in their faith in Christ, in their hope in Christ's promises, in their love for others out of love for Christ who first loved them. All of this is in keeping with the traditional Christian understanding of pastoral care. But the pope does not want bishops who are "ideologized." He proposes two examples of an "ideologized" bishop, saying one is "right-wing" and the other "left-wing," adding, "I mean homosexual." What he seems to be saying is that the traditional, conservative sexual morality preached by the archbishop of Philadelphia (with compelling eloquence, I might add) risks becoming an ideological category, a fixed idea over against the reality of individual souls, and in this sense is not "pastoral." Meanwhile, in a similar way, those who are promoting a "sexual revolution" and new evaluation of sexual behavior are also in danger of making their campaign into

an ideological one—becoming "ideologized" instead of
remaining focused on Christ, remaining pastors. Viganò
actually gives us a quite interesting insight into Francis's
mind in these few lines. Francis's words, as recalled by
Viganò, indicate that he opposes giving greater importance to politics than to pastoral care. But his concept
of the present ideological danger, which is in conflict
with the truly Christian pastoral activity he wishes to
promote, is of an "ideologized traditional morality" of
the "right" and an "ideologized non-traditional morality" of the "left" (the homosexual movement). The pope
did not have time to make these ideas precise and clear.
And Viganò himself admits that he did not understand
very well, saying, "of course, the logic of the correlation
between being left-wing and being homosexual escaped
me." The logic seems to be that the locus of the "ideolo-
gization" has moved during the past two centuries from
class, to race, to sexuality, gender, and family organiza-
tion without almost anyone understanding that each of
these in its own way stands over against the truly Christian view of reality, a view that the bishops must seek to
promote and defend.

> **Paragraph 48.** Immediately after, the Pope asked me in
> a deceitful way: **"What is Cardinal McCarrick like?"** I
> answered him with complete frankness and, if you want,
> with great naiveté: "*Holy Father, I don't know if you know
> Cardinal McCarrick, but if you ask the Congregation for
> Bishops there is a dossier this thick about him. He corrupted
> generations of seminarians and priests and Pope Benedict
> ordered him to withdraw to a life of prayer and penance.*"
> The Pope did not make the slightest comment about

those very grave words of mine and did not show any expression of surprise on his face, as if he had already known the matter for some time, and he immediately changed the subject. But then, what was the Pope's purpose in asking me that question: "*What is Cardinal McCarrick like?*" He clearly wanted to find out if I was an ally of McCarrick or not.

This is the key paragraph in the whole "Testimony." Finally, we come to the moment where the pope asks Viganò about McCarrick, at least in general terms, and Viganò answers. The pope asks, "What is Cardinal McCarrick like?" Viganò could have said something else other than what he said, perhaps, "Oh, McCarrick, he is a very capable fellow, well-connected with powerful political circles in the Democratic Party (who held the presidency at that time under Barack Obama) and in Republican circles as well, in the States, as would be expected by the archbishop of the capital city. He also is an effective fund raiser, inspiring in many wealthy Catholics a willingness to support the Church and the Vatican; for example, the members of the Papal Foundation, an important group of such benefactors, each of whom gives $1 million to join the group. So he is a capable man in many ways." If Viganò had spoken in this way, without mentioning McCarrick's alleged personal misconduct (I only say "alleged" because no trial has ever been held on these matters), who knows? Maybe this "Testimony" would never have been written. Maybe Viganò would never have called on Francis to resign. Maybe Viganò would never have gone into hiding. But Viganò did not speak in this way. He did not take the "diplomatic" line.

For Viganò, it was not "business as usual." It was speaking the truth. And here we have the heart of the matter: Viganò chose to speak very bluntly about the alleged personal misconduct of the cardinal. He did not consider that maybe Pope Francis was close to McCarrick. He did not consider that maybe McCarrick had helped elect Francis to the papal throne. Such considerations were not on his mind. Viganò, by fate or by providence, had personally seen the charges against McCarrick. They had crossed his desk in the Secretariat of State. Any other nuncio might have been ignorant about McCarrick. But Bertone had wanted him out of the Vatican, and Sambi was entering a hospital and dying, and the post of nuncio to Washington was opening up, so Viganò was sent to Washington, the city where McCarrick had been the archbishop and where he was still living. So Viganò answered Francis with the simple truth. "There is a dossier this thick about him" at the Congregation for Bishops, Viganò said. "He corrupted generations of seminarians and priests," and finally, "Pope Benedict ordered him to withdraw to a life of prayer and penance."

This was really Viganò's Rubicon. If he had not chosen to speak in this way about McCarrick, Viganò's history, his relationship with Francis, his role in the Vatican, his role in the Church, his role in history, would have been different. He would have been merely another time-server, willing to sugar-coat or cover up terrible truths. This was the moment when to his detractors, he became another Judas, while to his supporters, he became a hero.

We then hear of the pope's reaction to Viganò's words. The pope "did not make the slightest comment," he "did not show any expression of surprise," and "he immediately changed the subject."

So this is the situation. Viganò launched a powerful, devastating charge against McCarrick. And Pope Francis had—in Viganò's retelling of the conversation—no reaction at all.

We come to the final sentence: Viganò's interpretation of this. It is the most interesting sentence of the paragraph: "He clearly wanted to find out if I was an ally of McCarrick or not." It bears repeating: "He clearly wanted to find out if I was an ally of McCarrick or not."

This sentence is astonishing. It shows Viganò's mind clearly, as in the beam of a spotlight. Viganò is a lifelong curial figure of some stature, some experience, and in this sentence, we are privileged to enter a bit into this world. It is a world where the question of alliances is of the utmost importance because alliances are the means by which all projects are moved forward. One counts on one's friends and allies. One is blocked by one's enemies and opponents. So the important thing is to determine who is really a friend and who really an opponent. Because an opponent who gathers intelligence inside the inner circle of a group with a certain plan, or project, is a very dangerous thing. It can block the project, cause it to fail. So one first assesses a person, determines which side that person is on, and then knows what one can say and not say, what is safe to say and what would be dangerous to say.

In this case, Viganò interprets Francis as an ally of McCarrick(!), working on a "project" that is in harmony with the views of McCarrick, and interested in determining whether Viganò, too, can be an ally, along with McCarrick, in this project.

And what has Viganò done? He has just outed McCarrick in a frank statement to Francis. Speaking out of his own personal experience—the experience recounted in the first paragraphs in this "Testimony," where he received and forwarded letters regarding McCarrick and wrote up his own negative evaluation of McCarrick for his superiors—Viganò knows *as no other nuncio could possibly have known* that McCarrick has been accused of improper sexual advances since before the turn of the century, for decades (from the perspective of 2013, when this conversation occurred), which also means that McCarrick's career has never been sidetracked during all of those many years, because McCarrick was evidently, *for some reason*, an "ally" of other powerful figures in the United States hierarchy and in the Roman Curia.

Viganò is perplexed by the pope's lack of reaction to his revelations about McCarrick's corruption of seminarians. He says the pope reacted "as if he had already known the matter for some time." And he asks himself the question: "What was the Pope's purpose in asking me that question?"

You can see him turning over the entire situation in his mind. "It is my first meeting with the new pope. He has given me forty minutes. Perhaps these moments will enable me to enter into a good relationship with this new pope. Perhaps I can get off to a good start, after all the conflicts with Cardinal Bertone and others." (I am imagining what Viganò may have been thinking, what any person in such a position might have been thinking.)

And the very first question that Pope Francis asks him to open the meeting is: "What is Cardinal McCarrick like?"

Was this fate, destiny, providence? Viganò had been the man in the Curia who had processed the accusations against McCarrick. He had heard back from Cardinal Re that McCarrick had been disciplined by Pope Benedict. He had heard from his colleague in the nunciature that Sambi and McCarrick had had a shouting match when Sambi had told McCarrick about the restrictions he was being asked to accept. And now Pope Francis asks, first off, "What is Cardinal McCarrick like?" Viganò has half a second to think, and then he speaks, saying, essentially, that McCarrick was a corrupt and corrupting man.

**Paragraph 49.** Back in Washington everything became very clear to me, thanks also to a new event that occurred only a few days after my meeting with Pope Francis. When the new Bishop Mark Seitz took possession of the Diocese of El Paso on July 9, 2013, I sent the first Counsellor, Monsignor Jean-François Lantheaume, while I went to Dallas that same day for an international meeting on Bioethics. When he got back, Monsignor Lantheaume told me that in El Paso he had met Cardinal McCarrick who, taking him aside, told him almost the same words that the Pope had said to me in Rome: "**the Bishops in the United States must not be ideologized, they must not be right-wing, they must be shepherds. . . .**" I was astounded! It was therefore clear that the words of reproach that Pope Francis had addressed to me on June 21, 2013 had been put into his mouth the day before by Cardinal McCarrick. Also the Pope's mention "*not like the Archbishop of Philadelphia*" could be traced to McCarrick, because there had been a strong disagreement between the two of them about the admission to Communion of pro-abortion politicians. In his communication to the bishops, McCarrick had manipulated a letter of then-Cardinal Ratzinger who prohibited giving them Communion. Indeed, I also knew how certain Cardinals such as Mahony, Levada and Wuerl, were closely linked to McCarrick; they had opposed the most recent appointments made by Pope Benedict, for important posts such as Philadelphia, Baltimore, Denver and San Francisco.

In this paragraph, we enter fully into the "inside baseball" of the Catholic Church in the United States. We are introduced to (44) **Bishop Mark Seitz** of El Paso, Texas, and (45) **Cardinal Roger Mahony**, retired archbishop of Los Angeles.

We follow Viganò to Texas, to a conference on Bioethics in Dallas, and we find that Cardinal McCarrick has traveled to Texas as well, but to another city, El Paso, to attend the installation of the new bishop there, Seitz. Because Viganò cannot be in two places, he sends his aide, Lantheaume, to El Paso, and he attends the conference in Dallas. When Lantheaume meets up with Viganò, he tells him that he saw McCarrick in El Paso and that McCarrick had "taken him aside" and insisted to him that the men named bishops in the United States needed to be "non-ideologized" and "not right-wing" but "shepherds." Viganò tells us he had his "Eureka!" moment—he tells us, "I was astounded!" What was he astounded by?

By the fact that he seems to have finally understood that it was McCarrick who was guiding the agenda of

Pope Francis in choosing bishops for the Church! "It was therefore clear that the words of reproach that Pope Francis had addressed to me on June 21, 2013 had been put into his mouth the day before by Cardinal McCarrick," Viganò writes. "Also the Pope's mention '*not like the Archbishop of Philadelphia*' could be traced to McCarrick, because there had been a strong disagreement between the two of them about the admission to Communion of pro-abortion politicians."

In other words, Viganò has connected, in his own mind, the policy of the Francis pontificate with the careful maneuvering of the very same McCarrick, who, with a phrase here, a suggestion there, and occasionally a donation for a stalled initiative (anything to help forward the work of the Church—and his agenda) has managed to exercise enormous influence over Pope Francis himself!

The story is even more contorted and paradoxical: Viganò has come to conclude that this very McCarrick, the man Viganò had years before written a report about suggesting that he be removed from the cardinalate, had not only never been removed but had helped to elect Pope Francis and had now come to guide the thinking of the new pope on which men to choose as the new bishops in the United States, even though this was precisely the task of Viganò himself!

In short, Viganò has come to believe that not only is McCarrick not being restrained or punished in any way by Francis, he is in fact getting into the good graces of Francis in such an intimate way, if he was not already firmly ensconced there, that he is removing from Viganò's hands the very work that had been entrusted to him in

America by Pope Benedict: to choose the best young American Catholic priests to become the new bishops. A tangled web indeed.

> **Paragraph 50.** Not happy with the trap he had set for me on June 23, 2013, when he asked me about McCarrick, only a few months later, in the audience he granted me on October 10, 2013, Pope Francis set a second one for me, this time concerning a second of his protégés, Cardinal Donald Wuerl. He asked me: **"What is Cardinal Wuerl like, is he good or bad?"** I replied, *"Holy Father, I will not tell you if he is good or bad, but I will tell you two facts."* They are the ones I have already mentioned above, which concern Wuerl's pastoral carelessness regarding the aberrant deviations at *Georgetown University* and the invitation by the Archdiocese of Washington to young aspirants to the priesthood to a meeting with McCarrick! Once again the Pope did not show any reaction.

We learn here of a second face-to-face meeting between Viganò and Pope Francis, this one in October of 2013, four months after their June meeting. McCarrick does not seem to have come up at this meeting. Now the topic is the activity of Cardinal Wuerl, McCarrick's successor as archbishop of Washington. Viganò tells the pope of two things that Wuerl has done which suggest a "careless" attitude to "aberrant deviations." Wuerl is still inviting McCarrick to meet with young men aspiring to the priesthood. Business as usual, it seems. Viganò concludes: "Once again the Pope did not show any reaction."

Viganò is coming to believe that McCarrick, feeling confident of his close relationship with Francis, is forging ahead to bring men he likes into key posts across the United States. McCarrick is choosing the new bishops, acting, in a sense, as a nuncio ought to act, even exercising an authority like that of a pope. See the next paragraph.

> **Paragraph 51.** It was also clear that, from the time of Pope Francis's election, McCarrick, now free from all constraints, had felt free to travel continuously, to give lectures and interviews. In a team effort with **Cardinal Rodriguez Maradiaga**, he had become the kingmaker for appointments in the Curia and the United States, and the most listened to advisor in the Vatican for relations with the Obama administration. This is how one explains that, as members of the Congregation for Bishops, the Pope replaced Cardinal Burke with Wuerl and immediately appointed Cupich right after he was made a cardinal. With these appointments the Nunciature in Washington was now out of the picture in the appointment of bishops. In addition, he appointed the Brazilian **Ilson de Jesus Montanari**—the great friend of his private Argentine secretary Fabian Pedacchio—as Secretary of the same Congregation for Bishops and Secretary of the College of Cardinals, promoting him in one single leap from a simple official of that department to Archbishop Secretary. Something unprecedented for such an important position!

Here we are introduced to (46) **Cardinal Óscar Andrés Rodríguez Maradiaga** of Tegucigalpa, Honduras, in Central America, the influential member of a special "Council of Eight Cardinals" Pope Francis has set up to advise him, and we meet again the Brazilian (25) **Ilson de Jesus Montanari**, who, Viganò tells us, is "the great friend of his private Argentine secretary Fabian

Pedacchio." Made secretary, the number two post after the prefect (in this case, number two after Cardinal Ouellet) of the Congregation for Bishops—the office in Rome that chooses the bishops for the world—Montanari is extremely influential in "staffing" the future Church.

Viganò also claims that McCarrick is friendly with Maradiaga and worked in a "team effort" with him with regard to appointments to the episcopate in America. Moreover, McCarrick has positioned himself so that he is the voice most listened to in Rome in matters concerning Church relations with the US administration led at the time by (47) **President Barack Obama**. So McCarrick is influential on matters of Church and also on matters of state.

We also have a mention here of (48) **Cardinal Raymond Burke**. Viganò tells us that Burke, who had been a member of the Congregation for Bishops in Rome, and so had a vote on who would be made bishop in every diocese in the world, was ousted and replaced by Wuerl, McCarrick's successor in Washington. As of this writing, Wuerl, though in retirement, is still in that post in Rome.

> **Paragraph 52.** The appointments of **Blase Cupich** to Chicago and **Joseph W. Tobin** to Newark were orchestrated by McCarrick, Maradiaga and Wuerl, united by a wicked pact of abuses by the first, and at least of coverup of abuses by the other two. Their names were not among those presented by the Nunciature for Chicago and Newark.

Viganò here tosses a couple of verbal incendiary grenades, saying that McCarrick, Maradiaga (who is in the pope's Council of Eight), and Wuerl (who is on the Congregation for Bishops in Rome) were "united by a wicked pact" to choose the men to occupy two prominent sees and to become cardinals: (49) **Blase Cupich**, who is now a cardinal and the archbishop of Chicago, and (50) **Joseph Tobin**, who is also a cardinal and is the archbishop of Newark, New Jersey, where McCarrick was archbishop before he was named to Washington. Viganò gives us one specific point of information which some critics have contested and said is not true: he tells us that Cupich and Tobin "were not among those presented by the Nunciature for Chicago and Newark." In other words, the nuncio (who was Viganò himself) allegedly sent over to Rome a *terna*, or list, of three names for each diocese as suggestions for who should be chosen to be the bishop of Newark and of Chicago, but in Rome, the congregation decided to insert a name not on the list;—that is, to insert the names of Cupich and Tobin—and choose them. Viganò himself was responsible for presenting the "*terna*" of names, so one would have to believe he is lying when he says that the names of Cupich and Tobin were not presented by the nunciature. However, this point ought to be able to be proven, one way or the other, by a check of the archive of the Congregation for Bishops.

**Paragraph 53.** Regarding **Cupich**, one cannot fail to note his ostentatious arrogance, and the insolence with which he denies the evidence that is now obvious to all: that 80% of the abuses found were committed against young adults by homosexuals who were in a relationship of authority over their victims.

This paragraph seems a bit out of place in the "Testimony." It could perhaps have been written without the words "ostentatious arrogance" and "insolence" and merely present the fact that Cupich has denied the relevance of studies showing a link between homosexuality and cases of sexual abuse. Sentences like this one led Viganò's "Testimony" to be regarded as shrill and intemperate. In this instance, the critics may have a point. That said, when one considers the fact that we are talking about priestly sexual abuse of young people, which, as Viganò correctly noted, is largely a homosexual issue, the righteous indignation is better understood. In the next paragraph, Viganò, more calmly, sets forth some facts which do seem to suggest that Cupich should reconsider his position that clericalism and not homosexuality is a risk factor in cases of sexual abuse of young people.

> **Paragraph 54.** During the speech he gave when he took possession of the Chicago See, at which I was present as a representative of the Pope, Cupich quipped that one certainly should not expect the new Archbishop to walk on water. Perhaps it would be enough for him to be able to remain with his feet on the ground and not try to turn reality upside-down, blinded by his pro-gay ideology, as he stated in a recent interview with *America Magazine*. Extolling his particular expertise in the matter, having been President of the *Committee on Protection of Children and Young People* of the USCCB, he asserted that the main problem in the crisis of sexual abuse by clergy is not homosexuality, and that affirming this is only a way

of diverting attention from the real problem which is clericalism. In support of this thesis, Cupich "oddly" made reference to the results of research carried out at the height of the sexual abuse of minors crisis in the early 2000s, while he "candidly" ignored that the results of that investigation were totally denied by the subsequent Independent Reports by the *John Jay College of Criminal Justice* in 2004 and 2011, which concluded that, in cases of sexual abuse, 81% of the victims were male. In fact, Father Hans Zollner, S.J., Vice-Rector of the Pontifical Gregorian University, President of the *Centre for Child Protection*, and Member of the Pontifical Commission for the Protection of Minors, recently told the newspaper *La Stampa* that "*in most cases it is a question of homosexual abuse.*"

Here we are introduced to (51) **Father Hans Zollner**, SJ, vice-rector of the Gregorian University of Rome, an expert on questions of sexual abuse of young people by priests. Viganò attributes to him remarks which give the lie to Cupich's position.

> **Paragraph 55.** The appointment of McElroy in San Diego was also orchestrated from above, with an encrypted peremptory order to me as Nuncio, by Cardinal Parolin: "*Reserve the See of San Diego for McElroy.*" McElroy was also well aware of McCarrick's abuses, as can be seen from a letter sent to him by Richard Sipe on July 28, 2016.

We have here the unusual revelation of "an encrypted peremptory order" Viganò received in Washington. The revelation has been sharply criticized in the Vatican. Such "encrypted orders" should never be revealed under any circumstances, these Vatican officials say. For

Viganò to reveal the content of this encrypted note is characterized by his enemies as unprofessional on his part. An exhausted laity, still reeling from the revelations of widespread homosexual abuse and corruption in the Church, may be less troubled about such charges of "unprofessionalism" and more concerned with the seeming "packing of the episcopate" with bishops of a certain outlook. The note from Cardinal Parolin said, "Reserve the See of San Diego for McElroy." This refers to (55) **Bishop Robert McElroy**, a "reform-minded" prelate who graduated from Harvard College in 1975. Viganò was still the nuncio to the United States when, on March 3, 2015, McElroy was appointed bishop of San Diego by Pope Francis, succeeding the late Bishop Cirilo Flores.

> **Paragraph 56.** These characters are closely associated with individuals belonging in particular to the deviated wing of the Society of Jesus, unfortunately today a majority, which had already been a cause of serious concern to Paul VI and subsequent pontiffs. We need only consider **Father Robert Drinan, S.J.**, who was elected four times to the House of Representatives, and was a staunch supporter of abortion; or **Father Vincent O'Keefe, S.J.**, one of the principal promoters of *The Land O'Lakes Statement* of 1967, which seriously compromised the Catholic identity of universities and colleges in the United States. It should be noted that McCarrick, then President of the Catholic University of Puerto Rico, also participated in that inauspicious undertaking which was so harmful to the formation of the consciences of American youth, closely associated as it was with the deviated wing of the Jesuits.

In this paragraph, Viganò opens up a new theme, that of the Jesuits. The connection is that Bishop McElroy studied with the Jesuits and has written articles for the Jesuit magazine in the United States, *America*. Viganò speaks of "the deviated wing of the Society of Jesus" which "unfortunately today" has become "a majority." He introduces us to two new men (53) **Fr. Robert Drinan, SJ**, and (54) **Fr. Vincent O'Keefe, SJ**. He notes that Drinan was "a staunch supporter of abortion" and that O'Keefe promoted the *The Land O'Lakes Statement* of 1967, which he says "seriously compromised the Catholic identity of universities and colleges in the United States." Of course, Pope Francis is the first Jesuit ever to be elected pope. What is clear here is that Viganò has on his mind the idea that "deviations" in the Jesuit order have had negative consequences for the Catholic faith.

> **Paragraph 57. Father James Martin, S.J.**, acclaimed by the people mentioned above, in particular **Cupich, Tobin, Farrell and McElroy**, appointed Consultor of the Secretariat for Communications, well-known activist who promotes the LGBT agenda, chosen to corrupt the young people who will soon gather in Dublin for the World Meeting of Families, is nothing but a sad recent example of that deviated wing of the Society of Jesus.

Viganò devotes this paragraph to what he calls the "sad example of that deviated wing of the Society of Jesus," (55) **Fr. James Martin, SJ**. The words may seem harsh. Viganò's critics pointed to passages like this as evidence of his uncharitable vehemence. However, in Catholic teaching, the moral law of the Church is a way of salvation, and the ways of this world, when they conflict with that law, lead to misery and perdition. Viganò was vehement because souls are at stake and Martin himself is so unilateral in his way of presenting, many say distorting, Catholic moral teaching. Viganò was only summarizing a point of view expressed by many others in a more detailed way. In an August 29, 2018 article in *Catholic World Report*, for example, Fr. Steve Mattson wrote on Fr. Martin:

> The major theme of Fr. Martin's talks, tweets, and articles is a celebration of all things LGBT (including even Gay Pride events). . . . What Fr. Martin writes and says . . . is more aligned to the thinking of the World than the Word. . . . Despite his notoriety, Fr. Martin doesn't help us think deeply about the relevant questions. At all. That's because he doesn't talk seriously about chastity, or what it takes to live chaste lives. He focuses instead on feelings. . . . He simply does not think with the Church. I had long-suspected, as many have, that Fr. Martin has been propped up by gay-agenda promoting bishops and cardinals."[22]

So Viganò's apparent bluntness here is due to his concern for the salvation of souls.

**Paragraph 58.** <u>Pope Francis has repeatedly asked for total transparency in the Church and for bishops and faithful to act with *parrhesia*. The faithful throughout the world also demand this of him in an exemplary manner. He must honestly state when he first learned</u>

---

22    Fr. Steve Mattson, "Fr. James Martin is not thinking with the Church," *The Catholic World Report*, August 29, 2018, https://www.catholicworldreport.com/2018/08/29/fr-james-martin-is-not-thinking-with-the-church/.

**about the crimes committed by McCarrick, who abused his authority with seminarians and priests**.

In this paragraph and the next two, Viganò is summing up his "Testimony" in so far as it relates to Pope Francis. He is no longer giving us new evidence or new information. He is drawing conclusions. Here he asks Pope Francis to "honestly state when he first learned about the crimes committed by McCarrick." It is not yet a call for resignation. That will come.

**Paragraph 59. In any case, the Pope learned about it from me on June 23, 2013 and continued to cover for him. He did not take into account the sanctions that Pope Benedict had imposed on him and made him his trusted counselor along with Maradiaga**.

Viganò asserts the truthfulness of his account of the meeting he had with the pope on June 23, 2013—that he told the pope about McCarrick's misconduct. And he asserts that Francis nevertheless made McCarrick a "trusted counselor." He asserts that the pope continued "to cover for him." These are heavy accusations against the pope. At the outset, the "Testimony" had criticized the entire hierarchy, accusing many prelates of a kind of collective "culture of silence" with regard to abuse. Here, Viganò is becoming increasingly focused on Pope Francis, to the exclusion of those other prelates.

**Paragraph 60.** The latter [Maradiaga] is so confident of the Pope's protection that he can dismiss as "gossip" the heartfelt appeals of dozens of his seminarians, who found the courage to write to him after one of them tried to commit suicide over homosexual abuse in the seminary.

Here Viganò brings in a new accusation, but without any details, of abuse occurring in a seminary in Honduras under the authority of Cardinal Maradiaga.

> **Paragraph 61.** By now the faithful have well understood **Maradiaga's** strategy: insult the victims to save himself, lie to the bitter end to cover up a chasm of abuses of power, of mismanagement in the administration of Church property, and of financial disasters even against close friends, as in the case of the Ambassador of Honduras Alejandro Valladares, former Dean of the Diplomatic Corps to the Holy See.

Here we are introduced to a prominent lay diplomat from Honduras, now deceased, (56) **Alejandro Emilio Valladares Lanza.** Valladares served as the ambassador from Honduras to the Holy See and, in recent years, was the dean of the diplomatic corps to the Vatican, which includes more than one hundred ambassadors from around the world. There are rather vague allusions here to various problems in Honduras: "abuses of power," "mismanagement," "financial disasters." What is this about? In an April 6, 2019 article in the *National Catholic Register*, British Vaticanist Edward Pentin interviewed the widow of the late Ambassador Valladares, Martha Alegria Reichmann.[23] She had just published a book enti-

---

[23]   Edward Pentin, "Author Accuses Honduran Cardinal of 'Betrayal' and 'Cover-Up' in New Book," National Catholic Register, April 6, 2019, https://www.ncregister.com/daily -news/author-accuses-honduras-cardinal-of-betrayal-and -cover-up-in-new-book.

tled *Sacred Betrayal* (*Traiciones Sagradas* in the original Spanish) in which she accuses Cardinal Maradiaga of various "abuses of power" and "financial disasters." So it seems that these stories were circulating in diplomatic circles—circles where Viganò was very well-informed, having himself spent decades in the Vatican diplomatic service. Pentin writes:

> The widow of a former dean of the Vatican diplomatic corps has written an exposé accusing one of Pope Francis' closest aides of betraying her family and covering up for grave misconduct. Martha Alegria Reichmann, whose late husband, Alejandro Valladares, was the Honduran ambassador to the Holy See for 22 years, explains in the book, *Sacred Betrayal,* how they were once close friends of Cardinal Óscar Rodriguez Maradiaga, the longtime archbishop of Tegucigalpa. Her book, so far only in Spanish, chronicles how the cardinal, who is coordinator of the "council of cardinals" advising the Holy Father on Church reform, advised her to make a bad financial investment that caused her to lose her life savings. She also provides details of the cardinal's support for Bishop Juan Josè Pineda, who has been accused of sexual abuse of seminarians, living in active homosexual relationships and financial impropriety. Pope Francis accepted Bishop Pineda's resignation last July, but no details of any disciplinary measures have been revealed.

So this paragraph of Viganò's "Testimony" is a frontal attack on the credibility of Maradiaga. Still, the allegations, at least in the "Testimony," are presented without sufficient evidence to judge to what extent they are true. This would require further investigation and cross-checking everything. However, in her interview, the ambassador's widow makes this claim: "In the book there are very strong accusations and terrible revelations, but after everything, I give the evidence. So nothing is either invented or exaggerated. What is more, there are cases that are terrible and I did not include them because I do not have the evidence."

> **Paragraph 62.** In the case of the former Auxiliary Bishop Juan José Pineda, after the article published in the [Italian] weekly *L'Espresso* last February, Maradiaga stated in the newspaper *Avvenire*: "*It was my auxiliary bishop Pineda who asked for the visitation, so as to 'clear' his name after being subjected to much slander.*" Now, regarding Pineda the only thing that has been made public is that his resignation has simply been accepted, thus making any possible responsibility of his and Maradiaga vanish into nowhere.

In this paragraph, we are introduced to another high-ranking prelate from Honduras, (57) **Auxiliary Bishop Juan José Pineda**, who submitted his resignation to Pope Francis in the summer of 2018. Before that resignation, in an April 27, 2018 article in the *National Catholic Register*, Edward Pentin wrote:

> Despite serious allegations involving abuse of seminarians and financial misconduct leveled against him, Honduran Auxiliary Bishop Juan José Pineda Fasquelle of Tegucigalpa remains in position, and put in charge of the archdiocese during the frequent times Cardinal Oscar Andrés Rodriguez Maradiaga is away. Sources in the Honduran capital have told the *Register* that no action has been taken against Bishop Pineda, even though a papal investigation last year

contained accounts of sexual abuse allegedly perpetrated by Bishop Pineda against priests and seminarians, as well as allegations of extensive financial misconduct and corruption. The head of the investigation, retired Argentine Bishop Alcides Jorge Pedro Casaretto, was reportedly shocked by the testimonies, taken from more than 50 witnesses, including diocesan staff members and priests. The *Register* obtained affidavits from two of the seminarians who accused Bishop Pineda of sexual abuse.[24]

**Paragraph 63.** In the name of the transparency so hailed by the Pope, the report that the Visitator, Argentine bishop Alcides Casaretto, delivered more than a year ago only and directly to the Pope, must be made public.

In paragraph 63, Viganò mentions a document, which we may call **Document 11**, that Viganò says ought to be released to make clearer the ecclesial situation in Honduras. He also introduces us to the document's author, (58) **Alcides Casaretto**. The document is Casaretto's report on an inquiry he conducted into these problems in Honduras. He gave his report to the pope in 2017. Viganò is calling for this report to be made public.

**Paragraph 64.** Finally, the recent appointment as Substitute of **Archbishop Edgar Peña Parra** is also connected with Honduras, that is, with **Maradiaga**. From 2003 to 2007 Peña Parra worked as Counsellor at the Tegucigalpa Nunciature. As Delegate for Pontifical

---

[24] Edward Pentin, "Honduran Seminarians Allege Widespread Homosexual Misconduct," National Catholic Register, July 25, 2018, https://www.ncregister.com/daily-news/honduran-sem inarians-allege-widespread-homosexual-misconduct.

Representations I received worrisome information about him.

In paragraph 64, Viganò tells us that reports he received in his official role as delegate for pontifical representations in Rome contained "worrisome" information about (59) **Archbishop Edgar Peña Parra**, now the "*Sostituto*," or deputy secretary of state in the Vatican. In the spring of 2019, in his interview with the *Washington Post*, Viganò will speak about the Peña Parra case, but the *Post* will decline to print the "worrisome" information without confirming it on-site in Venezuela, where Peña Parra is from.

> **Paragraph 65.** In Honduras, a scandal as huge as the one in Chile is about to be repeated. The Pope defends his man, Cardinal Rodriguez Maradiaga, to the bitter end, as he had done in Chile with Bishop Juan de la Cruz Barros, whom he himself had appointed Bishop of Osorno against the advice of the Chilean Bishops. First he insulted the abuse victims. Then, only when he was forced by the media, and a revolt by the Chilean victims and faithful, did he recognize his error and apologize, while stating that he had been misinformed, causing a disastrous situation for the Church in Chile, but continuing to protect the two Chilean Cardinals Errazuriz and Ezzati.

In paragraph 65, Viganò tells us that a "scandal" is about to emerge in Honduras around Maradiaga "as huge as the one in Chile," where allegations of abuse were at first denied then affirmed after many years. Viganò criticizes the pope's slowness in believing the accusations of sexual abuse brought forward in Chile. We are introduced here to three of the Chilean prelates involved: (60) **Bishop Juan de la Cruz Barros**, who was disgraced after his abusive activity was finally revealed and made public, (61) **Cardinal Francisco Javier Errazuriz Ossa**, created cardinal in 2001 by Pope John Paul II and accused of covering up the acts of sexual abuse by Father Fernando Karadima (Errazuriz sent a priest to investigate the accusations and the priest told Errazuriz he considered "everything absolutely implausible," but the abuse seemingly had occurred; he served for five years on the "Council of Eight Cardinals" who were the closest advisors of Pope Francis), and (62) **Cardinal Ricardo Ezzati Andrello**, the successor of Errazuriz as archbishop of Santiago from 2010 to 2019, when he resigned; he was head of the Chilean bishops' conference from 2010 to 2016 and a defendant in a lawsuit against the diocese for the abuses of Karadima.

> **Paragraph 66.** Even in the tragic affair of McCarrick, Pope Francis's behavior was no different. He knew from at least June 23, 2013 that McCarrick was a serial predator. Although he knew that he was a corrupt man, he covered for him to the bitter end; indeed, he made McCarrick's advice his own, which was certainly not inspired by sound intentions and for love of the Church. It was only when he was forced by the report of the abuse of a minor, again on the basis of media attention, that he took action [*regarding McCarrick*] to save his image in the media.

This is Viganò's denunciation of Pope Francis for not acting on McCarrick.

> **Paragraph 67.** <u>Now in the United States a chorus</u>

of voices is rising especially from the lay faithful, and
has recently been joined by several bishops and priests,
asking that all those who, by their silence, covered
up McCarrick's criminal behavior, or who used him
to advance their career or promote their intentions,
ambitions and power in the Church, should resign.

Viganò attributes the call for resignations of "all those
who, by their silence, covered up McCarrick's criminal
behavior" to "a chorus of voices" rising "especially from
the lay faithful" in the United States. Viganò is about to
add his voice to theirs.

**Paragraph 68.** But this will not be enough to heal the
situation of extremely grave immoral behavior by the
clergy: bishops and priests. A time of conversion and
penance must be proclaimed. The virtue of chastity
must be recovered in the clergy and in seminaries.
Corruption in the misuse of the Church's resources
and of the offerings of the faithful must be fought
against. The seriousness of homosexual behavior must
be denounced. The homosexual networks present in the
Church must be eradicated, as Janet Smith, Professor
of Moral Theology at the Sacred Heart Major Seminary
in Detroit, recently wrote. "*The problem of clergy abuse,*"
she wrote, "*cannot be resolved simply by the resignation of
some bishops, and even less so by bureaucratic directives. The
deeper problem lies in homosexual networks within the clergy
which must be eradicated.*" These homosexual networks,
which are now widespread in many dioceses, seminaries,
religious orders, *etc.*, act under the concealment of
secrecy and lies with the power of octopus tentacles, and
strangle innocent victims and priestly vocations, and are
strangling the entire Church.

Viganò extends the indictment far beyond Pope Francis to "the homosexual networks present in the Church" which he says, quoting American theologian (63) **Dr. Janet Smith**, "must be eradicated."

> **Paragraph 69. <u>I implore everyone, especially Bishops, to speak up in order to defeat this conspiracy of silence that is so widespread, and to report the cases of abuse they know about to the media and civil authorities</u>.**

Viganò calls for complete transparency on these cases of sexual abuse.

> **Paragraph 70.** Let us heed the most powerful message that St. John Paul II left us as an inheritance: *Do not be afraid! Do not be afraid!*
>
> **Paragraph 71.** In his 2008 homily on the Feast of the Epiphany, Pope Benedict reminded us that the Father's plan of salvation had been fully revealed and realized in the mystery of Christ's death and resurrection, but it needs to be welcomed in human history, which is always a history of fidelity on God's part and unfortunately also of infidelity on the part of us men. The Church, the depository of the blessing of the New Covenant, signed in the blood of the Lamb, is holy but made up of sinners, as Saint Ambrose wrote: the Church is "*immaculata ex maculatis*," she is holy and spotless even though, in her earthly journey, she is made up of men stained with sin.

We have a reflection now on the mystery of the Church, "holy but made up of sinners," and after citing (1) **Pope Benedict**, he cites (64) **St. Ambrose of Milan**, Viganò's home city, who wrote that the Church is "holy though made up of men stained with sin."

> **Paragraph 72.** I want to recall this indefectible truth of the Church's holiness to the many people who have been

so deeply scandalized by the abominable and sacrilegious behavior of the former Archbishop of Washington, Theodore McCarrick; by the grave, disconcerting and sinful conduct of Pope Francis and by the conspiracy of silence of so many pastors, and who are tempted to abandon the Church, disfigured by so many ignominies. At the Angelus on Sunday, August 12, 2018 Pope Francis said these words: *"Everyone is guilty for the good he could have done and did not do ... If we do not oppose evil, we tacitly feed it. We need to intervene where evil is spreading; for evil spreads where daring Christians who oppose evil with good are lacking."* If this is rightly to be considered a serious moral responsibility for every believer, how much graver is it for the Church's supreme pastor, who in the case of McCarrick not only did not oppose evil but associated himself in doing evil with someone he knew to be deeply corrupt. He followed the advice of someone he knew well to be a pervert, thus multiplying exponentially with his supreme authority the evil done by McCarrick. And how many other evil pastors is Francis still continuing to prop up in their active destruction of the Church!

**Paragraph 73.** Francis is abdicating the mandate which Christ gave to Peter to confirm the brethren. Indeed, by his action he has divided them, led them into error, and encouraged the wolves to continue to tear apart the sheep of Christ's flock.

Viganò, in these two paragraphs above, is reiterating his denunciation of the lack of action and cover-ups in the McCarrick case. He says, "Francis is abdicating his mandate to confirm the brethren." In this sense, he is calling on Francis to be fully and powerfully the pope. He is calling on him to truly be (65) **St. Peter**, the first pope.

**Paragraph 74.** In this extremely dramatic moment for the universal Church, he must acknowledge his mistakes and, in keeping with the proclaimed principle of zero tolerance, **Pope Francis must be the first to set a good example for cardinals and bishops who covered up McCarrick's abuses and resign along with all of them**.

Here he calls on Francis to resign.

> **Paragraph 75.** Even in dismay and sadness over the enormity of what is happening, **let us not lose hope!** We well know that the great majority of our pastors live their priestly vocation with fidelity and dedication.
>
> **Paragraph 76.** It is in moments of great trial that the Lord's grace is revealed in abundance and makes His limitless mercy available to all; but it is granted only to those who are truly repentant and sincerely propose to amend their lives. This is a favorable time for the Church to confess her sins, to convert, and to do penance.
>
> **Paragraph 77.** Let us all pray for the Church and for the Pope, let us remember how many times he has asked us to pray for him!
>
> **Paragraph 78.** Let us all renew faith in the Church our Mother: "I believe in one, holy, catholic and apostolic Church!"
>
> **Paragraph 79.** Christ will never abandon His Church! He generated her in His Blood and continually revives her with His Spirit!
>
> **Paragraph 80.** Mary, Mother of the Church, pray for us! Mary, Virgin and Queen, Mother of the King of glory, pray for us!
>
> *Rome, August 22, 2018 Queenship of the Blessed Virgin Mary*

The last person he refers to is (66) **Mary,** "Mother of the Church . . . Virgin and queen, Mother of the King of glory."

## CHAPTER 13

# THE POPE'S SILENCE

*"You hate all evildoers. You destroy those who speak lies."*
—Psalm 5:5–6

POPE FRANCIS was asked about Viganò's public call for his resignation within hours. His response was to make no comment at all. "I will not say a single word on this," he told the world's journalists during an August 26 airplane press conference.

Viganò's "Testimony" was released to the world via various internet sites on the evening of August 25, 2018, and on August 26, Pope Francis was in his papal airplane flying back from a World Meeting of Families in Ireland. During the flight, as is his practice on such occasions, Francis agreed to take questions from the press.

Anna Matranga of CBS news, an American network, asked the pope:

> Good evening, Holy Father! I would like to return to the topic of "abuse" about which you have already spoken. In a document issued early this morning, Archbishop Carlo Maria Viganò says that in 2013 he had a personal conversation with you at the Vatican, and that in this meeting he spoke explicitly with you about the sexual abuse by former Cardinal McCarrick. I wanted to ask you if this is true. Another question I wanted to ask of

you: the Archbishop also said that Pope Benedict XVI had imposed sanctions on McCarrick, telling him not to live in the seminary, not to celebrate Masses in public and not to travel; the Church imposed sanctions on him. Can I ask you if these two things are true?

Pope Francis replied:

Just one thing. I would prefer—even though I will answer your question—that we speak about the trip [to Ireland] and then move on to other topics . . . but I will answer your question. I read the statement this morning. I read it and sincerely I must tell you, and all those who are interested: read it yourselves carefully and make your own judgment. I will not say a single word on this. I believe the memo speaks for itself, and you are capable enough as journalists to draw your own conclusions. This is an act of trust: when some time has passed and you have drawn conclusions, perhaps I will speak. But I ask that you use your professional maturity in doing this: it will do you good, really. That is enough for now.

The pope's council of cardinal advisors issued a statement on September 10 expressing their "full solidarity with Pope Francis in the face of what has happened in these last weeks"; namely, the accusation against him by Archbishop Viganò. They added that they were aware that the Holy See is preparing "the eventual and necessary clarifications" in response to the grave allegations Archbishop Viganò made in August. (As I write a year and half later, that response has not yet been forthcoming, though it has been rumored to be "imminent" for more than a year now.)

So did the archbishop not tell the truth about his

conversation with Pope Francis? Why did Pope Francis choose to say nothing about the conversation? If it wasn't true, why did he not say, "It isn't true, the conversation as the archbishop describes it did not occur." Or, perhaps, "The conversation did occur, the archbishop is correct. But I had my reasons for acting as I did, which I do not wish to discuss."

In May 2019, Pope Francis granted an interview to Mexican journalist Valentina Alazraki and made his first, and only, direct comments about the case of former Cardinal McCarrick. "About McCarrick, I knew nothing, obviously, nothing, nothing," Francis said. "I said it many times, I knew nothing, no idea."

When Alazraki asked the pope directly about the allegation made by Archbishop Carlo Maria Viganò that he had told the pope about Vatican-imposed restrictions against the former archbishop of Washington, Francis said, "I don't remember if he told me about this. If it's true or not. No idea! But you know that about McCarrick, I knew nothing. If not, I wouldn't have remained quiet, right?" Earlier in this book, the seemingly self-contradictory nature of this statement was pointed out.

CHAPTER 14

# AFTER THE "TESTIMONY"

*"Set a guard over my mouth, O LORD, keep
watch over the door to my lips."*
—Psalm 141:3

THE ARCHBISHOP published his "Testimony" on the
evening of August 25, 2018. Viganò described the corruption that he had witnessed in the leadership of the
Church and ended by calling on Pope Francis himself
to resign from the papacy. The text exploded within the
Catholic world with extraordinary force. Some Catholics, in their comments on the internet, expressed their
profound appreciation to the archbishop for finally
revealing the mechanism of this corruption and for
naming many names without fear or favor. "At last we
understand some of the background to this scandal,"
was the common judgment of these readers. But others had the opposite reaction. They said the archbishop
had really gone too far, naming names without providing
clear corroborating evidence of guilt, and had, unforgiv-
ably, offended the dignity of Pope Francis by calling for
his resignation in such a public way without any private
appeal to him in advance.

Dr. Massimo Faggioli, a prominent professor of
theology at Villanova University in Philadelphia,

Pennsylvania, born and educated in Italy, sharply criticized Viganò's "Testimony," saying it reflected a political battle within the Church. Viganò's indictment of Pope Francis with regard to McCarrick was therefore not balanced and worthy of belief, he said. "This letter has everything to do with factions in the Church that are vying for power and influence," he said.

But Cardinal Daniel DiNardo, president of the United States Conference of Catholic Bishops, released a statement declaring that Viganò's letter raised questions which "deserve answers that are conclusive and based on evidence. Without those answers, innocent men may be tainted by false accusation and the guilty may be left to repeat sins of the past."

Monsignor Jean-François Lantheaume, who had served as first counsellor at the nunciature in Washington, DC, stated that "Viganò said the truth" but declined to elaborate further. In his letter, Viganò had cited Lantheaume as the one who told him about the alleged "stormy" encounter between McCarrick and Archbishop Sambi in which Sambi informed McCarrick of the sanctions being placed on him.

Joseph E. Strickland, bishop of Tyler, Texas, said that he found Viganò's allegations "credible."

Bishop Athanasius Schneider of Kazakhstan stated that there was "no reasonable and plausible cause to doubt the truth content of the document." He demanded "transparency" in cleansing the Church of evils, particularly "homosexual cliques and networks" in the Curia.

Cardinal Gerhard Ludwig Müller, prefect emeritus for the Congregation for the Doctrine of the Faith, in an interview published on November 27, 2018, criticized Viganò's language against Pope Francis, saying, "No one has the right to indict the Pope or ask him to resign!" He said that these conversations "must take place in private, in the proper places, and without ever making a public controversy." Müller went on to say that such "attacks . . . end up questioning the credibility of the Church and Her mission." He added that he was convinced the pope "is doing everything possible" to resolve the abuse scandal.

In May 2019, Viganò gave a written interview via email to the *Washington Post*. Viganò argued that Pope Francis should not have defrocked McCarrick without a trial because a trial would have opened the way for other prelates who knew about McCarrick, or covered up for him, also to be indicted.

"Moreover," Viganò said, "having made the sentence definitive, the Pope has made it impossible to conduct any further investigation, which could have revealed who in the Curia and elsewhere knew of McCarrick's abuses, when they knew it, and who helped him to be named archbishop of Washington and eventually a cardinal." And he concluded, "Note, by the way, that the documents of this case, whose publication had been promised, have never been produced."

In September 2019, in the only interview McCarrick gave following the loss of his cardinal's position in 2018 and his laicization in early 2019, he still seemed to maintain his innocence of the charges. He dismissed Viganò's harsh denunciations of his conduct as politically based, saying, "He [Viganò] was talking as a representative of the far right, I think. I don't want to say he's a liar, but I think some of the bishops have said that he was not telling the truth."

Throughout the final months of 2018 and the first months of 2019, I maintained contact with Archbishop Viganò through a number of emails, but I had no idea where he was.

On October 1, 2018, I wrote a "Moynihan Letter" about the death of my mother, Ruth Moynihan, at the age of eighty-five on the Feast of St. Therese of Lisieux in Connecticut in the United States. I was at her side when she died. In the letter, I wrote:

> She had struggled for many months as a motor neuron disease took away her ability to walk, to talk, to swallow, and finally even to be, in this world. In her last hours today, we prayed a rosary. Yesterday, the parish priest visited, and anointed her, and gave her communion. As night came on, I read the *Book of Ruth* to her. As she grew weaker, she suffered greatly. Yet she was never demanding, self-centered, or impatient. Her greatest concern was always that my father, 92, have his eye-drops in the evening. She died as she had lived, for others.

In my email inbox the next day, I found this note from the archbishop, from wherever he was in hiding: "I offered a Mass for the eternal rest of your dear mother." Nothing more. But I felt thankful for this spiritual solidarity in a moment of sorrow.

\*\*\*

Again, the trajectory of Viganò's career took him up from a small town in northern Italy to the Eternal City of Rome, where he was promoted, step by step, through the Vatican's renowned diplomatic service to become one of a handful of men truly on the "inside" in the Church, devoting his life to the service of all of the recent popes, to whom he was ever the most loyal of sons—Paul VI, John Paul I, John Paul II, Benedict XVI, and then, yes, also Francis—until, at the very end, something happened. The man who for a time had run the day-to-day affairs of Vatican City, the man who rose each day to say his Mass at 7 a.m. in St. Peter's Basilica and then spent his hours attempting to streamline and better organize every facet of the administration of the Vatican—to the point where he was widely regarded as a heroic figure in the battle against every sort of financial corruption—was no longer "welcome" in the Vatican and was indeed in hiding in an undisclosed location. How did this happen?

Archbishop Carlo Maria Viganò became a hero to some and a pariah to others because, quite simply, he named names. Many names. He broke with the Vatican's "culture of silence" and spoke out about things more clearly than any other top Church leader in recent decades has ever done. Cardinal Joseph Ratzinger, just before he was elected Pope Benedict XVI in April of 2005, had lamented the "filth" that had covered up the image of Christ in the Church, that had harmed so many innocent young people and children. But Viganò explained the mechanism of that cover up: an interlocking network of corrupt ecclesial movers and shakers who mutually supported one another and hermetically sealed

off their evil actions from any scrutiny from the rest of
the world. Viganò prompted astonishment and outrage
on the "left" when he went so far as to call publicly for
Pope Francis himself to resign, saying Francis had not
done enough to expose and punish sexual abusers during
his pontificate, notably in the case of once-cardinal Theodore McCarrick.

Viganò's critics blasted him, saying he was not telling the truth, that his motives were not pure, that he
did not wish solely to purify the Church and protect the
innocent, but wished for revenge because he had not
been promoted to cardinal and was supporting a hidden
political, ideological agenda not rooted in the Catholic
faith but in worldly alliances. But Viganò said no, that
was false, that he was motivated by a desire to cleanse
the Church and protect the innocent from the horror
of abuse in order to prepare his own soul to meet his
Maker. In his late seventies, Viganò said, he knew he
would live only a few more years, and so he was acting
out of conscience, not calculation. In this line, Viganò
called on Francis to repent, publicly, of his omissions
and oversights. And Viganò himself stated that he himself is profoundly repentant for not having done enough
during forty years of a distinguished ecclesial career to
protect the innocent abused, to tell the truth, and so is
speaking out now in an effort to repair some of the harm
that his own inaction has caused.

Thus, one of the most significant ecclesial figures of
our time entered the consciousness of millions, Catholic
and non-Catholic, around the world. Viganò, overnight,
became the very special "truth-telling archbishop" who

had dared to speak out against abuse and cover-up even when all others held their tongues, whatever the cost to himself, even risking his safety and, perhaps, his life. ("When you have meetings with Vatican officials in the Vatican," he once said to me, with a little sparkle in his eye to show he was kidding me, "and you are offered a cup of coffee to drink, just politely decline." I replied, "Oh come on! You're kidding me, right?" And he laughed and said, "Sure. Just kidding." And then his tone changed, as if he were serious. "But still, don't take a coffee if it is offered to you.")

With his retirement into silence, Viganò became still more mysterious and intriguing. Who was this man? Why had he decided to speak out in this way? Where had he gone? Was he really afraid that the Vatican would find him and do him harm? What did he know about the corruption in the Vatican? Did he know more than he had revealed in his "Testimony"? And what had impelled him to break ranks with all of his long-time colleagues, naming names in an unprecedented way, one after the other, accusing many respected members of the hierarchy, and even Pope Francis himself, of not living up to their oaths of office, of not leading the Church with integrity, of not shepherding the flock with truthfulness and justice, but misleading the people, abandoning them to abuse and false teaching?

# CHAPTER 15

# FLAWED CHARACTERS

*"For the LORD knows the way of the righteous, but the way of the wicked will perish."*
—Psalm 1:6

I HAD long meditated on the Viganò affair because I knew and felt a certain sympathy for all of the main characters involved: for Viganò, now seventy-nine, for Emeritus Pope Benedict XVI, now ninety-three, for Pope Francis, now eighty-three, for many other leading Vatican officials, and even for former Cardinal Theodore McCarrick, now eighty-nine, and himself living in hiding and disgrace (it is rumored that he lives near Jacksonville, Florida, where Father Marcial Maciel, founder of the Legionaries of Christ, died in 2008).

I had crossed paths with McCarrick a number of times over the years. He had congratulated me in 2005 for my reflections on CNN on the meaning of the pontificate of John Paul II at the time of John Paul's death and funeral.

More than a decade later, I was in the Holy See's nunciature in Washington, DC, on March 13 in 2016 for the celebration of the third anniversary of Pope Francis's election to the papacy when I saw McCarrick, then eighty-five, suddenly collapse. He simply sagged to the ground as if the life-force had gone out of him. His face became pale white, and he was taken out, barely conscious, in a wheelchair, his head hanging to one side, his eyes still open but expressionless. I thought he had had a stroke or heart attack. At that moment, I felt a certain sympathy for the old man, reduced to such a pitiable state. (This was two years before the Archdiocese of New York in June 2018 made the first official public declaration of McCarrick's abusive activities.)

And I had felt sympathy for the precise, almost jauntily efficient Viganò, a man of great precision and integrity who had given his life to the service of the Church, always doing whatever job he was asked to do with passion, commitment, loyalty, integrity, and good humor. I had felt sympathy for him because he had fallen so far in the estimation of many Vatican observers and insiders. From being one of the handful of top officials in the Vatican—let us say, among the top ten in importance and influence—he had fallen year by year into ever more pronounced insignificance, until, that is, he became, through the publication of his "Testimony" one of the most significant figures in the Church. After his passionate allegations against Pope Francis in August of 2018, he had come to be regarded by key Vatican leaders in the circle of Pope Francis as a "Judas," a "betrayer of the pope." For the past eighteen months, whenever Viganò's name had come up in Rome, most people would simply shake their heads in a mixture of disapproval and pity, gesturing vaguely with their hands as if it were impossible to come to grips with the shocking thing Viganò had done—call for a pope to resign. It was as if he had been black-listed and his name had become a bad omen. To speak in Soviet terms, he had become, for the Vatican, a "non-person." He had even lost the Vatican apartment he had thought he would keep for life—Pope Francis in 2016 had unceremoniously kicked Viganò out after his return from the United States, telling him he could not live in Vatican City. (Reportedly, Francis also told Bertone to leave, but Bertone paid no attention and never left.) But almost no one had really tried to determine if what he had alleged was true or not.

I had felt special affection for the "Professor-Pope" Benedict, who had lived peacefully with his sister, Maria, until 1991, when she passed away. In the 1990s, Benedict (then Cardinal Joseph Ratzinger) had been courteous toward me, getting up and walking over to help me pull on a cumbersome winter coat over my suit jacket after an hour's interview in his office at the Congregation for the Doctrine of the Faith discussing time and eternity under the Providence of God and the true happiness of man. I had come to know him to be a man of intellect and spirit and a gentle, kind soul, but the world had depicted him as a cruel, unfeeling, almost sadistic man. It was the most false, unfair character assassination I had ever seen.

And I had also felt sympathy for Pope Francis, who had come from the streets of Buenos Aires to the halls of Vatican City in 2013 in that perplexing historical moment when the previous pope had resigned and after the tiller of the barque of the Church had been, for a decade or more, in the hands of two popes who were either quite ill (St. John Paul II) or quite ill-adapted to govern (Pope Benedict).

I had felt the pain in Viganò's voice when he had

spoken to me privately about how various lobbies of corrupt men had exploited and betrayed the Church in recent decades and how he had fought them valiantly but in the end, for the most part, in vain.

I had sensed that same pain and weariness in Pope Benedict's voice on many occasions as he had lamented both the rise in the world of the "dictatorship of relativism," not at all interested in the true good of men and women, and the rise in the Church of a type of corrupt careerism which had little to do with the Gospel of Jesus Christ.

I had sensed, on many occasions, a similar pain in the voice of Pope Francis as he lamented the reduction of the Church's message to a set of moral rules ("moralism"), neglecting, overlooking, forgetting the surpassing gift of grace freely given through Jesus Christ, who by his sacrifice had set mankind free from the chains of sin and death. That said, many faithful Catholics, including myself, have been confused and disoriented by this pope's statements as well as his silences.

And I had even sensed, with sadness, the pain in then-Cardinal McCarrick's voice, when, after a long lunch in Washington, DC, in 2013, he had spoken of his childhood, of how his father had died when he was three years old, of how he had stayed often with his cousins in different homes, sometimes a number of cousins sleeping on a sofa or bed, everything disorganized and improvised; yet he spoke about feeling a great deal of love at all times. And then McCarrick had summed up his theological-moral position as we were leaving the restaurant: "In the end, Bob, for us, for our Christian faith, it's all about the love, isn't it? That's what truly matters, after all. Don't you think?" I remember thinking, "Well, yes, it is about love, but so much depends upon how one defines the word."

I had also prayed together with Viganò, Benedict, and Francis: with Viganò in the chapel of the nunciature in Washington, DC, with Benedict at numerous private Masses over the years, and at his regular Thursday morning Mass in the Campo Teutonico, and with Francis in the chapel of the Domus Santa Marta.

And knowing something of the pressures under which these men must labor, I, like millions of Catholics around the world, have prayed for them all innumerable times.

# PART III

# FROM 2018 TO 2019
# . . . MORE LETTERS

# CHAPTER 16

# TESTIMONY 2 AND VATICAN RESPONSE

*"I will sing to the LORD as long as I live"*
—Psalm 104:33

ARCHBISHOP VIGANÒ was not quiet for very long after his initial "Testimony." One month later, in September 2018, he issued a second, very eloquent testimony, "*Scio Cui credidi*" ("I know whom I have believed") (2 Tm 1:12). This Scripture passage is Viganò's episcopal motto.

In its opening paragraph, Viganò reminded his readers of his motive for writing, a refrain he has come back to again and again: "As a priest and bishop of the holy Church, spouse of Christ, I am called like every baptized person to bear witness to the truth."

But he also reminds us that the truth is a source of joy, quoting Psalm 103 at the beginning of his text:

"I will sing to the LORD as long as I live;
    I will sing praise to my God while I have being.
May my meditation be pleasing to him,
    for I rejoice in the LORD"(Ps 104:33–34).

Then he delves into the roiling controversy caused by his decision to issue his first testimony, what he calls "the most painful and serious decision that I have ever made in my life."

"Well aware," he says, "of the enormous consequences that my *Testimony* could have, because what I was about to reveal involved the successor of Peter himself, I nonetheless chose to speak in order to protect the Church, and I declare with a clear conscience before God that my testimony is true."

After calmly pointing out that pontifical secrets only exist to "protect the Church," he assures his readers that they "are not binding when very great harm can be avoided" by divulging them. And he challenges the pope or any cardinals in Rome to deny the facts as he has presented them, as they had so far not done, and have not done yet. Then he comes to the meat of his testimony: "The center of my testimony was that since at least June 23, 2013, the pope knew from me how perverse and evil McCarrick was in his intentions and actions, and instead of taking the measures that every good pastor would have taken, the pope made McCarrick one of his principal agents in governing the Church, in regard to the United States, the Curia, and even China, as we are seeing these days with great concern and anxiety for that martyr Church."

Viganò took issue with the pope's comparison of him to the "Great Accuser"—Satan—in his September 11, 2018 homily[25] and challenged Francis to instead respond

---

25   "Pope Francis at Mass: Bishops must pray to overcome 'Great Accuser,'" Vatican News, September 11, 2018, https://www.vaticannews.va/en/pope-francis/mass-casa-santa-marta/2018-09/pope-francis-mass-great-accuser-bishops-scandal.html.

both to his charges and "the appeals by the faithful for accountability." The pope's refusals, Viganò said, "are hardly consistent with his calls for transparency and bridge building."

In the homily containing the "Great Accuser" reference, Pope Francis had said:

> In these times, it seems like the "Great Accuser" has been unchained and is attacking bishops. True, we are all sinners, we bishops. He tries to uncover the sins, so they are visible in order to scandalize the people. The "Great Accuser," as he himself says to God in the first chapter of the Book of Job, "roams the earth looking for someone to accuse." A bishop's strength against the "Great Accuser" is prayer, that of Jesus and his own, and the humility of being chosen and remaining close to the people of God, without seeking an aristocratic life that removes this unction. Let us pray, today, for our bishops: for me, for those who are here, and for all the bishops throughout the world.

Many observers, Viganò included, consider that the pope was referring to Viganò when he made mention of the "Great Accuser."

The pope, he maintained, was not only guilty of a cover-up of McCarrick's crimes; Viganò cited the cases of three other credibly accused abusers as well. He also criticized the pope's apparent brush-off of USCCB president, the archbishop of Galveston-Houston, Cardinal Daniel DiNardo, who publicly called for a Vatican investigation into McCarrick's doings.

Finally, Viganò issued a somewhat heartbreaking appeal to Cardinal Marc Ouellet, prefect of the

Congregation for Bishops in Rome and himself briefly
a candidate for the papacy in 2013, for whom Viganò
expressed "great esteem and affection": "You have at your
complete disposal key documents incriminating McCarrick and many in the Curia for their cover-ups. Your
Eminence," Viganò wrote, "I urge you to bear witness to
the truth."

Viganò also noted that Ouellet, who had at one time
been "courageous," had since "given up" when his task
of recommending candidates for the episcopacy were
thwarted by two homosexual "friends" of his dicastery,
whose recommendations were sent directly to Francis,
"bypassing the Cardinal."

"This is a time of repentance, of conversion, of prayers,
of grace, to prepare the Church, the bride of the Lamb,
ready to fight and win with Mary the battle against the
old dragon," he said, concluding with his reflection on
a mosaic from the Basilica of St. Mark in Venice: *The
Calming of the Storm*, in which the disciples are afraid
when a storm arises and Jesus is asleep in the boat.

"The scene is very timely in portraying the tremendous
storm the Church is passing through in this moment,
but with a substantial difference: the successor of Peter
not only fails to see the Lord is in full control of the boat,
it seems he does not even intend to awaken Jesus asleep
in the bow.

"Has Christ perhaps become invisible to his vicar?
Perhaps is he being tempted to try to act as a substitute
of our only Master and Lord? The Lord is in full control
of the boat!"

# CHAPTER 17

# OUELLET'S ODD RESPONSE
## (OCTOBER 7, 2018)

*"Your current position appears incomprehen-*
*sible and extremely deplorable to me."*
—Cardinal Ouellet to Viganò, October 7, 2018

AFTER ARCHBISHOP Viganò's letter of appeal to Car-
dinal Marc Ouellet appeared in the media, it was just a
few days before Ouellet's response was published by the
Holy See's Press Office, entitled "Open letter by Card.
Marc Ouellet on recent accusations against the Holy
See," October 7, 2018.

Cardinal Marc Ouellet wrote to "his fellow brother,"
Archbishop Viganò, saying he would respond publicly in
this letter to Viganò's accusations on the basis of his own
personal knowledge and documents in the archive of the
Congregation for Bishops and asks him to return to full
communion with the Successor of Peter.

Here follow excerpts of the "Open Letter" by Cardinal
Ouellet:

Dear fellow brother, Carlo Maria Viganò,
In your last message to the media in which you denounce
Pope Francis and the Roman Curia, you urged me to tell
the truth about the facts which you interpret as endemic
corruption that has invaded the Church's hierarchy even

up to the highest levels. With due pontifical permission, I offer here my personal testimony, as the Prefect of the Congregation for Bishops, regarding the events concerning the Archbishop Emeritus of Washington, DC, Theodore McCarrick, and his presumed links with Pope Francis, which constitute the subject of your sensational public denunciation, as well as your demand that the Holy Father resign. I write this testimony based on my personal contacts and on archival documents of the aforementioned Congregation, which are currently the subject of a study in order to shed light on this sad case.

First of all, allow me to say to you with complete sincerity, by virtue of the good collaborative relationship that existed between us when you were the Nuncio in Washington, that your current position appears incomprehensible and extremely deplorable to me, not only because of the confusion that it sows in the People of God, but also because your public accusations seriously damage the reputation of the Successors of the Apostles. I remember the time in which I once enjoyed your esteem and confidence, but I realize that I stand to lose the dignity you recognized in me for the sole fact of having remained faithful to the guidelines of the Holy Father in the service that he entrusted to me in the Church.

What follows is a kind of theorizing about the probability that the accusations in Viganò's "Testimony" could be true, despite the fact that Cardinal Ouellet introduces the main body of his text with the sober declaration, "Let us get down to the facts."

Let us get down to the facts. You say that you informed Pope Francis on 23 June 2013 on the McCarrick case during the audience he granted to you, along with the many other papal representatives whom he then met for the first time on that day. I imagine the enormous quantity of verbal and written information that he would have gathered on that occasion about many persons and situations. I strongly doubt that McCarrick was of interest to him to the point that you believed him to be, since at the moment he was an 82-year-old Archbishop Emeritus who had been without an appointment for seven years. In addition, the written brief prepared for you by the Congregation for Bishops at the beginning of your service in 2011, said nothing about McCarrick other than what I told you in person about his situation as an emeritus Bishop who was supposed to obey certain conditions and restrictions due to the rumors surrounding his past behavior.

So, it turns out that Ouellet uses the words "I imagine" and "I strongly doubt"—hardly the stuff of "facts." And he confirms Viganò's claim that McCarrick was under "certain conditions and restrictions," though he takes pains to say the measures were not "sanctions," presumably meaning "canonical" sanctions that carried canonical penalties—something Viganò had never claimed.

After re-examining the archives, I can ascertain that there are no corresponding documents signed by either Pope, neither is there a note of an audience with my predecessor, Cardinal Giovanni-Battista Re, giving Archbishop Emeritus McCarrick an obligatory mandate of silence and to retire to a private life, carrying canonical penalties.

Then, Ouellet returns to speculation, saying McCarrick's case "would have been the object of new disciplinary measures" had his dicastery been provided with decisively incriminating information. And he goes on to theorize as to why McCarrick was allowed to rise to the lofty heights he did: McCarrick "knew how to defend himself very skillfully."

> It seems unjust to me to conclude that the persons in charge of the prior discernment are corrupt even though, in this concrete case, some suspicions provided by witnesses should have been further examined. The prelate in question knew how to defend himself very skillfully regarding the doubts that were raised about him.

After again expressing that Viganò's accusation of papal malfeasance are, Ouellet believes, "incredible and unlikely," he goes on to note that he "had never heard Pope Francis allude to this self-styled advisor" in the matter of appointing US bishops. Ouellet reproves Viganò's audacity in "casting doubt on his faith," saying the pope deals with his duties "very charitably, mercifully, attentively and seriously, as you yourself have experienced."

> Reading how you concluded your last message, apparently very spiritual, mocking and casting doubt on his faith, seemed to me to be really too sarcastic, even blasphemous! Such a thing cannot come from God's Spirit.

And then Ouellet lets fall a telling plea: he urges Viganò to "come out of hiding." It seems not unreasonable to conclude after reading Ouellet's letter, so full of opinions and speculations, and so short on actual "facts," that he might have been "put up to" writing the letter, not to clarify the issues at hand, but as an attempt to persuade

Viganò to surrender to whatever procedures of censure, and silencing, some in the Vatican may wish, may even be desperate, to impose.

> In what other way can I respond to your request other than to say: come out of hiding, repent from this revolt and retrieve better feelings toward the Holy Father, instead of exacerbating hostility against him. How can you celebrate the Holy Eucharist and pronounce his name in the Canon of the Mass? How can you pray the Holy Rosary, the Prayer to St Michael the Archangel, and to the Mother of God, condemning him whom She protects and accompanies every single day in his heavy and courageous ministry?

# CHAPTER 18

# TESTIMONIES 3 AND 4: VIGANÒ RESPONDS TO OUELLET'S LETTER AND OFFERS AN EXHORTATION TO THE BISHOPS OF THE UNITED STATES

*"I am an old man, one who knows he must soon give an accounting to the Judge for his actions and omissions."*
—Archbishop Viganò to Cardinal Ouellet, October 19, 2018

## VIGANÒ RESPONDS TO OUELLET

TWELVE DAYS later, on October 19, 2018, Archbishop Viganò, sounding at this point as if he was wearying of the accusations and counter-accusations which he knew would come and calling himself an "old man," issued his third testimony—a firm response to Cardinal Ouellet's letter of October 7.

But Viganò's response also seems to reveal another side, another texture to his decision to speak. Speaking about a crisis of "confusion and division" over Church doctrines, he says, "When he [the pope] then exacerbates the crisis by contradictory or perplexing statements about these doctrines, the confusion is worsened. Therefore I spoke."

So the call to account he has issued previously to the pope, in this "third Testimony," now seems to have expanded in scope of purpose: the silence Viganò condemns in the pope is not only silence about McCarrick and others involved in sexual aberration but silence over appeals of the faithful over questions of doctrine which are also causing confusion.

Viganò's letter of response to Ouellet appeared "on the Feast of the North American Martyrs," October 19, 2018. In it he wrote:

> To bear witness to corruption in the hierarchy of the Catholic Church was a painful decision for me, and remains so. But I am an old man, one who knows he must soon give an accounting to the Judge for his actions and omissions, one who fears Him who can cast body and soul into hell. A Judge who, even in his infinite mercy, will render to every person salvation or damnation according to what he has deserved. Anticipating the dreadful question from that Judge—"How could you, who had knowledge of the truth, keep silent in the midst of falsehood and depravity?"—what answer could I give?

After reasserting his original testimony that Pope Francis had to have been aware of McCarrick's misdeeds, he goes on to once again defend his public avowal of what he knows to be true. He then "restates" the "key points" of his "Testimony" (all of these bullet points are cited from Viganò's letter):

- In November 2000 the U.S. nuncio Archbishop Montalvo informed the Holy See of Cardinal

McCarrick's homosexual behavior with seminarians and priests.

- In December 2006 the new U.S. nuncio, Archbishop Pietro Sambi, informed the Holy See of Cardinal McCarrick's homosexual behavior with yet another priest.

- In December of 2006 I myself wrote a memo to the Secretary of State Cardinal Bertone, and personally delivered it to the Substitute for General Affairs, Archbishop Leonardo Sandri, calling for the pope to bring extraordinary disciplinary measures against McCarrick to forestall future crimes and scandal. This memo received no response.

- In April 2008 an open letter to Pope Benedict by Richard Sipe was relayed by the Prefect of the CDF, Cardinal Levada, to the Secretary of State, Cardinal Bertone, containing further accusations of McCarrick's sleeping with seminarians and priests. I received this a month later, and in May 2008 I myself delivered a second memo to the then Substitute for General Affairs, Archbishop Fernando Filoni, reporting the claims against McCarrick and calling for sanctions against him. This second memo also received no response.

- In 2009 or 2010 I learned from Cardinal Re, prefect of the Congregation of Bishops, that Pope Benedict had ordered McCarrick to cease public ministry and begin a life of prayer and penance. The nuncio Sambi communicated the Pope's orders to McCarrick in a voice heard down the corridor of the nunciature.

- In November 2011 Cardinal Ouellet, the new Prefect of Bishops, repeated to me, the new nuncio to the U.S., the Pope's restrictions on McCarrick, and I myself communicated them to McCarrick face-to-face.

- On June 21, 2013, toward the end of an official assembly of nuncios at the Vatican, Pope Francis spoke cryptic words to me criticizing the U.S. episcopacy.

- On June 23, 2013, I met Pope Francis face-to-face in his apartment to ask for clarification, and the Pope asked me, "*il cardinale McCarrick, com'è* (Cardinal McCarrick -- what do you make of him)?"-- which I can only interpret as a feigning of curiosity in order to discover whether or not I was an ally of McCarrick. I told him that McCarrick had sexually corrupted generations of priests and seminarians and had been ordered by Pope Benedict to confine himself to a life of prayer and penance.
- Instead, McCarrick continued to enjoy the special regard of Pope Francis and was given new responsibilities and missions by him.
- McCarrick was part of a network of bishops promoting homosexuality who, exploiting their favor with Pope Francis, manipulated episcopal appointments so as to protect themselves from justice and to strengthen the homosexual network in the hierarchy and in the Church at large.
- Pope Francis himself has either colluded in this corruption, or, knowing what he does, is gravely negligent in failing to oppose it and uproot it.

I invoked God as my witness to the truth of my claims, and none has been shown false. Cardinal Ouellet has written to rebuke me for my temerity in breaking silence and leveling such grave accusations against my brothers and superiors, but in truth his remonstrance confirms me in my decision and, even more, serves to vindicate my claims, severally and as a whole.

- Cardinal Ouellet concedes that he spoke with me about McCarrick's situation prior to my leaving for Washington to begin my post as nuncio.
- Cardinal Ouellet concedes that he communicated

to me in writing the conditions and restrictions imposed on McCarrick by Pope Benedict.

- Cardinal Ouellet concedes that these restrictions forbade McCarrick to travel or to make public appearances.
- Cardinal Ouellet concedes that the Congregation of Bishops, in writing, first through the nuncio Sambi and then once again through me, required McCarrick to lead a life of prayer and penance.

What does Cardinal Ouellet dispute?

- Cardinal Ouellet disputes the possibility that Pope Francis could have taken in important information about McCarrick on a day when he met scores of nuncios and gave each only a few moments of conversation. But this was not my testimony. My testimony is that at a second, private meeting, I informed the Pope, answering his own question about Theodore McCarrick, then Cardinal archbishop emeritus of Washington, prominent figure of the Church in the US, telling the Pope that McCarrick had sexually corrupted his own seminarians and priests. No Pope could forget that.
- Cardinal Ouellet disputes the existence in his archives of letters signed by Pope Benedict or Pope Francis regarding sanctions on McCarrick. But this was not my testimony. My testimony was that he has in his archives key documents – irrespective of provenance – incriminating McCarrick and documenting the measures taken in his regard, and other proofs on the cover-up regarding his situation. And I confirm this again.
- Cardinal Ouellet disputes the existence in the files of his predecessor, Cardinal Re, of "audience memos" imposing on McCarrick the restrictions already mentioned. But this was not my testimony. My testimony is that there are other documents:

for instance, a note from Card Re not ex-Audientia SS.mi, signed by either the Secretary of State or by the Substitute.

- Cardinal Ouellet disputes that it is false to present the measures taken against McCarrick as "sanctions" decreed by Pope Benedict and canceled by Pope Francis. True. They were not technically "sanctions" but provisions, "conditions and restrictions." To quibble whether they were sanctions or provisions or something else is pure legalism. From a pastoral point of view they are exactly the same thing.

In brief, Cardinal Ouellet concedes the important claims that I did and do make, and disputes claims I don't make and never made.

Viganò then goes on to note "two dramatic silences": "The first silence regards the plight of the victims. The second regards the underlying reason why there are so many victims, namely, the corrupting influence of homosexuality in the priesthood and in the hierarchy. As to the first," he says, "it is dismaying that, amid all the scandals and indignation, so little thought should be given to those damaged by the sexual predations of those commissioned as ministers of the gospel."

And with regard to the "second silence," Viganò names it out loud: "the scourge of homosexuality." He says:

This very grave crisis cannot be properly addressed and resolved unless and until we call things by their true names. This is a crisis due to the scourge of homosexuality, in its agents, in its motives, in its resistance to reform. It is no exaggeration to say that homosexuality has become a plague in the clergy, and it can only be eradicated with spiritual weapons. It is an enormous hypocrisy to condemn the abuse, claim to weep for the victims, and yet refuse to denounce the root cause of so much sexual abuse: homosexuality. It is hypocrisy to refuse to acknowledge that this scourge is due to a serious crisis in the spiritual life of the clergy and to fail to take the steps necessary to remedy it.

"You too are faced with a choice," he concludes, addressing Cardinal Ouellet.

You can choose to withdraw from the battle, to prop up the conspiracy of silence and avert your eyes from the spreading of corruption. You can make excuses, compromises and justification that put off the day of reckoning. You can console yourselves with the falsehood and the delusion that it will be easier to tell the truth tomorrow, and then the following day, and so on.

On the other hand, you can choose to speak. You can trust Him who told us, "the truth will set you free." I do not say it will be easy to decide between silence and speaking. I urge you to consider which choice-- on your deathbed, and then before the just Judge -- you will not regret having made.

These last two paragraphs are striking in that they constitute a direct challenge to a cardinal of the Church to gird his loins and speak the truth. His rhetoric is that of an Old Testament prophet or a Father of the Church. He would shortly thereafter use similar language in addressing the United States bishops, seemingly asking them, too, to gird their loins and be courageous in their roles as shepherds. Given the timing of his brief message, it seems certain that he was asking the US bishops to take firm action on the sexual abuse crisis even if Rome was asking them to wait for the results of an upcoming February 2019 summit on the subject in Rome.

## Testimony 4: Viganò to US bishops, Nov. 13, 2018

On November 13, 2018, on the website of the magazine I edit, *Inside the Vatican,* we published a brief message from Archbishop Viganò to the bishops of the United States. Two and a half months had now passed since he had published his "Testimony."

> Dear Brother Bishops in the US,
>
> I am writing to remind you of the sacred mandate you were given on the day of your episcopal ordination: to lead the flock to Christ. Meditate on Proverbs 9:10: The fear of the Lord is the beginning of wisdom! Do not behave like frightened sheep, but as courageous shepherds. Do not be afraid of standing up and doing the right thing for the victims, for the faithful and for your own salvation. The Lord will render to every one of us according to our actions and omissions.
>
> I am fasting and praying for you.
>
> *Arch. Carlo Maria Viganò*
> *Your former Apostolic Nuncio*
>
> *November 13, 2018*
> *Saint Frances Xavier Cabrini*

# HOW HAD IT COME TO THIS?

*"Why do the nations conspire, and the peoples plot
in vain? The kings of the earth set themselves,
and the rulers take counsel together, against the
Lord and his anointed, saying, 'Let us burst their
bonds asunder, and cast their cords from us.'"*

—Psalm 2:1–3

So I asked myself: How had it all come to this? What
had happened to the Catholic Church?

How had it come, first of all, to the startling, seemingly
unplanned, and rather chaotic resignation announce-
ment of Pope Benedict XVI on February 11, 2013? How
had it come to Benedict himself living "hidden away" for
the past seven years, almost as if Benedict were a type of
Viganò himself, hiding from the stressful duties of the
papacy that he had devoted himself to carrying out with
great energy for eight years. Why had Benedict also chosen to go into hiding, living a "hidden life" in a small
convent in the Vatican Gardens, with almost no public appearances and not many guests? What did it mean
that we Catholics had a pope in hiding to go along with
a visible pope and an archbishop in hiding? Was there
some profound dysfunction somewhere in the Church?
Where, precisely?

Then, how had it come to Viganò's denunciation of Pope Francis and his call for Francis's resignation? How had it come to pass that a respected archbishop of the Church, highly honored, should have chosen to go into hiding because his friends thought he might be harmed, or sequestered, by his brethren in the Church hierarchy or their agents in order to keep him silent? What was the real root of the denunciation? Did it have any basis, or was it "over the top," an emotional exaggeration?

And then, Pope Francis himself. How had it come to pass that a newly elected pope would not live in the residence of the popes for the past five hundred or six hundred years? What was the real reason he had chosen to live in a guest house designed not for popes but for monsignors working in the Vatican and pilgrims passing through Rome—usually bishops and monsignors but sometimes even people like myself, a Vatican journalist and organizer of small pilgrimage groups to Rome and central Italy? And how had it come to pass that this new "people's pope"—for that is how the world's press characterized him, as a pope of the people, of the poor and marginalized and discarded—had come to declare that he wanted to transform the Church, reform the Curia, end corruption, as if the Church led by John Paul II and Benedict had been in some way gravely deficient in all these areas? Had it been? Was he in fact signaling that he wished to break with his predecessors as some argued? Very few Catholics would fail to agree that the Curia needs to be reformed and that the corruption in the Church needs to be rooted out. But was that not what Viganò, through his entire career, strove to do? Truth be told, as urgent as is the need to address corruption, the culture of cover-up, and individual cases of abuse, what is truly at the heart of the crisis in this time of tremendous uncertainty in the Catholic Church is the question "What does Francis mean when he says he wants to transform the Church?"

# PART IV

# FINDING VIGANÒ

CHAPTER 19

# THE CALL

*"What does the LORD require of you but to do justice, and to love kindness, and to walk humbly with your God?"*
—Micah 6:8

MY CELL phone rang. I saw the name, a special code name I hadn't seen appear on my phone screen for a year or more, since before August 25, 2018, the day Archbishop Carlo Maria Viganò published his eleven-page "Testimony" denouncing the cover-up of sexual abuse in the Church and calling on Pope Francis to resign his office for his alleged complicity in the cover-up, then went into hiding. It was July 2, 2019.

"Ah," I thought. "Here it is. Viganò is finally calling."

I was in America, about to fly to Rome, then to Moscow (those were still the innocent days before the virus when we would travel freely in this breathtakingly beautiful world, from the solemn monuments of Washington to the marble palaces of the Vatican, to the golden-domed churches of the Kremlin.) Archbishop Viganò had been "in hiding" for ten months.

Viganò had disappeared from public view like a ghost, like a mist, at the end of August 2018. Rumors soon floated around the internet that the Vatican was evaluating the preparation of serious charges against the archbishop for breaking a vow all Vatican officials take not to disclose pontifical secrets and had even activated secret agents to track him down, arrest him, and bring him back to Vatican City to put him on trial.

During the weeks and months that followed, from his hiding place, Viganò had occasionally issued new texts via email, which were duly published by a number of Catholic websites and then circulated on the internet. But he had never appeared in public, and no one knew where he was.

On June 27, 2019, I sent an email using a coded email address that we had used on occasion in years past.

"Dear Archbishop," I wrote. "I have a proposal I would like you to consider. I have read the text that you emailed to me of your long interview you sent to the *Washington Post* on May 2. (*Note*: Later the archbishop would tell me, 'You have no idea what it cost me to write out all that text. It was an enormous amount of work that took a great deal of my strength over many days.')

"There you write something I particularly appreciated. You said: 'We can all learn from our mistakes. I myself regret not having spoken publicly earlier. . . . I had truly hoped against hope that the Church could reform itself from within. But when it became clear that the successor of Peter himself was one of those covering up the crimes, I had no doubt that the Lord was calling me to speak up, as I have done and will continue to do. . . . As a Christian and bishop, I have the duty to witness to the truth without fear. . . . No pope can dispense from that duty, and if a man faithfully fulfills it, he cannot be rebellious in any but an honorable sense. Dishonorably rebellious are those who presume to break or change the perennial tradition of the Church."[26]

I continued in my email: "I would like to go farther and have an extended dialogue with you on the challenges facing the Catholic Church and Catholic faith today. This project would aim to elevate your profile even higher than it is now as a defender of the innocent and abused, as a lover of the truth, as a man of courage, as a disciple of Christ, as a defender of the Faith—as 'a man of the Church.' I would very much like to come to visit you, to carry out this conversation over three or four days. If I send you a more detailed outline, would you consider my proposal?"

That same day, the archbishop wrote back to me: "Yes, of course. Waiting for your text."

I prepared an outline and emailed it to him.

"Here is a summary of my proposal," I wrote to him.

"*Possible title*: 'Final Testament.'

"*Possible subtitle*: 'How to Face the Current Crisis and Renew the Church'

"*Main thesis*: An ecclesial culture of cover-up, developed to protect the good name and mission of the Church, has catastrophically harmed thousands of young people who have been sexually and spiritually abused. It has also profoundly damaged the moral authority of the

---

[26] "Archbishop Carlo Maria Viganò gives his first extended interview since calling on the pope to resign," *The Washington Post*, June 10, 2019, https://www.washingtonpost.com/world/europe/archbishop-carlo-maria-vigano-gives-his-first-extended-interview-since-calling-on-the-pope-to-resign/2019/06/10/00205748-8b79-11e9-b08e-cfd89bd36d4e_story.html.

Church, with ruinous consequences for her mission: the proclamation of the Gospel and the salvation of souls. This culture of cover-up must be changed.

"An effort at reform has been made, but the resistance is entrenched and powerful, and extends to circles in the Vatican immediately around Pope Francis, who has himself recognized that he did not act promptly in a number of cases, especially regarding Chile.

"Healing will require: 1) acknowledging wrongs done and crimes committed, 2) expressing contrition, 3) facing the legal consequences, and 4) instituting Church procedures to protect the innocent, not cover up for the guilty.

"If this is done, this crisis can lead to a profound repentance, conversion, and renewal in the Church. With repentance, contrition and a change in Church culture, this long 'passion' of the Church, which has caused so much pain and suffering, can be followed by a type of resurrection and vibrant new life.

"We could discuss the Church in the time of the Council (1960s), the corruption of the Jesuit order under Arrupe, the confusion and massive laicization under Paul VI, the rather 'lax' attitude of Pope John Paul II toward Father Maciel, the breaking of the 2002 abuse scandal in Boston, the election of Pope Benedict in 2005 (his denunciation of '*sporcizia*' in the Church), Vatileaks I, the investigation of Herranz, Tomko and De Giorgi (the white box!²⁷)—and your testimony for that investigation,

---

27  The "white box" is a large white cardboard box seen in photographs and videos sitting on a coffee table between the new pope, Francis, and his predecessor, Benedict XVI, at their first

which Pope Francis asked you about—then the pontificate of Francis, his dismissal of your words to him about McCarrick, the years from 2013 to 2018, Vatileaks II, the summer of 2018, the decision to publish the *Testimony* after the allegations against McCarrick in June and the Pennsylvania state's attorney's report in August, the decision to go 'into hiding' . . . your months of prayer and reflection . . . and your decision now to publish a more complete report on the source of the problem, and the need to heal the Church via repentance and renewal, for which you (perhaps!) ask Francis to also repent, and lead the renewal, even at this very late hour. . . .

---

meeting at Castel Gandolfo outside of Rome on March 23, 2013, ten days after Francis was elected pope on March 13, 2013.

The box is believed by many to have contained the documents and conclusions of a secretive, year-long investigation of "lobbies" in the Roman Curia, ordered in 2012 by Pope Benedict XVI and conducted during the final year of his pontificate.

More than 150 Vatican officials were interrogated on multiple occasions, then their testimony was cross-checked with the testimony of other officials to enable the pope to understand the intricate networks of friendships and alliances in the Roman Curia. The investigation was entrusted to three senior cardinals: Cardinal Salvatore de Giorgi of Palermo, Sicily, now eighty-nine; Spanish Cardinal Julian Herranz, now ninety, one of the leading canon lawyers in the Church; and Cardinal Jozef Tomko, now ninety-six, a Slovak who has spent a lifetime in the Roman Curia and was a close advisor of Pope John Paul II.

This is the sense in which I used the term "white box." However, it is not certain that the "white box" did actually contain these documents, because the Vatican never officially confirmed what were the contents of the box.

"So, that is the proposal. Could we talk later today? Robert"

Viganò responded, "I have given some thought to your proposal. I can send answers to questions you send to me."

"I would appreciate that," I replied. "But I really think it will be necessary for me to come to where you are and meet with you personally."

I did not want to converse through emailed questions only. I wanted to see the man in person, see where he was living, sit across from him and ask him questions, observe his face as he gave his answers, follow up the answers with other questions in a real dialogue. I wanted to see the expressions on his face as I asked my questions and as he answered. Facial expressions can sometimes give more information than the spoken words themselves. And facial expressions do not pass through emails. I wanted to hear the tone of his voice, see if he was bitter, or repentant. Not just read his written answers to emailed questions. (In the end, I was right in wishing this, because in our talks, on at least five occasions, I would see the archbishop weep, or nearly weep, when speaking of his work in the Roman Curia, his relationships with "Uncle Ted" McCarrick and with Pope Francis, and his relationships with his own father and brother.)

So I continued, "I would like to come to see you in person. I would like to sit down with you and go through everything. I will come to wherever you are, even if it requires airplane flights, and we can sit down for several days and talk everything through."

"I will need some time to think it over," the arch-bishop said.

"Just give me a call if the time seems right," I said.

And now the phone was ringing. Viganò was call-ing from wherever he was in hiding. I hit the icon and accepted the call.

"Hello!" I said in a friendly way.

"Hello Robert," the archbishop replied, his voice calm. "How are you? Are you well?"

"Very well," I said. "And you, how are you?"

"I am well, thanks be to God," Viganò said. "I am well. And I think I am ready for you to come to me where I am, to have the conversation you proposed to me some time ago. Do you still want to talk with me?"

"Yes," I said.

"Ok," Viganò said. "But I have to ask you to be very prudent. Can you agree?"

"Yes," I said.

But then I was the one who had to temporize.

"I have one problem," I said. "It can't be immediate. I have a pilgrimage scheduled, we are meeting in Rome then flying to Russia and Ukraine then to Hungary to meet with Cardinal Erdo. I won't be back in Rome until July 22 if all goes well. Then we will stay for four days in the Domus Santa Marta. After that, I will be free. On about July 27."

"Alright," he said. "Come see me at the end of July then. I will be in touch to give you exact details of where to go and how we will meet."

"Ok," I said.

"And why don't you give this message to Metropolitan

Hilarion when you meet with him: tell him to continue to criticize the excesses of the Western Christians and to preach the faith of all time. To remain orthodox.

"I will tell him you said that."

\*\*\*

And so the deal was made. I would go to find Viganò where he was in hiding and talk with him for several days. This would be my chance to question him at length and to clarify the various obscure, contested points of his "Testimony" and of his position on Pope Francis, the Church's sexual abuse crisis, and the general crisis of faith facing the Church.

I began again to study all the many texts and news reports connected with the priestly abuse scandal: Viganò's "Testimony" and everything else he had published between August 2018 and July 2019, the allegations made by victims of McCarrick, the action (or inaction) of Popes John Paul II, Benedict XVI, and Francis to address this terrible scandal. Some of the matters, like so much connected with the Vatican and the Church, seemed mysterious, hard to understand, and sometimes I felt frustrated and at a loss as I read claim and counter-claim. Who was telling the truth? Had St. John Paul II and his collaborators been to blame for not exercising sufficient control in their government of the Church during the last years of his pontificate when John Paul was ill and weak? Had Pope Benedict been to blame for being a "theologian pope" and not a "man of government" (that was what Curia officials commonly said about him in Rome during his pontificate), allowing problems to fester that should have been solved? Was Viganò right that Pope Francis had turned an indulgent eye on reports of McCarrick's improper behavior with seminarians? Or were those around Pope Francis right that Viganò, perhaps in conjunction with obscure and powerful forces in and out of the Church, had used the McCarrick case as a pretext to "strike the Shepherd" (Pope Francis) for ideological reasons, because Viganò was a "reactionary" and Francis a "reformer"?

So it was agreed. In late July of 2019, I was to set out to find Archbishop Viganò to ask him several days' worth of questions: Had he reconsidered his call for Pope Francis to resign? Did he have documents to prove his allegations? If he did, would he give them to me? Did he have information about other cases of the hierarchy's cover-up of cases of clerical sexual abuse, not just the case of Cardinal McCarrick?

What I did not realize at the time was that the priestly abuse scandal and the allegations of a cover-up of such misconduct by many members of the hierarchy was only one aspect of Viganò's concern for the Church.

I would find that my search for Viganò was not just a long geographical journey but also a complex psychological and spiritual one as well. I slowly came to understand that if I misinterpreted or misunderstood things, much harm might be caused to many: to Viganò, to Pope Francis, to the Church, even to myself.

So, from early in July of 2019, I knew I would be meeting within the month with the archbishop who had denounced Pope Francis and called on him to tender his resignation.

# CHAPTER 20

# "I AM BACK IN ROME"

*"The LORD will keep you from all evil; he will keep
your life. The LORD will keep your going out and your
coming in from this time forth and for evermore."*
—Psalm 121:7–8

So, IN July of 2019, I traveled to Russia, then to Ukraine via Hungary (because in 2019 there were no direct flights between Russia and Ukraine), spending several days in Lviv, then back to Hungary to spend a day with Cardinal Erdo, then to Rome, where I and several pilgrims traveling with me, including my son, Christopher, were guests in the Domus Santa Marta, the residence of Pope Francis. It was now July 24.

The next day, I spoke again with Archbishop Viganò on what I felt was a safe line of communication.

"I am back in Rome, staying in the Domus Santa Marta," I said. "I have some meetings here, and then I will be able to come to see you, wherever you are."

"Very well," he said. "This is what you will need to do."

And then, for the first time, he told me where he was.

He gave me an address where I needed to go. I would have to travel a long way, rent a car when I arrived, then drive a considerable distance to where he was.

Our rendezvous would be in front of a certain hotel in a certain small town where Viganò felt safe. He would meet me when I arrived in the parking lot outside the hotel.

"So in the end we will not meet in some mountain castle, but in a hotel parking lot," I thought. "Classic."

Viganò had it all worked out. We would talk, Viganò said, have dinner, I would stay the night in the hotel, and then we would travel together in my rented car to a small monastery where we would spend several days living with the monks. He told me where the monastery was and how appreciative he was that the abbot there had decided to offer us hospitality.

"Are you sure it will be safe?" I asked the archbishop.

"Quite sure," the archbishop replied.

I made a calculation based on travel times and connections and told him when I thought I might arrive.

"Good," Viganò said. "That will be fine. I will come to meet you there in the parking lot when you arrive. Send me a text message if you are delayed or have any problem. I look forward to seeing you. Safe travels. Be careful."

So now the trip to find Viganò was "on."

I wondered what I would learn that I didn't already know. What type of story would it turn out to be? What kind of mood would he be in? Would his months in hiding have changed his personality? Would he have grown even more radically opposed to Pope Francis? Or would he be less insistent, perhaps even repentant, about his call for Francis to resign? Would he have a briefcase full of documents from the Vatican's files? What would I do with such documents if he was willing to share them with me? In any case, I thought, one way or the other, there will be a story here if he is really willing to speak freely.

CHAPTER 21

# MY FATHER

*"As a father pities his children, so the
Lord pities those who fear him."*
—Psalm 103:13

I called my father's house in Connecticut where I grew up. The phone rang three times and then . . .

"Bob!" exclaimed my father, William Moynihan, then ninety-two years old. "How are you? Are you back in Rome?"

"I'm fine, Dad," I said. "Yes, I'm in Rome, in the Domus. How are things in Storrs?"

"I'm getting old," my father said. Born in Haverhill, Massachusetts, he had grown up in the Great Depression, almost dropping out of high school before a wonderful nun, Sister Eucharita, took him under her wing. His two older brothers were already in the US armed forces and in combat in the South Pacific. She wanted Bill to complete high school. She persuaded him to enroll for two years in St. Joseph's Seraphic Seminary run by the Franciscans at Callicoon, New York, not far from St. Bonaventure University, from age sixteen to eighteen so as not to be drafted. After the war, he left the seminary and joined the US Marines, serving for four years in Washington, DC, at the commandant's office in the color guard. Then he married, finished his college degree on the GI bill, had me and my sister and my brother on his way to having seven children, of whom I am the eldest, finished a doctorate in English at Brown University, became a professor at the University of Connecticut, then head of the English Department there for twenty-five years. He retired in the early 1990s, and in his retirement, he began to assist me as a kind of assistant editor for *Inside the Vatican* magazine, writing many pieces that were published under the name Inside the Vatican Staff. He made several trips to Rome to meet with me, and we attended the private Masses of Pope John Paul II and Pope Benedict, met with many journalists, theologians, priests, and bishops and cardinals, and even with the daughter, Miriam, and the granddaughter, Maura, of the deceased Chief Rabbi of Rome in the 1930s and 1940s, Eugenio Zolli, who converted to Catholicism in 1945, in part out of appreciation for the courage displayed by Pope Pius XII (Eugenio Pacelli) in hiding several thousand of Rome's Jews after the Gestapo round-up on the morning of October 16, 1943. My father and I appreciated our conversation with Miriam and Maura so much that ever after we would always refer to it as one of our most profound encounters in Rome. My father had wanted to pay for our dinner together, but Miriam had said, "Here I am the *Matrona* (a noble Roman woman). You are my guests. I will take care of the bill, and not another word about it."

"How are things in Rome?" my father asked.

"Well, I have some news, good news I think."

"Tell me."

"Viganò has agreed to see me."

"That *is* good news. Congratulations! When will you see him?"

"In a couple of days. He told me I can go to where he is and interview him."

"Wonderful! He's an important figure. That's great."

"But I have some concerns."

My father was silent.

"I don't know what he may tell me," I continued, "and I don't know what effect it all may have on the Church if I publish what he says."

"Well, these are things you can't predict," my father said. "They are out of your control. You just have to go forward as you have in the past, without fear or favor. Give him a hearing. Let him speak. That's the fair thing to do. See what he has to say."

"But what if what he tells me is devastating?" I said.

My father interrupted me. "Don't put the cart before the horse," he said. "First, go see him. Prepare yourself well. You have waited for this moment. Now it has come to you."

"I am not sure I'm ready. So many issues are so complex, and there are so many factions, it's hard to know who to believe. People have lined up on both sides of every question."

"Take a breath. You are going into this with a right intention. You are trying to get at the truth. You are well-prepared to do it. Your whole life has prepared you for this. Now just go forward."

"Well, there are a lot of pitfalls on the path. I could fall on my face."

"It was ever so. Just watch your step. And if you do stumble, get up again. I'll be praying for you."

"But it touches on the pope himself."

"All the more reason to go forward. The forces ranged against the Church are counting on creating divisions. Your task is to do something no one else could do. You have to find a way to square the circle, to keep unity while not betraying truth. You'll find a way. This book will be an important work in your life. You will be judged on how you handle the various aspects of this present crisis. But you have been prepared for a challenge like this. Don't hesitate now. As Krishna said to Arjuna on the field of battle, 'Fare not well, fare forward.'" (He was citing lines he always cited from T. S. Eliot's *Four Quartets, The Dry Salvages.*)

"Consider the future and the past with an equal mind," I cited back to him.

"Yes," he said. "Here, between the hither and the farther shore." (Meaning, in the midst of this life, between birth and death.)

"Ok," I said. "I understand." I was silent for a moment. "Are you getting out to walk every day?"

"Almost every day."

"And you are eating well? Your appetite is good?"

"Well. I just finished a big bowl of granola and fruit."

"Good. Better than me."

"Get yourself on a regular schedule and get enough sleep! Sleep knits up the raveled sleeve of care."

"Ok, Dad. Thanks for the advice."

He growled back at me, "My mother would always say, whenever I left her, 'Billy, go with God.' I have nothing better to say to you than that: *Vai con Dio*. Go with God. That is the way. Call me whenever you can. Great to hear that you got that meeting with the archbishop. Let me know how it goes."

"Thanks Dad. I will. And keep up your daily walk. That's important."

# TWO POPES AT CHRISTMAS

*"Know that the LORD is God. It is he that made us, and we are his; we are his people, and the sheep of his pasture."*
—Psalm 100:3

ON THE morning of December 27, 2013—the first Christmas of Pope Francis in Rome, just nine months after his election—I was in the Domus Santa Marta, staying as a guest with a group of pilgrims, standing by the reception desk when I looked up and saw Pope Benedict's shock of white hair coming in the front doorway above.

Benedict was arriving from his residence in the Vatican Gardens, about three or four hundred yards away, to pay a Christmas visit to Pope Francis and to have lunch with him. It was the first time he had come to the Domus since Francis's election; perhaps it was the only time he ever came to the Domus, I do not know for sure.

There was a sudden flurry of activity as when wind gusts stir up a pile of leaves in autumn, and a Swiss Guard whispered to me, "Benedict is coming." I looked back, blankly, not sure what I should do. "Please," he said *sotto voce* (in a whisper), "move down the entrance hall toward the manger scene there at the end so the two of them can be alone when Benedict comes down the stairs."

Francis appeared from his elevator, and above, against the light shining through the Domus doors, I saw Benedict's white hair almost as if on fire in the sunlight. I turned and walked slowly away, toward the end of the hall, to the manger scene. I looked back and saw the two popes greet each other, embrace, smile. They spoke for a moment, then they both turned and began walking toward me, toward the manger scene. The same Swiss Guard caught my eye and motioned to me to step aside from the manger scene. Now I had nowhere to go except into the Domus Chapel around the corner. I turned, pulled open the chapel door, and entered the chapel. It was completely empty. I closed the door behind me and walked over to a chair in the middle in the very last row. I looked up toward the altar and read the Latin inscription above it: "*Veni Sancte Spiritus, Reple Corda Tuorum Fidelium*" ("Come Holy Spirit, fill the hearts of your faithful"). I think as I read the words, I whispered them almost as my own prayer.

A minute or two passed, and then, unexpectedly, I heard the chapel door opening. I glanced over and saw both Pope Francis and Pope Benedict entering the chapel, both dressed in papal white. I met their eyes for the barest instant, and they recognized me, and then I looked again to the front of the chapel. They had finished looking at the manger scene and had come to the chapel to pray a Christmas prayer together for a moment.

They walked to the middle of the chapel, stopping just behind where I was sitting, perhaps a yard behind me. I heard the barest whisper of a prayer, two murmurs, the slightly German and the slightly Spanish accent indicating the differing origins and histories of the two men. "What could this mean?" I thought, "that I am here alone with the two popes, at Christmastime?"

I did not hear any words distinctly. They were just barely murmuring. I, silent, joined my hope to their intentions, whatever they might be. They were so close behind me that I could hear their breathing, but I did not even turn my head.

In that moment, I asked silently that I might be granted the chance to be able to do something to support the Church, besieged on all sides, and even from within, and even due to my own defects, limitations, and sins.

Then I did hear a distinct word. They ended their prayer with a common "Amen," softly spoken, half-German, half-Spanish, then turned and walked out of the chapel, leaving me alone.

# CHAPTER 22

# FRANCIS ENCOUNTERED
# AT THE BUFFET

*"Grace to you and peace from God our
Father and the Lord Jesus Christ."*
—1 Corinthians 1:3

DURING HIS first few months living in the Domus, Pope Francis took his meals at a table in the very middle of the main part of the dining hall in full view of everyone. We were told that he wanted everything to be "normal," so we should not stand when he entered or exited the room. We should just stay seated in our chairs. Some of the pilgrims almost had nervous breakdowns over this policy, for as soon as they saw the pope, they would rise half out of their chair, automatically, and I would have to glance at them and shake my head, "Not necessary, not wanted." But still the person would remain halfway out of his or her chair for a second or two, so strong was the feeling that it was improper to remain seated while the pope walked by. As the months passed, the pope evidently felt that the center of the room was too exposed, or too much of a burden for guests, so he moved his table to the very far corner of the dining hall to the far left as one walks in the main doorway, separated from everyone, though still easily visible from throughout the dining hall. But he would sit with his back toward the room, facing the wall. Thus, the only way to see him "up close" was to encounter him at the buffet when he would go up to fill his plate a second time with salad.

I felt it would be only fair to tell Pope Francis that it was my intention to go to find Archbishop Viganò in just a few days. But I knew I did not have much time to ask for an audience, which might take days or weeks to obtain. I even hoped that the pope might ask me again, as he had with my sons in August of 2013, to stop and talk with him for a minute or two on the matter. But the protocol of the Domus impeded me from going over to the table where the pope was sitting with his secretary, Father Fabian Pedacchio, and a friend.

So I bided my time and waited. The pope got up from his seat and, carrying his own plate, went up to the salad bar, laid out on a long table that separates the dining room into two parts, one part for the pope and the Vatican monsignors who live in the Domus year round, another part reserved for guests and pilgrims.

I also got up from my table and walked toward him from the other side of the buffet. When I got close, I began to fill my plate with shredded carrots, lettuce, cherry tomatoes, and pieces of artichoke *alla Romana* to make a salad. I thought, "I will catch his glance then say to him, 'Good evening!' and then, 'I am planning to go meet with Archbishop Viganò and I wanted to tell you.'"

I watched as he put a bit of lettuce on his plate, and then he glanced up at me. "*Buona sera!*" I said.

But instead of recognizing me and nodding, he simply stared back at me. I looked into his eyes and saw no sign there either of acknowledgment or of irritation. Just his grey eyes staring back at me. I could not read anything in his look. Did he feel I had taken Viganò's part and had become his enemy? Or had he so many other things on his mind that he had simply forgotten who I was?

In that fixed gaze, I was uncertain of what to say. I hesitated for a second, thinking, "I will wait until he says *'Buona sera'* back to me, then I will tell him I am going to see Viganò." A second passed, and he did not say a word. Then he looked down at the table and added another leaf of lettuce to his plate.

I said to myself, "Well, it would be impolite to keep insisting. I had better remain silent." So I waited another second, then he finished with the salad bar and, turning away, started to walk back toward his table, walking with one leg moving more awkwardly than the other. I turned, too, and walked back to my place, not having said the words I had intended.

# CHAPTER 23

# ARCHBISHOP GAENSWEIN

*"No one can serve two masters; for either he will
hate the one and love the other, or he will be
devoted to the one and despise the other."*
—Matthew 6:24

THAT SAME evening, I emailed Archbishop Georg
Gaenswein, the personal secretary of Emeritus Pope
Benedict and prefect of the Pontifical Household. I
asked for a meeting. I told him I intended to go find
Archbishop Viganò and hoped I might speak with him
urgently.

He wrote back almost immediately. "You may come
to the Prefecture at 11 a.m. tomorrow. GG."

I prepared my things for my planned trip and went into
the Vatican at 10:30 a.m. A Swiss Guard escorted me
from St. Anne's Gate to the Bronze Doors, then up the
wide staircase which leads to the Cortile San Damaso.
The offices of the Prefecture, which is in charge of everything having to do with visitors to the pope, are through
a door off of the first landing of the massive stairway. I
was escorted to a large reception room and sat there alone
for a couple of minutes. I had often met here during the
pontificate of John Paul II with Monsignor James Har-
vey, an American, now a cardinal, a friend dating back

to the 1980s when he was chief of the English language section in the Secretariat of State.

"So," I thought, "I think I will tell Archbishop Gaenswein that I am going to find Viganò. Then, at some future time, he can help possibly set up a meeting with Emeritus Pope Benedict, or with Pope Francis, or with both."

Archbishop Ganswein entered the room.

"Good morning, Bob."

"Good morning," I said. "Thanks for making this appointment with such little warning. I wanted to discuss the case of Archbishop Viganò."

"Ah!" he said. "Yes, Viganò. You said you want to go find him, but no one knows where he is."

"I know," I said. "And I plan to go to see him and talk with him. I want to ask him about his 'Testimony.'"

"You know where he is?" he asked.

"Yes," I said.

"Really? Did you speak with him? How does he seem to you?" he asked. "You know, is he in good spirits? Balanced in his thinking? We are all a bit worried about him . . . the impression is that he is quite isolated, you know."

"He seems well enough," I said. "In good spirits, but of course quite concerned about the situation of the Church."

"Well, that is good to hear," the archbishop said. "I do think he has spoken out courageously. This present situation is weighing on us all." He looked upward and lifted both hands into the air. "So much confusion! No clear doctrinal line. And the situation of the Church in Germany!"

We began to discuss the situation of the Church in Germany, the tens of thousands of people leaving the Church each year for many years now, and then we spoke for a moment of America. Then I asked again what he thought about Viganò and his "Testimony."

"When he describes his meeting with Francis on June 23, 2013," the German archbishop said, "either it's true, and so then the pope knew, or it's a lie. And we've been waiting to see the pope say that it's a lie, but he has never said it's a lie.

"Regarding the corruption in the hierarchy that he condemns, I think he has said many true things which will require reform, but I think he went too far in calling for the resignation of Pope Francis," he said. "That was too much!"

"I was thinking that perhaps it might be a good thing to arrange a private meeting between Archbishop Viganò and Pope Francis," I said. "Do you think it might be possible?"

"With Francis?" he said, looking at me in puzzlement.

"Or with Emeritus Pope Benedict. Do you think he might agree to receive Viganò?"

"Would Viganò want such a meeting?" the archbishop asked.

And then I realized that I did not know the answer to that first, elementary question.

"Actually, I don't know," I said. "I will have to ask him."

"Well, you will have to tell me what Viganò would like to do. If he has clear ideas about what he wants, let me know and I will see what I can do." The archbishop said he did not know if any such meetings might be possible, but he asked that I stay in touch in case it seemed there might be a real desire for such a meeting.

"Well, I appreciate you giving me this time," I said. "My best wishes also to Emeritus Pope Benedict."

"I will convey your wishes," he replied. "So, when are you setting out to find Viganò?"

"Today," I said. "Now. As soon as I leave you."

"Today!" He arched his eyebrows in surprise. "Well then," he said, "have a safe journey! Godspeed. And send me word when you return to Rome."

## CHAPTER 24

# FINDING VIGANÒ

*"There are friends who pretend to be friends, but there is a friend who sticks closer than a brother."*
—Proverbs 18:24

I LEFT Vatican City and went to my apartment on the Janiculum hill. I quickly packed one small bag and a second computer bag containing my laptop computer, a small tape recorder, a phone charger, some notebooks and pens, a printout of Viganò's biography from the Wikipedia page on the internet, and a copy of his "Testimony" of August 25, 2018. I took bus 75 across Rome to Termini station, the central station for all the trains in Italy, walked across the parking lot and into the station, bought a bottle of water, a cornetto and a *caprese* (mozzarella, tomato, and basil) sandwich, located the *binario* I was looking for, and boarded my train. The great wheeled beast departed without a sound, pulling out of the busy station on one of some two dozen different tracks which come together in Termini from all over Italy and beyond. I was soon traveling across the flat, wide expanses of Lazio and beyond at speeds touching three hundred kilometers (two hundred miles) per hour.

"Well," I thought, "if all goes well on this journey, I will finally again be with Viganò. I wonder what that will be like? What has this year in hiding been like for him? Will he be in good spirits? In good health? Will he show me new documents which prove the cover-up of sexual abuse by the Church leadership? And if so, what will I do with those documents? What does he really hope to accomplish through our meetings? What will I do with whatever he tells me?"

Eventually, though I would rather not say how long the trip was, the train pulled into the station of a city. I got off and walked through the station to an office where I rented a car. I took the keys, loaded my two bags, and checked the route to my destination on my cellphone. I started the car and began to drive.

I love to drive in Europe. Many people find that surprising because European drivers can be unpredictable for those used to driving in America. Europeans often drive "outside the lines," creeping up on the right, or the left, even in a seemingly off-limits breakdown lane—at a stoplight, for example, or an intersection where many lanes funnel down into one. The rules of the road are merely suggestions for many European drivers. This can be disconcerting, but it also can be in some way freeing—with flexible driving rules, one can make one's way by taking opportunities when they present themselves, like a football player seeking a hole to run through in the defensive line in front of him. One can feel free driving in Europe, always moving toward open space, always toward an opening in the traffic, unconstrained by everyday rules.

Traveling quietly and with certain precautions so that, if it were possible, I might not be easily followed, using cash instead of my credit card to purchase tickets, I drove toward the place where Viganò had indicated he would be waiting to meet me. I looked every so often in my rear-view window to see if someone might be following me. I stopped twice to rest and to see if any vehicles would stop within my range of vision. I did not notice anything that suggested that I was being followed.

I arrived in a small, quiet village. Neat, clean houses, clean streets, no congestion, everything quiet. A pretty little town, like so many little towns around our world, infants in strollers, young people standing and talking, old people in cafes. There was a little church in the town center and a fountain flowing with water.

I drove to the parking lot of the hotel where I would be staying, as Viganò had told me to do. I parked the car.

I looked around me. I didn't see anyone who looked like Viganò. Then I noticed someone walking toward me, a slender, elderly man with a large white beard, his head covered by a white baseball cap and wearing dark glasses. Something in his springy step reminded me of the archbishop, and I said to myself, "Could that be him?" I did not recognize him, bearded and with his head covered as he was, but I sensed his energy, which I had come to know during our many prior conversations over the years.

I was still sitting in my car. Evidently, he had seen me drive up. He walked toward the vehicle and stood by my window. "Robert," he said. "Did you recognize me with my beard?"

"I thought it was you," I said, "but I wasn't sure."

"That is all I wanted from this disguise," he said. "So welcome. Let us get you settled after your long journey."

We went to a room the archbishop had reserved for me in the hotel, paying with cash, not a credit card, and I put my bags down.

"Well," I said. "Great to see you. Do you want to talk now?"

"Sure," he said. "Let's talk."

We began to speak. I placed my little tape recorder on the side-arm of the sofa I was sitting on and asked if I might take a photograph to document this historic moment.

"No photographs," he said.

# PART V

# FACE TO FACE WITH VIGANÒ

# CHAPTER 25

# FIRST MEETING, JULY 27, 2019

*"I received some warning that I was not safe where I was."*
—Archbishop Viganò, July 27, 2019

I SAT down with the archbishop in a hotel room in a little out-of-the way town in an unnamed country, placed my tape recorder on the arm of the chair between us, and we began to talk. My intent was to ask about the past year, where he had been and what he had done, and how he now regarded the things he had said in his "Testimony." I wanted the archbishop to speak freely on the issues facing the Church today.

**Well, it is great to see you. You look well. Thanks for allowing me to visit you. There are so many things I want to ask you.**

Archbishop Viganò: Sure. But you must be tired after all of your travels. Perhaps you should rest and then we can talk later?

**Thank you, but I feel fine. Let's talk for a few minutes, and then we can take a break and have something to eat. Ok?** (*He nodded.*) **Well, my first question is: Do you think the Vatican police are really trying to find you?**

They are trying right now. (But then Viganò smiled broadly at me, as if to tell me that he was really joking with me, and that he did not really take the threat of being tracked and found very seriously. So, with a certain sense of relief, I changed the tack of my questioning.)

**Well, everyone wants to know one thing: why have you gone into hiding?**

Well, at a certain moment, I received a warning from friends that I was not safe where I was. So they sent a person to travel just up and down from the capital where I was—not in Italy—just to bring me to another country. So, practically, just a few weeks or a few days after I made my first testimony, I flew to that country, hoping to get there and that they would not stop me at the airport when I arrived.

(The archbishop seemed calm and composed. As he talked, I wanted immediately to repeat my first question, to ask him again about his reasons for going into hiding, but I decided to follow the course of the conversation. Interviewing is always a mixture of following a plan and discarding the plan. Any living conversation demands a living response, not pre-scripted. These conversations had a plan. Each time I sat down with the archbishop, there were ten or twelve questions I wanted to work through. But these conversations were also free-flowing, moving from point to point like any ordinary conversation. That was my goal as well: to engage the archbishop in a free-flowing exchange and, in this way, to come to understand him and his motives more fully. In his first answer, he was talking about passing through passport controls in that country, not focusing on what I asked—his reasons for staying "in hiding"—but I felt I had to stay with him on his journey, not switch the topic.)

**That had to be nerve-wracking. Were you worried going through passport control?**

Well, I was, but I never took it that seriously. The other people took it more seriously than I did. It is true, the first thing that I didn't want to happen was to expose anyone to any risk. So I avoided contact with most other people. But one person traveled with me. After, I was brought to a place to stay with a very nice family. Just elderly people, a couple of elderly people who were very well-introduced in the cultural field in that country, in the university and so on. And they were living in a place very much isolated. So practically from almost the beginning of August, yeah, I think the beginning of August.

(I wanted to ask who was the person who traveled with him, but he was speaking of the beginning of August, while his "Testimony" was from August 25, so I needed to quickly make the chronology of events clear.)

**Your "Testimony" was published . . .**

At the end of August. So it was the beginning of September, for six months. After six months, in March, I had to leave.

(I suddenly felt the need to somehow record this "historic" moment of our first meeting, Viganò's first meeting with anyone of a "public" nature after a year in hiding. I decided to ask him if I could take a photograph. I didn't want to risk offending him by taking a photo without asking, but really wanted to record the moment.)

**Excuse me, may I take a photograph?**

(*Sternly, lifting his hand, laughing.*) Wait.

(His answer was clear. He had his own sense of timing about his emergence from hiding—and perhaps did not wish to emerge at all, but to remain hidden, even though he had agreed to meet with me. I realized the situation was still delicate, that he had his own timetable about when and how to emerge from hiding.)

**Okay.**

My face is invisible for the moment. Sorry about that! I know that you are a writer, but you are also a journalist, so . . . no. No photo for the moment.

**Just words, no photos. Ok.**

Because I have something else in mind. Maybe it's going beyond my capacity, what I'm able to do, but I was thinking of finding a monastery where I might go. I don't know. I am seventy-eight, almost seventy-nine now, so I cannot wait too long. And maybe . . . I did find a monastery where the abbot was willing to receive me, all the papers were settled.

(This startled me. Viganò entering a monastery? I smiled to myself. I imagined Viganò in a monastic setting, in a monk's robes, passing his days in prayer, chanting the Divine Office. The picture in my mind didn't seem to come quite into focus. But where was he planning to lead this monastic life? Now the interview had quickly gotten completely off track.)

But then I thought, "There are too many people in a monastery, especially that one." And there was also their school not far away. So it would have been only a matter of time; I could not just have presented myself with another name. Once the news would have come out that I was there, I would have had no peace anymore. So, practically, before taking the final step for that monastery, I hesitated. I was sorry, because the abbot was very, very kind with me. He was preparing everything that was necessary, giving me a status also as a teacher, *etc.* But I said, "No, better not take such a risk."

So in spite of the advice of some of the family who said, "You're taking a risk to fly," I took the risk. I took the risk, and I flew back again, and I was able to stay with another family in another country. And I remained there practically from the beginning of March, until maybe two weeks ago.

(I understood now where he had been all year. He first went into hiding in late August or early September of 2018. He spent six months in hiding—September,

October, November, December, January, February. Then, in March, he went to another country, but to which one?)

**Can you say which country?**

Say which country? (*He paused.*)

(But now he was telling me that he went to another country because he had left his car there. So at some point, evidently, he had driven his car from Italy to that country? This trip, too, was part of the puzzle. When had he done that?)

**In that country?**

I abandoned my car in that country, and it has remained there for a year practically. It has been kept working, *etc.*, but now I have made a gift of this car.

(So he had driven to that country about a year before and had left his car there for the whole year. Conclusion: immediately after he published his "Testimony" and said goodbye in Italy to the two Italian journalists who helped him, Aldo Maria Valli and Marco Tosatti, he had hopped into his car and driven from Rome to that country. He had stayed there only briefly, perhaps a few days, before someone from another country had told him he might not be safe where he was and might be safer in this other country. So he had flown to this other country, in haste, but then he had left that country, sometime in March of 2019, had come back to where he had left his car, and had stayed with a family there for about four months, until early July. Then he had left that family and come to the little village where we were meeting, just fifteen or twenty days before we met.)

**So you need a car.**

I need a car, sure for that, I feel very much handicapped, because I was . . . With a car I can . . .

**You're free.**

I am free; I can go everywhere in Europe. This place where I am . . . (*He sighs.*) Ah . . . It may not be completely safe.

**But you must feel lonely.**

No, not at all. I have my daily readings and prayers, and correspondence, and I feel continually supported by emails and calls from friends and members of my extended family.

**But now, at least physically, you are completely alone.**

I'm completely alone.

**So does this make you regret having published your "Testimony"?**

No. It was something I had to do.

# CHAPTER 26

# MONASTIC VOCATION?

*"For my father and my mother have for-
saken me, but the LORD will take me up."*
—Psalm 27:10

**AND NOW, you would like to go to a monastery?**

Archbishop Viganò: Yes, I met this abbot a year or two ago, probably in 2016, at the end of 2016 or early in 2017. I spent a week in another Benedictine monastery in France. There is a Benedictine abbot whom I met for the first time in Washington. At one of the first "March for the Family." I went there and I found that there was no bishop from the United States at the march, and just one French bishop. The one who had organized a demonstration of one million persons in Paris in defense of the family.

I met the abbot there in Washington—it was probably in 2015—and fortunately, there was a group that came from Brooklyn, mainly they were Evangelical, no Catholic bishops. So when I went home, I called some of the American bishops and said, "Why, why didn't you prepare, why didn't you inform the diocese they should have been here? I was alone with one French bishop. Where

248

were you?" There was nobody from Washington. Anyway, I met him there.

So I spent a week with him in France. And in the monastery, I was following the strict old rule, praying Matins at 3:30 in the morning. (*He laughs.*) All the hours and following the old rite of the liturgies.

(In these sentences, I felt Viganò was telling me a number of important things. First, he revealed another stop on his itinerary of "hiding"—he had stopped in France. He up to a monastery in France, spending a week there, following the monastic cycle of daily prayer. And he also gave an insight into his experience as Nuncio in the United States from 2011 to 2016. He had found himself alone in publicly demonstrating support for the family, with not even one American bishop present. I found it significant that he mentioned that detail.)

**This was in France?**

This was in France.

**So then you came here. Then I contacted you to ask if I could come talk to you, and finally you said, "Okay." And then you made the plan to meet me and for us to go together to this abbot's monastery. You wanted me to come here and pick you up because you have no car.** (*I laughed.*)

Yes. I want to visit this abbey. Though it is certainly still premature to take any decision where to stay.

**Do you really want to become a monk?**

(*He made a determined face, the type of face one makes before stepping into icy water.*) I have to test myself if I am able to. (*He laughs.*)

(All of this was unexpected for me. I had imagined that after determining where Viganò had been for a year, we would begin talking about cases of sexual abuse and cover up, and the various stages of Cardinal McCarrick's career, and any evidence he could provide for his allegations that Vatican officials, up to Pope Francis himself, were complicit in "covering up" for McCarrick for two or more decades. Instead, we were talking about Viganò's discernment of his monastic vocation—traveling to a monastery in France and now to another one, tomorrow, attempting to discern where he might spend the last years of his life. "If he really becomes a monk," I thought, "he will truly be 'hidden' from the world, no longer engaging in Vatican diplomacy or in polemics between 'progessives' and 'conservatives,' but living his life in daily prayer, from dawn until dusk, even from before dawn." For the monks wake up at 3 a.m. to pray, as he had said.)

**This is amazing to me. You, in a way, seem to be taking a path similar to that of Pope Benedict.**

Well, Pope Benedict is, in spite of many who have been criticizing him . . .

(He paused; I had thought, because he used the words "in spite of many who have been criticizing him," that he was about to praise Benedict for his spirituality, but in mid-thought, it seemed that he had changed his mind.)

Certainly, he has been too weak . . . too weak. Like Pope Francis told me regarding Dezza and Pittau: "They were too weak! Too weak!"

(Again, our conversation jolted sideways. I suppose I should have kept the conversation strictly focused on Viganò and his year of hiding. But I was struck by this "news" that Viganò was considering entering a monastery and living in monastic silence. This alone seemed to me to refute all of those speculations that Viganò was acting out of rancor, that he had been "crushed" when he was not made a cardinal, that his writings were his way of "lashing out" at the Church hierarchy, and the pope, out of frustration and bitterness. If he was considering becoming a monk, none of these interpretations made sense. And that meant that there was something else behind Viganò's "Testimony" and other writings: not personal rancor but, perhaps, a desire to reform the Church and diminish patterns of corruption in the Church's life.

Moreover, I was struck by what seemed to me a similarity between Viganò's plan and the decision of Pope Benedict to step aside from all of the "activities" of a pope and move to a monastery, the *Mater Ecclesiae* monastery in the Vatican Gardens, and to live a kind of "monastic" life there. *Note*: that monastery began to be renovated in November 2012. This means that already by November of 2012, Pope Benedict had taken the decision to step down from the papal throne. He then announced the decision on February 11, 2013, stepped down on February 28, went for two months to live in Castel Gandolfo, then moved into the monastery on May 2, 2013. He has never left the place ever since[28]—stability of life. He lives there accompanied by a few assistants with their domestic needs cared for by a small community of women belonging to a secular institute called *Memores Domini* (literally, "Rememberers of the Lord"), part of the Communion and Liberation movement.

Anyway, now Viganò in his answer was mentioning four names: Benedict, Francis, Dezza, and Pittau. This was his first mention of Benedict, and he added a critical judgment: "Too weak." Then he remembered that Pope Francis had uttered a similar judgement, "Too weak," but with regard to two leaders of the Jesuit order who had been chosen by Pope John Paul II in the early 1980s to attempt to keep the increasingly restive modern Jesuits "in line," especially in regard to "leftist political activities" in Latin America: Father Paolo Dezza and Father Giuseppe Pittau. And the judgement was: "Too weak."

For Vigano, Bergoglio's answer with reference to Father Dezza and Father Pittau as "too weak" had a sarcastic tone and intention because the Society of Jesus had been irritated by the decision of John Paul II to intervene in the government of the Society of Jesus by appointing Dezza and Pittau, suspending the power of Father General Arrupe. So Viganò's thought moved in this way:

---

[28]  This is no longer true as he did go to Germany recently to visit his brother Georg shortly before the latter's death.

from Benedict, to Benedict being "too weak," to Francis, to Francis speaking of Dezza and Pittau as "too weak." In this, Viganò's first "assessment" of Francis, I found it interesting that Viganò and Francis shared a judgement of other men in positions of Church leadership: "too weak." So I chose to be provocative.)

# CHAPTER 27

# J'ACCUSE!

YOU KNOW, I sometimes wonder if Pope Francis is actually also too weak, that he only seems strong, but that those around him are doing many things he cannot control, sometimes even using him. But you think he is strong?

Archbishop Viganò: I don't think so. I think he suffers from *delirium omnipotentiae*. This is evident.

(And suddenly, here we were: Viganò's position on Francis. We had been talking for less than ten minutes, and the archbishop was no longer speaking about his travels, his hiding places, his own situation, but about Francis. He was telling me, without any qualifying clauses, that Pope Francis suffers from a psychological "delirium" of "omnipotence," that he feels "all-powerful." Viganò punctuated this diagnosis with three blunt words: "This is evident." My problem was now directly before me. I had just been a guest in the pope's house. I had, in 2013, written a favorable book about Pope Francis. Pope Francis had asked me personally to pray for him, and I had said I would.)

Well, I was a guest with pilgrims in the Domus these past few days, and one day, Francis was getting his insalata at the buffet, so I made some insalata and I looked at Francis and I said, "Buona sera." No word. He didn't say a word to me.

At the beginning, it was not like this.

He was more . . . I brought my book to him . . .

You gave your book to him?

Well, in 2013, Msgr. Xuereb, Alfred, said, "The pope will receive you now." Alfred Xuereb from Malta.

Ah, Xuereb, yes. Now he's nuncio in Korea.

(I noted that Viganò always placed his Vatican friends and colleagues according to their posts. It was as if he had a grid in his mind, and on the grid was every member of the Vatican hierarchy, some moving, some staying at their posts. It was an institutional mind, a hierarchical mind.)

Yes. So I came over to his table and he stood up and he took my hand and he said, "Thank you so much for your book," very nicely. And then he said, "I would like to ask you one thing: Remember to pray for me." I thought it was because the title of my book was *Pray For Me*, but now I know that he always asks that of everyone he meets. Anyway, I am not sure if Fr. Pedacchio

**was there in those first months, I don't recall, but Pedacchio has become quite influential.**

He is terrible. Arrogant. I saw the first approach of Pedacchio to me on that twenty-third of June in 2013.

(Pedacchio became the second private secretary of Pope Francis in the spring of 2013, first working alongside the first secretary, Monsignor Xuereb, then, after one year, in the spring of 2014, taking over the role of first private secretary after Francis promoted Xuereb to be general secretary of the Council for the Economy. Pedacchio, like Pope Francis, is from Argentina. In a *Catholic News Agency* report dated July 19, 2013, a well-informed Italian journalist, Andrea Gagliarducci, wrote, "In a December 26, 2011 report, an anonymous informant wrote in the Argentinian portal *Intereconomia* accusing him (Pedacchio) of being 'a spy of Cardinal Bergoglio in Rome' within the ranks of the Congregation of Bishops. The report insinuated that Msgr. Pedacchio used to inform Cardinal Bergoglio 'of any document or letter that reached the Congregation, sealed documents included.' The report also asserted that 'when the issue at stake is very important, Msgr. Pedacchio also sends faxes to Bergoglio with all the documentation required' by 'his boss.'")[29]

---

[29]   Andrea Gagliarducci, "Pope Francis' shadow: Monsignor Pedacchio Leaniz," *Catholic News Agency*, July, 19, 2013, https://www.catholicnewsagency.com/news/pope-francis-shadow-monsignor-pedacchio-leaniz.

# CHAPTER 28

# VIGANÒ'S HEALTH

*"The LORD sustains him on his sickbed; in
his illness you heal all his infirmities."*

—Psalm 41:3

**LET ME ask you about your health. Your physical health?**

Archbishop Viganò: My physical health is good. In some
way, I am feeling more secure for some months, because
. . . I don't know if I told you that I have implanted one
transmitter? No?

**You did not tell me, no.**

So in 2017, I was in New York, and without having any
kind of warning, I fainted.

**You fainted?**

I was eating with my nephews, and suddenly I fainted.
So it was a kind of, how do you say, a collapse. So I was
brought to a hospital close by. They kept me for a night
in the emergency room. They made me take I don't know
how many exams; they didn't find anything. So what was
my problem? I had bradycardia. I had a very slow beat of

the heart. When I was sleeping, it would slow down to thirty-five beats a minute. But this was not affecting me at all. This question of collapse was the fact that there is a break . . .

**An arrhythmia . . .**

. . . of a certain number of seconds, so I collapsed. But they told me that I have no mis-function of valves, so the rhythm is correct, it's just slow, and from time to time I may faint. Then it happened to me a second time. So in this hospital, at the end, they told me, okay there is now like a small battery, very small; they have removed it now, that is lasting five years, it's just connected like a cellular phone, but branched on the cable, and from here during the night is transmitting the electrocardiogram of the last forty-eight hours. So this is connected with an international system, Medtronic; it is a very big American firm.

So a doctor is in charge of monitoring your heart. And I am able to tell him, for example, to call and say, "Look, I think I felt something wrong." They look at it and they can see, "Yes, you have a break for four seconds." So, that happened to me now, when I fainted like this. I was seated, and just talking as I am now, and I went like this. (*He lets his head slip down limply as in a fainting moment.*)

**So two times you have fainted?**

I fainted twice. But I returned to normal after five or six seconds without any kind of message or anything. But

I consulted two or three cardiologists; they told me it's better that you put in a pacemaker. So they put in a pacemaker. In a wonderful way, a wonderful hospital with the attention that I couldn't have certainly in Rome, or even in New York, with so many people around. They kept me, just for security, one night inside. They gave me the same pacemaker that they would have given me in America. And since then, if my heart rate is going down below fifty, it's giving an impulse. So now I can see from this, for example, during the night it's stabilized on fifty, the minimum. On some occasions, it can go a little bit lower than that. But you know, normally it doesn't. And this device will last for ten years.

**And your blood pressure is good?**

My blood pressure is okay. Absolutely.

**So you take no medicines?**

No, practically not taking any other medicine.

**Your exercise?**

I have to walk. Today I've already (*looks at his watch*) walked more than six kilometers. Just around. But here I don't want to show myself too many times at the same place, because after all, it's a small town.

********

**So I am here, after so many months, and we can talk . . .**

I'm very happy you are here. Very happy. I think it was okay that you were able to stay in Rome to visit such an important person now.

(I thought, "Well, he has at least retained his sense of humor through all of this.")

**Well, I'm asking people what they think about the situation, people at a high level . . . such as Gaenswein.**

Where did you see Gaenswein, inside the Vatican?

**Yes, in the Prefecture. I asked about Benedict, how is Benedict, and I asked about how he is working with Francis. And then I asked about this Synod on the Amazon Region that's coming up. And I said . . .**

What did he say about that?

**Well, he said it's based on a sort of natural earth mother, not so much on revelation in Scripture, just as Brandmueller has said and as Mueller has said. The synod seems to risk departing from traditional Catholic teaching in some ways, and they are definitely trying to lobby for a change in the priesthood, first in the Amazon, then in Germany, then throughout the world, almost like an Eastern-rite Catholic Church, married priests and just celibate monks.**

So he is very much concerned about the Synod?

(In the months leading up to the October 2019 Synod on the Amazon region, many press reports suggested that the synod would push strongly for the acceptance of married priests in order to respond to the shortage of priests in the region, and also for the ordination to the diaconate of women, despite or perhaps because of the fact (depending on what motivations you want to ascribe to those in favor) that the diaconate has traditionally been seen as the first rung on a ladder that leads to priestly ordination. The synod was also seen as likely to speak favorably about many of the beliefs of the indigenous peoples of the Amazon region, especially their devotion to a "Mother Earth" goddess. At the synod, there were considerable efforts made to support these goals, culminating in a controversy over the appearance in St. Peter's Basilica and in a Catholic church on via delle Conciliazione, St. Mary in Traspontina, of "Pachamama" images, images of a naked woman revered by the indigenous Indians. But many traditional Catholics felt it was inappropriate and sacrilegious to host images of what was thought to be a pagan earth goddess in a Catholic church. The images were famously removed from the church by a young Austrian man, Alexander Tschugguel, early in the morning of October 21 and tossed from a nearby bridge into the Tiber River. A few days later, Pope Francis said the images were never intended to be idolatrous, only examples of indigenous religiosity.)

**He is. And then I asked him what he thought about everything to do with you. I said, "What do you think**

about the Viganò case and his 'Testimony'?" And he said, "He said certain things that were true, and it is duty to speak the truth when there are crimes and abuse, but he probably should not have asked for the resignation. This was too far."

Yes, this was also the position of Cardinal Mueller. But you know I asked the second time in my last "Testimony" if he [Francis] will not convert, and confirm his brothers, and if he is not willing to do that, then he should resign. But now I am going much further than that.

**You think he has not acted?**

Yes, because this so-called Amazonian culture, which is pagan culture, this is the field where the devil is working. All this kind of, how do you say, magic? This is the devil. This is the field where the devil corrupts the people and is killing and is making all kinds of slavery and so on. It is not different in Africa; they are using masks, there are secret sects controlling the situation and imposing the law. This is the kingdom of the devil. The pagans and the kingdom of the devil.

(This may sound strange to many modern secular readers, but Catholics do believe the devil exists, a malevolent spiritual being who, as Scripture says, "roams about seeking the ruin of souls." A century ago, such a comment would have been considered unremarkable; that it is perceived as strange today is perhaps testament to the success of the devil in his greatest trick: that of convincing the world that he does not exist.)

**Well, what everyone always wants to know is why is Archbishop Viganò alone, why have no other cardinals and bishops really spoken out and said, "We are with him?" You seem to be a lone voice.**

But did Gaenswein say that he believed that I am telling the truth?

**On your "Testimony," he said, I think . . . We talked for about ten minutes, so I'm trying to remember. He said, "When he describes the meeting on June 23, either it's true and the pope knew or it's a lie. And we've been waiting to see the pope say that it's a lie, but he has never said it's a lie." But in the latest interview the pope gave about three weeks ago to a Mexican journalist, he says, "I didn't know and I never understood." In a way, he's negating, somehow. He didn't specifically say that you didn't tell him or you are telling a lie. Prior to that, he never considered it worthy of any comment. Now Pope Francis has made a comment, which is sort of a half-denial, but . . .**

So, he's lying all the time, so he is, how do you say, habituated to lying.

# WHAT IS AT STAKE FOR CATHOLICS

*"My soul also is sorely troubled."*
—Psalm 6:3

## Two Conflicts of Conscience

THERE ARE two great conflicts of conscience at the center of this book. Both are conflicts between two loyalties. Both are conflicts similar to those many of us face in our daily lives: Should we hastily complete a task to meet a deadline even if it requires cutting some corners or should we take all the time needed to do the job right even if one cannot finish in the time promised? Should we obey a problematic or even unjust law in our country we love because we are patriots and love our country, and disobeying laws can lead to anarchy, or should we disobey the law because we perceive, and are loyal to, a "higher country" in which that unjust law would never have been passed?

The two conflicts concern the need to choose between two conflicting claims, two conflicting loyalties. How does one make such a choice? What principles may guide a man who feels loyalty to two good principles, or institutions? What are the deep roots in a man's experience of life which determine the choice he will make? When those two principles come into conflict, which does one choose? Each man chooses differently, and the difference of the choice reflects the character and soul of the man who makes the choice.

The man at the center of this book, the Archbishop Viganò, for better or for worse, has made his choices—as each of us must as we work out our salvation in this fallen and confusing world.

The first conflict is between one's loyalty to an institution—in this case, loyalty to the Roman Catholic Church—and one's loyalty to truth.

To restate more precisely, it is the conflict between a loyalty to the Church, in its institutional structure and procedures, and a loyalty to the truth about very ugly matters happening within that structure which human weakness and corruption would prefer to avoid or cover up.

The second conflict is similar but more narrowly focused: it is between loyalty to a pope, as a particular man, and loyalty to the "essence" of who the pope is, the successor of Peter and vicar of Christ; that is, the man who, no matter what his faults and weaknesses (Peter denied Christ three times), finally, through his virtues and strengths (assisted by the Holy Spirit) "turned and confirmed his brothers," acted as Peter acted to confirm the fearful and uncertain in their faith. Viganò has dared to ask the question, "What if the pope fails to confirm his brothers?" Not to put too fine a point on it, but on the answer to that question and the one which it begs—Has

Francis failed to confirm the faithful? Has he confused them?—everything depends.

For Catholics, loyalty to the pope is a central, supporting column of the faith, as loyalty to one's father is a central, supporting column of any family. The pope is literally the "father" (the "*papa*," the Italian word for pope) of the family that is the Church. All members of the Church are "brothers and sisters" in Christ, so to call the Church a "family" is not improper. And yet, when Jesus taught his disciples to pray, he began with these words: "Our father, who art in heaven." So for the Church, there is "our Father in heaven" who is our father, God the Father of all. The pope then is the father of the Church on earth, but he is a son in relation to God the Father of all.

The conflict comes down to this: between one's loyalty to an institution one believes was founded by Christ and which one pledges to support with one's work and vision and one's loyalty to the truth as a supreme good which must be told if the institution one admires and supports is in the deepest sense to be honored and protected.

## THE SUPREME LAW OF THE CHURCH

The Church is essentially parental, both fatherly and motherly at once: seeking to protect, nourish, instruct, and save her children.

The Church is a parent in this world—a father, a mother—for the souls entrusted to her. She is a "soul-saver." Even, or perhaps especially, in terrible times of disaster, war, famine, plague, disease.

Her essential mission is to care for and *save* souls. This mission is a *spiritual* not a *material* one. Such a mission has material consequences, of course, but it is, first and foremost, *the care of souls*, not of bodies.

The mission is to instruct, protect, nourish (on spiritual food, on every word that issues from the mouth of God), and through all of this, to *save souls*, threatened not by bodily hunger or disease but by sin, by everything that distances the soul from the perfect holiness of God: actions stemming from pride, self-centeredness, lack of love.

In his 2008 homily on the Feast of the Epiphany, Pope Benedict XVI recalled that the Father's plan of salvation had been revealed in the mystery of Christ's death and resurrection. That plan, that salvation, needs to be welcomed in human history, which is always a history of fidelity on God's part and, unfortunately, also of infidelity on the part of us men, he said. The Church, the depositary of the blessing of the New Covenant, is holy but made up of sinners, as St. Ambrose wrote: "*immaculata ex maculatis,*" holy and spotless even though, in her earthly journey, she is made up of men stained with sin.

In Catholicism, *salvation* is the saving of the soul (we moderns, for whom the old language of faith seems to have worn out in recent decades, might speak of the saving of "the person" rather than "the soul") from sin and its consequences.

Salvation is "deliverance" or "redemption" from sin and its effects.

And salvation is brought about *through God's grace*, which means it is freely given, not merited, not earned.

In view of this central mission, Canon Law, the law of the Church, proclaims that "the *suprema lex* (supreme law) of the Church is *the salvation of souls*."

In essence, this means that saving a human soul is *more important* than anything else.

Saving a soul "trumps," as it were, every other law, custom, and activity of the Church. All ecclesial life, all Church rites and rituals, all canon law, all bureaucratic rules—such as those enjoining the "pontifical secret" with regard to certain matters which might "harm the reputation" of the Church if revealed—serve this one ultimate purpose: the saving of souls.

So, how does one choose if one is confronted with the choice between breaking a Church law or custom and harming a soul, or many souls?

In such a crisis of conscience, the answer must always be: *choose the souls.*

Choose the path that will shed light on the evil that is harming souls so as to allow the good to bring justice and healing where there has been injustice and wounding. Only in this way may a soul, or souls, be saved.

So, if breaking an oath of secrecy about some matter is necessary to save the soul of even one person, it is not only permissible but required—according to this supreme law—to break that oath. (Note: I am not referring here to the seal of sacramental confession. Sacramental confession, in which grave, mortal sins are confessed by a penitent, is always sacred because it is a moment in which the fate of a guilty soul hangs between eternal life and eternal death. The object of the confessor is to receive, in the place of Christ, the confession of a soul seeking forgiveness. This is always an inviolable moment. However, every priest then has the right and, I would imagine, the duty to say to the penitent that, having confessed, having been forgiven, there are other steps to take, other duties to fulfill, including but not limited to making reparation for the wrong, the abuse, that has been done. Not to break the seal of confession but to urge the penitent to turn himself in voluntarily to authorities to show that the repentance for the sin, for the crime, is real. C. S. Lewis famously wrote something to the effect that the proper course of action for a Christian who commits murder is to turn himself in to be hanged.)

According to this reasoning, it would seem, one may defend the controversial and (in the Vatican) much-criticized decision of Archbishop Viganò in 2018 to reveal in his "Testimony" what he knew about *the improper conduct of many in the hierarchy* of the Catholic Church with regard to the sexual abuse crisis of recent decades, *even if some of the things he revealed he had learned in the course of his years of delicate Church work*, which normally would have required him to keep those facts secret.

Viganò, in this crisis of conscience, *chose to follow the supreme law of the Church*: to defend souls, even if that required him to transgress a boundary of secrecy that he had sworn to uphold, and had upheld, during a lifetime of service to the Holy See.

In Viganò's own words:

Bishops and priests, abusing their authority, have committed horrendous crimes to the detriment of their faithful, minors, innocent victims, and young men eager to offer their lives to the Church, or by their silence have not prevented that such crimes continue to be perpetrated. To restore the beauty of holiness to the face of the Bride of Christ, which is terribly disfigured by so many abominable crimes, and if we truly want to free the Church from the fetid swamp into which she has fallen, we must have the courage to tear down the culture of secrecy and publicly confess the truths we have kept hidden. We must tear down the conspiracy of silence with which bishops and priests have protected themselves at the expense of their faithful, a conspiracy of silence that in the eyes of the world risks making the Church look like a sect, a conspiracy of silence not so dissimilar from the one that prevails in the mafia."[30]

The second conflict of conscience implicit in the actions of Archbishop Viganò, discussed above, is that which sets loyalty to the pope against loyalty to the supreme law of the Church, the salvation of souls.

In the Catholic Church, the veneration for the pope is profound. The pope, successor of Peter, is "the rock" upon which the Church finds her stability. Vatican diplomats, who spend their lives in the service of the Church, are required to take an oath of fidelity to the pope when they enter their service. Archbishop Viganò took that oath. He swore to abide by all Vatican procedures and regulations in devoting his mind and skill and energy to the service of the universal Church, governed by the pope. He told me once that he took that oath with pride and carried it out for many decades serving under Pope Paul

30    Viganò, "Testimony," August 22, 2018.

VI, Pope John Paul I, Pope John Paul II, Pope Benedict XVI, and Pope Francis.

However, the Church has never "divinized" the man who becomes the pope. The Church has never regarded any pope as anything other than a man whose essential task and mission is *to confirm his brothers in the faith of the ages*, that faith handed down from the apostles which speaks about Jesus Christ and brings salvation. So it has always been believed that the pope, being human, may commit sins. In fact, being human, the pope cannot, by definition, be anything other than a sinner, as all men are sinners. And it has also always been believed that a pope may err in his judgments on what are called "prudential matters." So any pope may be imprudent. Any pope may err in all sorts of ways in matters of daily life and in such things as his political and economic judgments. These papal judgments can never be *de fide* (of the faith, binding in faith), as are the clauses of the Creed.

Where does this leave the question of papal infallibility? And where does it leave the belief, based on the words of Jesus, that "the gates of hell shall not prevail" against the Church?

With regard to infallibility, the Church did define at the First Vatican Council in 1870 that the pope, when teaching *in accord with all prior Church tradition*, speaking solemnly and after considerable reflection and meditation *from his throne* (this is call speaking *ex cathedra*, "from the chair," or "from the throne"), defines a Church's teaching, he is protected from error and teaches infallibly.

*The Catechism of the Catholic Church* deals with these points in paragraphs 882, which declares the supreme authority of the pope in matters of doctrine, and 890 and 891, which stress that this authority is given to remain faithful to a teaching which has been already given, so it is not given to alter the tradition but to preserve and defend it.

Paragraph 882 reads: "The Pope, Bishop of Rome and Peter's successor, 'is the perpetual and visible source and foundation of the unity both of the bishops and of the whole company of the faithful.'(402) 'For the Roman Pontiff, by reason of his office as Vicar of Christ, and as pastor of the entire Church has full, supreme, and universal power over the whole Church, a power which he can always exercise unhindered.'(403)"[31]

On only two occasions, once before the First Vatican Council, in 1854, when the dogma of the Immaculate Conception was proclaimed, and once in 1950, when the dogma of the assumption of Mary into heaven was proclaimed, this "infallible" charism was exercised by the pope. It has never been used on any other occasion— and some are of the opinion that it may not be used again, because of the considerable risk of confusion both among Catholics and among Orthodox and Protestants about what such declarations really are and really mean. To avoid that confusion, the popes may decide not to exercise their prerogative of defining doctrine infallibly.

The important point is: what the pope teaches on such occasions is what the Church has always taught and believed. Nothing more. Nothing new. Nothing

---

[31]   https://www.vatican.va/archive/ccc_css/archive/catechism/p123a9p4.htm.

"innovative." Nothing "trendy." Only a definition of something already believed "from the beginning" by Christians everywhere.

So this doctrine of infallibility does not apply to any innovation or addition to Church teaching. It applies only to the expression of the perennial teaching in a way that is clear and understandable to those to whom the teaching is addressed; that is, to the Catholics of our time.

All of this is to say that there may arise a situation when a pope (or any other religious superior)—perhaps upon the counsel of his closest advisors, who all may have their own special motives and aims—may act, or fail to act, in a way such that his action or inaction harms, or could harm, souls or cause scandal to souls.

In such a situation, even a Catholic who is profoundly loyal to the pope, profoundly obedient to him, even a Catholic who is truly a "faithful servant" of the Holy See and of "Peter" as the custodian of that See, must confront a dilemma: Should I speak out in such a way as to end the harm to souls or should I remain silent?

Each man and each woman may face such a dilemma during a lifetime, and it would be a tragedy for the Church if we were to limit or lessen in any way the freedom of Catholics to speak their minds when grave matters affecting the salvation of souls are in question. We are free men and women in the Church, and we must speak in accord with our consciences on behalf of the truth and on behalf of the "little ones" who may suffer abuse of body or mind or heart or soul.

So the fact that Archbishop Viganò issued a

"Testimony" in August of 2018 denouncing Pope Francis for not acting more vigorously in the matter of then-Cardinal McCarrick's alleged acts of sexual molestation and calling for his resignation is not *tout court* an act of mutiny against Francis. It is an appeal for truth, for the end of cover-ups, in a matter of profound importance for souls, and so for the Church. It cannot be that a "whistle-blower" in the Church is *ipso facto* ("by that very fact") regarded as a traitor to the pope. In fact, he is providing the pope with an opportunity to come face to face with his duty to take action and confirm his brothers in the faith. Those who do not advise the pope to take action in this way are the truly disloyal ones, the ones who truly *are not faithful to the pope*. Still, in Rome, Viganò has tended to be sharply criticized, and the wagons around Pope Francis have been drawn up in a circle.

The "*suprema lex*," the "supreme law" of the Church, makes clear that, at the Church's core, her vision has an *eternal*, not a *temporal*, horizon. Salvation may begin in this world, but it is intended for eternity. For the Church, we human beings live "unto eternity," not "unto time." This means that, for the Church, what is to be feared, as Jesus taught, is not what can kill the body but what can kill, or damn, the soul. We must do whatever we can to avoid the loss of souls, the wounding and confusing and rendering hopeless of souls. We must provide healing to souls, and the clarity of truth, and the balm of hope, in view of eternal life.

Since, as St. Irenaeus taught, "the life of man is the vision of God," the loss of the vision of God—a characteristic of our time often lamented by Emeritus Pope

Benedict and more recently lamented by the West African Cardinal Robert Sarah—leads to the loss of the life of men. That vision of God may be lost, the Church teaches, through sin, through the transgression of the holy commandments of God. The restoration of that vision comes through the forgiveness of sins, the healing of spiritual wounds, the comforting of souls tempted by the demons of pride, concupiscence, despair, and the other deadly sins—and through the spiritual healing of those who have suffered from abuse, especially the innocent who have suffered from sexual abuse.

But how can there ever be such healing if the sins and crimes are never made public, if they forever remain shrouded in a realm of silence and cover-up? And what of justice? Should wrongdoers not be exposed and punished, especially when one is talking about crimes as egregious as the sexual abuse of minors?

This was the burden of the teaching of Jesus, who forgave the sins of sinners but never told the sinners that the things they had done were not sins. The teaching of holiness as the path toward Christ, toward blessedness, toward eternal life, has been the message of the Church since her foundation and must be her message until the end of the world.

Both holiness of life and the vision of God may be lost. Holiness of life may be lost through yielding to the temptation to sin, and the vision of God may be lost through a defect in teaching the truths of the faith. So it becomes the mission of the Catholic Church, and especially of the leaders of the Church, the bishops, the cardinals and the pope, to do everything in their power to teach and support holiness of life and orthodox teaching of the truths of the faith, preeminently the truth that Jesus Christ is the sole savior of the world and that through him, the entire world, the entire creation, which had been languishing in the shadow of death, has been redeemed. Through teaching holiness of life and orthodoxy in doctrine, the Church has prepared and preserved many souls for eternity with God.

Still, throughout her history, the Church has often wrestled with challenges to the clear teaching of the truths of the faith, and this has also been a real struggle in recent decades, as pope after pope has warned of the dangers of modernism, relativism, a false (because syncretistic) ecumenism, and a general tendency to accept the standards and teachings of "the world" rather than to hold fast to the perennial teachings of the faith.

For Christians, the essential doorway to salvation, to eternal life, is Jesus Christ, born in time in Bethlehem, who nevertheless overcame death itself, "trampling death by death," as it says in the Byzantine liturgy. If the Church no longer teaches clearly this and every truth about Jesus Christ, faith in Jesus Christ may be impeded, or made problematic, or impossible. In this way, false or confusing teaching can become a grave danger to souls because it can become a cause for loss of faith in Jesus Christ.

The energy or power of Christ's conquest of death is holiness, for it is sin that leads to death, sin that produces death ("for the wages of sin is death, but the free gift of God is eternal life in Christ Jesus our Lord," St. Paul writes in Romans 6:23). The holiness of Christ means that he is, in fact, incorruptible, not subject to corruption—death has no power over him, nor over those who share in his holiness and life.

# CHAPTER 29

# HOPE AMIDST THE CRISIS AND PRIESTLY MEMORIES

*"When I had my first private meeting with him, I was very confident and straightforward. I opened my heart."*
—Archishop Viganò, recalling his June 23, 2013 meeting with Pope Francis

THE INTERVIEW continues, and Viganò gave me the key to understand his own mind and this entire book: that he views the present crisis in the Church as being one not just of physical sexual abuse, but one, too, of intellectual and spiritual "abuse."

In his view, this second type of abuse takes the form of bishops and priests, including, on some occasions, the bishop of Rome, the pope, for whatever reason failing to teach effectively, without any ambiguity, traditional Catholic doctrine.

Rather, Viganò maintains, many Church teachers are promoting an altered, "modernist" version of the faith.

In other words, false teaching.

In the process, they are endangering innumerable souls—including their own. However, Viganò also speaks movingly of God's forgiveness, of the unfailing character of Christian hope, of the maternal tenderness of the Blessed Virgin Mary, and of what the laity can do during this time.

The key that opened the way to understand that the "crisis" was not simply physical sexual abuse and its cover up but also spiritual abuse through the confusion caused by ambiguous teaching was Viganò's revelation that in their famous June 23, 2013 conversation after the pope's question about Cardinal McCarrick, there was a "second question." That "second question" concerned the Jesuits. Over months and years of reflection, Viganò had come to believe that the "second question" was of fundamental importance for the entire Church, a question which will be examined more fully in the follow-up volume to this book.

Despite the perilous state of the Church in this time of confusion and what he considers to be widespread apostasy, Archbishop Viganò is a man of hope. Below, he discusses the source of that hope.

**What is your hope now for the crisis in the Catholic Church?**

Archbishop Viganò: My hope now? (*thinks a moment*) Since the beginning, as I had the news that Pope Francis was elected, I had a lot of confidence in the pope. The pope could have been John Paul II, certainly. I spent a lot of years close to him. Pope Benedict also. But the new pope was Francis. So my entire confidence and affection was given to him from the beginning.

For that reason, when I had my first private meeting with him, I was very confident and straightforward. I opened my heart. He asked me about McCarrick and I said, "I don't know if you know McCarrick; here's what he has done."

If I had not trusted him in some way, if I had been in some way apprehensive regarding Francis, I never . . . I should have been more careful and perhaps said, "I don't know exactly."

So, I opened my heart, my mind. I told him what I knew from my previous job at the Secretariat of State. And in fact, after I told him, my trust was always complete after that. I had no reason not to trust him.

So, my hope certainly, at certain moments, was shaken, because I realized that my duty was to continue to bear witness to the truth.

I cannot but be a witness to the truth in spite of any kind of consequence. The truth is a light. And the light of the truth cannot be hidden. It would come out, as St. John tells us in the last Gospel. The dark cannot win over the light. Never.

So the truth is a winner. So that . . . Because of my education, because of my faith, because of my trust in the Church and in Mary, mother of the Church, I think that I have been a witness for the truth.

In spite of everything, I have full hope for the future of the Church. Why? Because the Church is protected. The Church is the bride of the Lord. How could the bridegroom abandon the bride? Can the mother of the Church abandon the Church?

In spite of all the human drama of a very disordered kind, I still understand more and more that our time is now the time of the Mother. This is the time of the

Mother of the Church. She asks, she has been entrusted to protect the Church. How is she going to do this? In this, we have to have faith in Jesus, the only Savior—the only Savior, there is no other. There is no other Savior. Through the grace of the sacraments, and by returning to the Mother who will protect us in this battle, as it has been entrusted to her, to lead the fight against the devil.

What we see now is certainly a terrible freedom that God has permitted to the devil to show that he's the victor, but he's not; he's the one who is defeated.

Of course, what has happened to the Church? The Church, the path of the Church could not be different than the path of Jesus. There's no other path than the path of the cross. The cross is the throne of the Risen Lord. He's already glorious. The victor is Jesus.

But the Church has to pass through the same persecution, the same cross, the same path of Jesus Christ. There's no other way than the way of the cross.

So, I do think we are approaching this time of persecution. There are so many signs now. The loss of the faith in a great part of Europe. Not everywhere. You can see for example the great mystery of how the faith has been still strongly alive in many vocations, more than there used to be before—in Spain, for example. In some regions of the south of Italy, where there was the tradition, for example, of the confraternity. This is so rooted deeply in the family. You can see people who have been making many sacrifices all along the years. Just in order to keep alive this tradition of the devotion to our Lady, to the suffering Jesus, to Christ carrying the cross. A specific example is our Lady of Macarena,[32] just to mention one of the devotions that is protecting the Church in the sacred heart, the maternal heart of Mary.

I must say that since I finished my service to Washington, of course, I've been challenged, because I have had to find a new home. But I was never abandoned. I was never scared by anything. So, I will continue to proclaim the truth as far as I think that it is necessary to do so.

My hope is with Our Lady, she will lead the Church in the battle against the devil. A time will come very soon. This is my feeling. The Church may lose [its status] as a temporal leader. But we have the one to whom the Church has been entrusted since the beginning, since the first chapter of Genesis.

Our Lady will crush and defeat the devil. So she's victorious. She has been during the history of the Church, several times, for example, when the Church was threatened to be battered by the Muslim armies. And sometimes, it is true, when the Church has been persecuted, it was because the Church was in a state of corruption. Not only at the time of St. Damian in the eleventh century, but also the times of the sack of Rome. The corruption was very much spread and the Church and the Holy See was almost completely destroyed. Also,

---

32    The Virgin of Hope of Macarena (Spanish: *Virgen de la Esperanza de Macarena de Sevilla*) is a title of the Blessed Virgin Mary associated with a pious seventeenth-century wooden image of the Blessed Virgin venerated in Seville, Spain. https://en.wikipedia.org/wiki/Virgin_of_Hope_of_Macarena.

the apostolic palace was in ruins because of the corruption of the Church.

One prominent person, a convert from Judaism in fact, with whom I interact has said to me, "You know, why, when Jesus was condemned by the Sanhedrin, why was he condemned to death? Because the Sanhedrin was deeply corrupt. They were not able to recognize the visit of Jesus as one of them. Now, the corruption of the Holy See is very great, as was the corruption at that time, now as then. So this is a sign for me as a former Jew that the time is very near for the second coming of Jesus."

**What should people do during this time?**

The people should be confident and pray, as was suggested by Our Lady of Fatima and in many other apparitions of Our Lady in which this was always the very strong and prominent message. Convert yourself. Pray the Rosary. Ask for the protection of Our Lady. She will be the leader of the Church. Don't be scared.

So, I would say that devotion to Our Lady has always been reassuring me. My devotion to the Blessed Mother continues today. When I was appointed to the Secretariat of State, I think I was one of the first when the Basilica was opening at seven o'clock in St. Peter's. I was able to choose the altar dedicated to Our Lady Mother of the Church, the new chapel going on the left.

**The one in the back on the left? The chapel "Mater ecclesiae"?**

Yes, also called the Chapel of Our Lady. If that was already taken by somebody, I was going to another chapel at the tomb of St. Gregory Nazianzus, where there is also a little chapel dedicated to Mary. I have always sought out a chapel dedicated to Our Lady.

**What does it mean to you to celebrate Mass?**

Well, to celebrate Mass is my first intention and desire every morning. So that is what keeps me able to serve the Church, forgetting myself. At the Secretariat [during the many years when he worked in the Secretariat of State in the Vatican], I began every day with personal prayer, preparation for the Mass, the celebration of the Mass, giving sufficient time, then going back to the office. So, this was the Mass, to offer the sacrifice of Christ for the Church, for the pope whom I had been serving so closely for many years. This is something that has given me always serenity in spite of the challenges. I was never afraid. This was not a virtue; it was a feeling of security, a feeling to be safe.

**Do you feel Our Lady is close to you and protecting you?**

Absolutely. Yes. I can't presume, and I know it's very difficult to say if that is coming from a kind of psychological attitude or from a real spiritual grace. But certainly, I never was afraid in my life. I was never afraid when I crossed the desert throughout the night from Baghdad to Beirut alone. I did that several times, sometimes in a very weak car. Of course, there was no ISIS then, there was not the war in Iraq at that time, but crossing eight hundred kilometers of the desert from Baghdad to Damascus, it's not a joke. There is not a single tree. But I was not scared.

Similarly in Nigeria. I did what I had to do. If I'm doing something for the mission, no one will stop me.

**You felt safe.**

I always thought if I'm doing that for a mission, I'm not scared. I did not go out for dinner in the city when I knew that there was a risk for armed robbery in Nigeria, but for pastoral visits, nothing would stop me. With prudence, I'd arrive at a destination before dark. Of course, I was very much protected because during the many miles I traveled in difficult countries, I never met any particular risk, being attentive and so on.

**When you made these travels, you were working for the Church and for the Gospel, you were trying to reach out to people. You were reaching out to give hope and faith to people. Is this the vision of your task?**

I would never impose my program, my own vision, when I was a nuncio. I was trying to respond to the request of the local Church. I would plan, for example, to have a week to visit a diocese. Going around to the different villages, the people were welcoming the representative of the pope with great enthusiasm. Of course, I was never alone. I would make those pastoral visits with one of the priests, sometimes it was a local missionary, always there was someone with me. I tried to share my visit with each one of the personnel working with me. And of course, I was visiting the seminary; there was a major seminary in the diocese. I was summoning all the priests to have a meeting with me, and all of the religious sisters.

So I tried to contact all the community in the villages. And it was extraordinary. As I was able to see how the Church was alive and that gave me strength and still gives me strength today. From my experience, I think the future of the Church in Africa is really great. The time that I spent, especially in Nigeria, was the most beautiful experience of my life. I remember I even said to John Paul II when he appointed me to Nigeria, "Well, you are taking a great risk. You're sending somebody to the most populous country in Africa and somebody who has never been in Africa before." But I did go, and I was very much encouraged by, of course, Cardinal Arinze. He was a great support to me and a wonderful collaborator. I had many wonderful collaborators in Nigeria.

**While you were there, did you ever face illness, sickness? I think you once or twice had malaria? And so the task to serve the Church was sometimes difficult . . .**

Almost just at the beginning, I received very good advice before going to Nigeria from an old lady, an American lady from Chicago, who was a friend of my brother priest who was serving in Chicago at the Oriental Institute. This lady was a widow. She was almost one hundred years old. But she had lived for some time in India with her husband and she gave me a bit of advice. And this advice was simple. It was, "Don't put on your socks in the morning without turning them inside out. You may find there is a scorpion inside."

**And that was a metaphor for everything in those countries, and even in the United States?**

Yes. Be very careful. She also told me that one thing that you need to be very careful of is malaria. So before leaving for Nigeria, I read some literature regarding malaria and I learned that there was a different kind of malaria. Some that is cyclical, which was present also in Italy, even in the north of Italy, but especially in areas where there was stagnant water, like the area of Fiumicino where Maria Goretti died.

So I learned there are different types of malaria. In particular, there was one that was a deadly malaria. The one was named plasmodium falciparum because the virus that caused it could be recognized by its shape under the microscope. You can see the shape of the cell, the one attacking you. It was kind of a "*falce,*" how do you say, a sickle.

**Yes, like a sickle or a scythe.**

So at some point during the first years I got a very high fever. There was a small clinic in Lagos, close to the west quarter, run by *Memores Domini.* And one of them, who by chance I had met when I was in London because she was sent to London to have a nursing degree approved by the British that would be recognized also in their former colonies, she told me, "You have malaria." So, I answered to her, "This is not sufficient for me, I want to know which kind of malaria I have." So there was a laboratory there. She went to this laboratory and she brought the small (*pauses, groping for the word*) . . .

**The little slide.**

Yes, the little slide. There I could see this was plasmodium falciparum. So, I brought with me the medicine that was the specific one for the plasmodium falciparum. The name of the drug was lariam, but the chemical was mefloquine.

So I took doses of that. My fever was over 40 degrees centigrade [about 104 degrees Fahrenheit]. So the effect of this Lariam was horrible—a nightmare in the sense of all the world running around in your head. So that I felt that I was losing my senses. But this medicine was able to completely destroy this plasmodium falciparum. So I was cured.

I know where I got this mosquito, this bite, this *plasmodium falciparum*. Because almost . . . This can be checked. But John Paul II visited Benin Republic—it's very close to the border to the south of Nigeria—in November, so I asked for authorization to join the visit. It was just perhaps a hundred kilometers [sixty miles] to go there. So we crossed the border with the Benin Republic, but I didn't find any accommodation, other than in a very, very dirty hotel, full of mosquitoes. Probably I caught the malaria there. But I was happy to be there anyway.

So one of the great impressions that I got during my

visit in Nigeria was the enormous growth of priestly religious education, full seminaries, sometimes several hundred major seminarians all behaving in a very good formation. A new seminary was founded when I was there. So that it gives them a great hope for the future of the Church in Africa, especially because Nigeria was, I must say, probably the most important country in Africa. What I saw then and now I can see clearly is that certainly the Church in Africa is giving great hope, in spite of many challenges. We have been living an incredible quick decline of the faith due to the secularization in Europe, the loss of faith, no vocations. But the great impression of my experience in Africa remains this: an impression of hope.

I was very much comforted seeing that the leaders of the Church, the bishop and the cardinals in Africa, are still strong in the faith and fight for the truth. They had an incredibly strong formation through the missionary work.

**When did you leave Nigeria?**

I left in '98. But Our Lady was always present, and I was comforted in the last months that I was in Nigeria by the visit of John Paul II in March 1998. He visited Nigeria, and it was he himself who called me back to the Secretariat of State, offering me the post of delegate for Pontifical Representations.

(Note: The archbishop's service during the years between 1998 and 2011 is covered earlier in the book.)

**Your final post was in the United States from 2011 to 2016. How did you like the United States of America? What do you think of the Americans?**

So, I remember that before going to the United States, of course, I was always very much impressed by the great testimonies of the American martyrs. The first Jesuits who went there—St. John de Brebeuf and also the other one.

**Isaac Jogues.**

Isaac Jogues. On one occasion I privately visited Canada. In Montreal, I think it was, I visited a college dedicated to John de Brebeuf. And, of course, I heard the story of the North American Martyrs, the Jesuits, so I feel incredible closeness to them, especially having seen how terrible the climate was in Canada. How those people could survive that weather! I remember my first visit to Quebec City in winter.

**Oh, it's cold.**

I rented a car alone and drove from Montreal to Quebec City. From the place where I was able to park the car, I wanted to visit the cathedral.

I was not able to continue. I had to stop in a bar to take something hot because I was freezing. My face was completely freezing. So the climate was impossible.

So, thinking of the North American Martyrs, in fact, after I accepted my appointment to the United States, I chose as the date of publication, their feast, 19 of October. So, on the feast of the North American Martyrs, my appointment to the nuncio of the United States was published. So I really felt they were my protectors.

That was one of the reasons why I was deeply scandalized by the decision of the American Jesuits to abandon the shrine in Auriesville. [The Shrine of Our Lady of Martyrs is located in the hamlet of Auriesville in Fultonville, New York. Once the seventeenth-century Mohawk village of Ossernenon, it is now a Roman Catholic shrine dedicated to three Jesuit missionaries who were martyred there and to St. Kateri Tekakwitha, a Mohawk/Algonquin woman who was born there. The Jesuit Order announced in mid-2015 that it would leave the Shrine of Our Lady of Martyrs. Shrine spokesman Joey Caruso said the Society of Jesus was "consolidating Jesuit orders," and the three priests now at the shrine will be leaving. "The shrine is not closing. The active ministry of the Jesuits will move on to serve other parts of the order," Caruso said.]

When I visited Auriesville, I found an old father had just died; it was just a mess. It is a tragedy. I found just close to the shrine an exact copy of Our Lady of Fatima in bronze, exactly the same that I used to visit in the Vatican Gardens. Just after the grotto, you go on the right.

**In these months, since your "Testimony," how have you lived your life? How have you been living?**

This time was certainly difficult. I do not take unnecessary risks, but I was advised that I was risking myself. I don't know if that was real. But I think the timing has been providential in some ways. I have had the possibility to dedicate myself more to private prayer than what I had the opportunity before.

Additionally, I have found a lot of friends who give me, for example, the possibility of having a permanent chapel with the Blessed Sacrament. So with them, we used to have many hours of the adoration of the Blessed Sacrament.

Later on, it was suggested that I should change my residence a couple of times. Always, I had a lot of time for praying, for praying the entire Rosary, the twenty mysteries, including the new mysteries of light. Every day, of course, the adoration of the Blessed Sacrament. And more time also to be kept informed of what was going on in the Church. It was my duty also to know about that. This year has passed quickly, in serenity, supported by friends, by messages, by those responding to my witness and believing that I was saying the truth. When you're saying the truth, truth will come out.

**Have you been afraid?**

Well, I don't know, maybe it's a sign that I am a little bit crazy. But this was kind of unconscious, but I have always had a deep sentiment of, as everybody has of course, that we are immortal. Nobody can kill us. I can talk for myself. So, nobody would kill *me*; they would kill *my body*, but my mind is surviving, *my soul is surviving*. So what is there to be frightened of?

## You believe in the immortality of the soul?

Of course. Not because I am unaware of my mortality. I know I am growing old. I'm feeling, especially during the last year, my strength is not the same. I realize that as the years are passing, this is coming faster and faster. So, you perhaps can be like your father over ninety, but I don't think that anybody in my family has been able to reach such an age. My father died very young; he was sixty-three and my mother was seventy-seven. Of course, the previous generation, because the progress of medicine was not so good, certainly life was not as long as it often is now.

So I consider the fact that I have reached past seventy-eight years old not normal for my constitution. I feel, for example, the strength of my legs is not anything like it was before. Maybe two, three years ago I was still able to run. So now, for example, the genuflection is not without a certain pain, so I said to myself that this is the sign that now it is a question of taking care of what is more necessary for the soul.

## So how do you take care of your soul?

Since I retired, and especially in this past year, I have realized the moment has come for me to give more time to prayer, to reflection, to the adoration of our Lord. I have been reading an Irish Benedictine, I don't know if he's English or Irish, you may know that. He has written a book, *In Sinu Jesu: A Personal Dialogue with Jesus*. You know the name of this book? So during this time, the first six months after publishing my "Testimony," I have been meditating on this book.

**Really?**

It is about the importance of adoration. The need for adorers of the Eucharist.

**What does "adoration" really mean?**

Adoration means that you are in the presence of and united with Jesus. You may listen to him, just keep quiet and serene and the Lord of the world is there with you, protecting you. Sometimes you have to express your desire, your thanks for what you have been given during this life, the grace that you have received. That, to me, is adoration—feeling the presence of Jesus. Jesus is here. What greater thing can there be on earth? You're looking at the sky or all the beauty of nature—all this is nothing without the Lord's presence.

**Do you feel that he is close to you?**

Well, yes, I feel that.

**What is your message to everyone who reads this?**

My message cannot be different from what you know. First of all, I am assuring everybody that I am in good health. Thank God I continue to have a normal life in the sense that I can do what I was able to do before. And of course I recommend to everybody to look at the faith you received since the beginning, persevere in what you have been taught since your youth, and remember what was the first mission that St. John Paul II told us: don't be afraid; the light and the truth, they are the witness. So, keep steadfast in all you have been told from the beginning and continue to believe. Let them say what they want—new doctrine, new paradigms. The only "new" we have received is the command we proclaim in the Ambrosian Rite at the end of the consecration of the body of Christ: "Preach my death."

Before the word of the consecration of the first canon, the Ambrosian Rite has these words: "And I give you another command: Preach my death, announce my resurrection, wait with confidence for my Second Coming. Trust my return when I come back to you from heaven."

**And do you feel that we are in that time?**

This is the spirit in which we have to continue to believe, especially now, while we wait with confidence his coming again from heaven.

**And the preservation of the true faith, the depositum fidei. Is it possible it is in danger?**

Of course, this has been threatened since the beginning. We can feel now the faith is being threatened by the world, and I would say that never has it been threatened so much as now. Now practically we are not able to receive confirmation of our faith by those who in fact have the duty to do so, from bishops, from priests and also from the supreme head of the Church. So the expectation of the second coming of Jesus is becoming more and more close to us. The signs are the . . .

**What are the signs?**

The signs are deviation, the impression that the Church is abandoned to herself. And many new doctrines, many new paradigms.

**An example of such new paradigms?**

New paradigms have been preached. Also, there's an article that during the Mass in St. Peter's at ten o'clock yesterday the one who was presiding, who preached, made an allusion that Sodom and Gomorrah were not destroyed at all, because the Lord listened to Abraham's invocation. That is a new paradigm.

**You told me you went recently to confession. Why did you go to confession?**

Because I need to confess myself. I cannot stay hidden to the extent that I do not receive the sacrament of confession. I felt that I should confess myself. If a priest would recognize me, I would say, "You are under the seal of confession."

**Do you feel you have done something that you repent of doing?**

Not regarding my witness. As every human being, I may have temptation, I was maybe not quick enough to refuse the temptation. It was maybe the weakness that everybody has, but certainly not regarding what I have testified. Because this I did for the Church, to fight the corruption, to reveal those who were part of that corruption from inside the Church at this time. In fact, also Pope Francis, in one of the last documents after the meeting in February [the Vatican summit with the world's bishops on the clerical abuse crisis, February 21–24, 2019] said, "You should denounce those who are corrupted in the Church."

**What does it mean to you to love the Church?**

Well . . . Can you love the Church without loving the truth? The truth is Jesus. Can you love the truth without loving Mary? I mean, she has given light to the truth.

# PART VI

# VIGANÒ ON THE CRISIS IN THE CHURCH

*"But this is the last movement, because something is going to happen."*
—Carlo Maria Viganò, July 27, 2019

# CHAPTER 30

# HOMOSEXUALITY AS KEY

**So LET's begin with your first testimony and then-Cardinal McCarrick.**

Archbishop Viganò: Going back to the twenty-third of June 2013 [Viganò's meeting in Rome with Pope Francis] and saying, restarting from what I said, regarding the question, and stressing again. Many people are writing, "I talked about McCarrick." This is not the point. I had been asked a question about McCarrick. Why was I asked that question? And I told what I answered, what in conscience I knew. Now, the pope is obliged to observe the eighth commandment, is he not? [The eighth commanment is "Thou shalt not bear false witness against thy neighbor."] Because he lied. And he lied and also made a calumny. And he continues to this day.

**So, "do not bear false witness"?**

Don't bear false witness. So, it is a grave matter. Because this is treason, and he is destroying everybody who is saying the truth.

**What can I say to make the people understand that this is the situation?**

I will repeat on McCarrick. This has been going on and
there is a lie. And you know, more and more every day
there is a new homosexual who is protected or is coming
out through new investigations, and I have denounced
some others, but nobody is touching them. Nobody is
catching them. On the contrary, they are being privileged, pushed to the fore in other words. For example,
there is Zanchetta coming back again.[33]

---

[33]  In a June 11, 2019 *MercoPress* article, Zanchetta's history and
the Vatican's response was discussed. "The Vatican had been
denying that the Pope had any knowledge of this as late as January, stating that they only learned of the allegations in 2018;
however, Fr. Juan José Manzano, Zanchetta's former vicar
general, has contradicted this denial saying that he reported
Zanchetta to the Vatican in 2015 and 2017.

   "'In 2015, we just sent a "digital support" with selfie photos
of the previous bishop [Zanchetta] in obscene or out of place
behavior that seemed inappropriate and dangerous,' Manzano
said. 'It was an alarm that we made to the Holy See via some
friendly bishops.'

   "'The nunciature didn't intervene directly,' he continued, 'but
the Holy Father summoned Zanchetta and he justified himself
saying that his cell phone had been hacked, and that there were
people who were out to damage the image of the Pope.'

   "After Zanchetta met Francis in 2015, the Pope permitted
Zanchetta to continue as bishop of Orán for another two years.
Then, in 2017, as mainstream media began covering the story,
Zanchetta suddenly resigned as the bishop of Orán, disappear-
ing for months.

   "He reappeared in Rome as an 'assessor' — a position Francis
seems to have invented — for the Administration of the Patrimony of the Apostolic See (APSA), the Vatican office that
oversees millions of dollars in Church real estate." "Argentine
homosexual bishop criminally charged for sexually abusing
seminarians," *MercoPress*, June 11, 2019, https://en.mercopress.

Why is Pope Francis not talking with clarity, with firmness, on the first and the principal cause of the sexual abuse of the clergy, homosexuality, on the abominable sin of sodomy? And why would he not confirm without prevarication the teaching of the Catholic Church? Why continue to keep silent and keep close to himself in the great responsibility of governing the Church persons who are notoriously homosexual or in favor of homosexuality, men like Archbishop Vincenzo Paglia and the very well-known Jesuit James Martin, to mention just a couple? Mainly people are asking themselves how was it possible that McCarrick was promoted to be cardinal archbishop of Washington.

To this question, I give already a substantial answer in my first testimony, being that the case of McCarrick was not different from the one of Father Maciel. How is it possible that Pope Francis has not answered?

## CHAPTER 31

# INCREASING CONCERNS ABOUT FRANCIS AND HIS CIRCLE

LET US return to the more general topic of the crisis playing out in the Church today.

Archbishop Viganò: It did not begin today or even yesterday. Many people have written to say that it is not just sixty years but much longer, centuries. They are centuries, certainly. But what was started really in our time came after the Second Vatican Council.

On the contrary, I hope that my message would be followed also by some people in positions of responsibility, like Cardinal Parolin, who is a traitor to the Church. I see China, I see Vietnam . . . all are secret agreements. Why secret? The Catholic people don't have the right to know? Then why are the Chinese Catholics suffering? And why are they destroying the Church in China, and now, with a new agreement which is also secret in Vietnam? Why is he trying to make a secret agreement? It is secret to the faithful in China, not only to us in Europe! And the faithful in China, do they have no right to know if a guillotine is poised above their head because it is secret? Parolin is a traitor.

**Why do you think Emeritus Pope Benedict does not say anything if all of this corruption is so clear?**

Certainly, I am not approving at this moment that he is keeping silent. He has made some . . . somebody has said that also his last answer to the German theologians was made to defend himself, to defend his government of the Church, of course. But he is more courageous in theological debate than in government; this has always been his weakness. He delegated his government to Bertone. That was the beginning of the disaster.

**And how did Bertone handle the government?**

Well, Bertone handed the government over to corruption. Absolutely. You can see from what has come out: promoting his friends in order to allow himself to govern and not Benedict, in order not to expose corruption when he knew about it.

With the Enemy—with a capital letter, I mean with the devil—there cannot be dialogue, one should be quick to run away or to fight. The Enemy should only be fought against and defeated, you cannot persuade the Enemy of his error, because he knows the truth very well and better than ourselves.

**When you celebrate Mass, you have in the liturgy a prayer also for the bishop and for the pope. Do you make such a prayer?**

In the Ancient Rite, the priest pronounces the words of the Canon in secret, under the voice. This is also the secret of my conscience. I pray for Pope Francis and Pope Emeritus Benedict. For both of them.

**Again, what do you say to those who attack you for attacking, for there is no other word for it, the decisions and actions of this pope?**

It's not an attack on the Church, but a service given to the Church to testify to the truth, because only the truth may protect from the attack of the one who's treacherous, who puts us in danger constantly, the father of lies. This successor of the Apostle Peter is not exempt from the attack of the devil. On the contrary, he may be the one most disposed to be targeted by the enemy, for to hit the head, the chief, would be an exceptional achievement for the devil because if you hit the pastor, the sheep will be dispersed—Matthew 14.

For this reason, all the faithful have the obligation to pray for the pope because he's most exposed to the attack of the devil. The sheep, how can they follow the pastor, how can they listen to his voice if it's not talking to them in truth?

If he will not speak clearly, if he uses ambiguous language, if he leaves fundamental doctrines exposed to the opposed interpretation, if he's not correct, the pastors and the faithful are confused and they may follow paths contrary to the teaching or the tradition of the Church that lead them to the scene of eternal death. The door of the sheepfold is open to all. No one is excluded, but it should remain well-secured and protected when the sheep are exposed to the attack of the wild beast or the brigand. Yes, the shepherd must go in search of the lost one, but also must not in so doing expose the ninety-nine to danger.

**That opens up a whole series of additional questions, but it is getting late. Perhaps we can explore that question in greater detail later. We need to go to dinner.**

Yes. There is a self-service place where we can go. We will not be alone so we will not be able to talk too much.

\*\*\*

We went to the self-service place, but it had no food that seemed appetizing, so we did not stay. The archbishop walked around, still wearing his baseball cap.

We then drove down to a little restaurant and had a lovely dinner, really delicious. The archbishop seemed to enjoy himself. He ordered his food and ate it with great enthusiasm. We spoke with our waiter about his family, his three small children.

"My children," he said, "are the most important thing in the world to me. Everything I do, I do for my children."

"You are a good man," the archbishop said.

# PART VII

# TO THE MONASTERY

CHAPTER 32

# A CONVERSATION IN THE CAR

*"Monsignor Viganò looks tired. He
should go back to Rome with me."*
—St. Pope John Paul II, in Nigeria in 1998, where
Viganò was the nuncio. Later that year, Viganò was back
in Rome in an important post in the Secretariat of State

THE NEXT morning, we drove to a small monastery,
though whether near to or far from where I had first met
Viganò must remain unsaid. We spoke in the car as we
drove.

As we drove, I did not want to talk about McCarrick
and child abuse but about Viganò's decades of work for
the Vatican. I wanted to form an idea of his character. I
wanted to hear about other challenges he had faced and
about his relationships with other men in the Church
besides McCarrick and Francis. So I turned on the tape
recorder and set it on the console between us.

On April 3, 1992, when Viganò had just turned fifty-
one, Pope John Paul II decided to make him a bishop.
Viganò would receive the Titular See of Ulpiana with
the rank of archbishop. (A titular see is a see which was
occupied in past centuries but no longer functions due to
historical changes. So an ecclesiastic whose work is not
in a diocese but in some other area, like diplomacy, is

311

made a bishop and given a see that does not require him
to be present and act as a dicocesan bishop; it is a way to
give the title of bishop without the actual task and activity of an ordinary bishop.)

At the same time, Viganò would also become apostolic pro-nuncio to Nigeria. So Viganò was consecrated
an archbishop on April 26, 1992, in St. Peter's Basilica
by Pope John Paul II with Polish Cardinal Franciszek
Macharski and Italian Cardinal Angelo Sodano, then
secretary of state, serving as co-consecrators.

"I was assigned to be nuncio in Nigeria in 1992,"
Viganò began. "By 1998, I was ending my time there as
Pope John Paul II was visiting Nigeria."

**That trip was historic.**

Archbishop Viganò: John Paul was already walking with
a cane and he was red in his face; it was very hot. The
pope stopped by me and said, "Monsignor Viganò looks
tired. He should go back to Rome with me." So from
Abuja we took a plane, to go from Abuja to Enugu, for
the beatification of Father Tansi.

**Blessed Tansi was the bishop who ordained Cardinal
Arinze?**

Father Cyprian Michael Iwene Tansi, OCSO, who was
beatified, was not a bishop. He was a simple priest (born
in the diocese of Onitha where Arinze was born, who
was baptized by Tansi). Tansi subsequently entered a
monastery, in the Cistercian Order, in England. And

so, on the plane, Cardinal Sodano called me and said, "Come, sit close to me." And he said, "The pope wants you to be the new delegate for Pontifical Representations. Do you accept?"

**But why did he want you to have that post? It's a very important post.**

Monsignor Monterisi, until then delegate for the Papal Representations, had been promoted to archpriest of the basilica of San Paolo Fuori-le-Mura. Since I had been working for eleven years as secretary of the substitute, they talked about me. That's why.

**And the substitutes for whom you worked were?**

The substitutes were first Caprio, then Martinez Somalo, and then it was the first year of Cassidy.

**Ah. Edward.**

Cassidy. He wanted to send me . . . before going to an audience with John Paul II, he told me, "I want to tell the pope that I want to send you to Taiwan." (*He laughs.*) But I didn't say anything. So he went, and when he came back, he told me, "You know what the pope told me, John Paul II? Why do you want to send him so far away? He will think I don't love him!" (*He laughs.*) That was around December of 1988, I think. So when Strasbourg was free, he sent me to Strasbourg.

**Not so far.**

Not so far. It was, I think it was in May 1989, just before the Berlin Wall fell. One of the first visitors was Gorbachev, to the Council of Europe, in the beginning of July.

**Great times. So those were the years, the 1980s were the years when you consolidated your knowledge and experience of the entire working of the Vatican because you were in charge, under the substitute, of all . . .**

If the substitute trusts you, you can see many things. Practically all the things that are going into the pope are passing through the substitute.

**Right. And so . . . so you know the Vatican very well, and you know the various people, their characters.**

(Further conversation led us to the question of incorruptibility. Viganò offered a couple of examples of the ways in which subtle pressures can be applied to one within the Vatican walls.)

Once, I was walking in the Cortile San Damaso, and I met, it was the second man in charge at the Vatican bank, I don't remember his name now, he was made prelate later on.

**De Bonis?**

Yes, Donato de Bonis [an Italian prelate who worked in the Vatican bank, born in 1930, died in Rome in 2001]. At that moment, Italy had just released the new five hundred lire coins in two metals, five hundred lire. [Similar in value to an American quarter.] So he took out from his pocket one of those coins and he gave it to me. "Have you seen the new coins?" he asked. So he gave it to me. I looked. It was very nice; it was made of two metals. And then I returned it to him, to this de Bonis. I knew him. So he insisted two or three times, saying "No, keep it, keep it, this is for you." So I stopped walking, walking together, and I told him . . .

**Right in the Cortile San Damaso?**

In San Damaso, on the side, just close to the lift, just close to the elevator, and I stopped, I looked in his eyes. I said, "Monsignor"—he was not yet a bishop at that time—"this is not my problem." And I gave the coin back to him. It was just five hundred lire. But I knew how he was with the people visiting him. He had a drawer filled with money. And he would say, "This is for you to say Mass for this poor fellow." This was the heritage of Cardinal Di Jorio.

**The heritage of Cardinal Di Jorio . . .**

Who was in charge of the bank before Marcinkus.

**But these are small amounts really. This is less than a dollar.**

It was a small amount, but it was symbolic. It was nothing, just five hundred lire, but the way that he insisted was also symbolic. He was testing me.

**He wanted you indebted to him?**

Yes, something little, but starting . . . I was the secretary of the substitute, and I didn't want to be indebted to anybody. So for example, when Monsignor Gianni, what was his name? He recently died. He was the secretary general of the Governatorato.

**Danzi?** (Archbishop Gianni Danzi, Archbishop Prelate of Loreto, Italy, lived from 1940 to 2007)

Yes, Danzi. He would call me and say, "I am Monsignor Danzi, Gianni." And I would say, "Yes, Monsignor." The same thing I was doing with Stanislaw [Dziwicz].

**I don't understand. What do you mean?**

He was trying to give me the "*tu*" or to have me give him the "*tu*." [The familiar form of address in Italian used between close friends.] I said to Stanislaw, "No, Monsignor, you're the secretary of the pope." So I said to Danzi, "Yes, Monsignor." I was keeping my distance in order not to be involved.

**You didn't wish to become too intimate too quickly?**

Okay. (*He nods his head in agreement.*)

**All right. You mentioned Marcinkus. What do you know about that time? What did they think about Calvi?[34]**

We don't know. We remember that we had some visitors that came that when it was finished, it was a question of this Carboni in the middle, there was a question also of a Father, a Jesuit Father who claimed that he had the briefcase of Roberto Calvi, that it had been given to him.

**Was this Hnilica?**

No, no.

---

[34]   Roberto Calvi became a close collaborator with the Vatican Bank. He managed to take control of the traditionally Catholic bank of Milan called the Ambrosiano. The two banks made investments in many areas which ended disastrously with the collapse of the Banco Ambrosiano and a debt of 1.3 billion dollars. When Calvi asked Marcinkus to save him from this debt, Marcinkus said the Vatican had supported him all along but had never agreed to be responsible for his debts. Calvi proceeded to London to seek financing, and on June 18, 1982, was found hanging dead from the arch of Blackfriars' Bridge in that city. In the Freemasonic tradition, to die by flowing waters with bricks in your pockets is a sign of punishment for treachery or betrayal. Marcinkus told me that I should come to talk to him before he died, and he would tell me things about the Vatican and this case that would curl my hair. "And your hair is pretty curly," he said. I made an appointment to meet him in February 2006 in Sun City, AZ, but as I was preparing to go see him, I read in the newspaper that he had died.

**Do you remember, Bishop Hnilica appeared again in the 1990s and said he had some access to that bag? The bag of Calvi.**

No. The one that was claiming to have the bag of Calvi was an Italian Jesuit who was at a house close to Grottaferrata.

(The conversation continued and took turns, this way and that, seemingly mirroring our own journey by car. Eventually, we arrived at our destination, a monastery where we would be staying and conducting the bulk of the interview.)

# CHAPTER 33

# A SHOCKING STATEMENT
# AT THE MONASTERY

*"And he brought inside the Conclave this face of Christ
of Manoppello and the article of this journalist."*
—Archbishop Carlo Maria Viganò, July 28, 2019

ONCE WE had met with the abbot of the monastery and
taken our bags to our rooms, we met in a large meeting
room with a coffee machine in the corner. We would use
that machine each morning, and sometimes in the afternoon and evening, during our stay. Our schedule was
the celebration of morning Mass, a light breakfast, then
conversation throughout the morning, then a lunch with
the monks, an hour or two siesta, then more conversation until late in the afternoon, then a little walk, then
dinner with the monks, and then another hour or two
of conversation into the evening. The archbishop would
then go to sleep, and I would stay up writing my "Letters" and taking notes on what had been said, and not
been said. In this way, we covered many topics in the
life of the archbishop and of the Church over these past
seventy years.

On our first morning at the monastery, we first sat
quietly for many minutes as we looked through emails
and text messages that had reached us from around the

world. I saw that the archbishop was reading something carefully and began our conversation.

**What are you reading?**

Archbishop Viganò: I am reading this prophecy of Malachy, where he writes that, after the pope, Benedict, the "Glory of the Olive," the City of Seven Hills will be destroyed. That God will judge his people. The end. I believe we are just there.

(I was perplexed. I did not know how serious Viganò was about the Malachy prophecies. But he seemed to be taking them, or at least some of the general ideas contained therein, seriously. This line of inquiry will be explored further in the coming volume.)

**May I take a photograph?**

No. I don't want a picture to exist. It is not because I don't trust you. But a mistake can happen.

(I understood the archbishop's reluctance. However, I felt it was necessary. I told him that we could take the photograph without showing his face. Doing it that way would not expose him to discovery but would comfort many of those who were worried about him. Finally, he agreed. We went outside and found a place to take a photo. We took several, but then he said that the walls themselves might reveal where we were. "Let's stand in front of an olive tree," I said. "It's a sign of peace. My face will be seen, but yours will not be, and no one will be able to tell from the tree where we are." So we stood in front of an olive tree and took the photo. That evening, I wrote a letter including the photo and told the world in this way that Viganò was no longer invisible. In this sense, it marked the end of one period in his journey. I did not know it at the time, but from this moment, he would begin with renewed energy to study and to write about the modern crisis in the Church.

CHAPTER 34

# VIGANÒ IS MOVED TO TEARS

AFTER WE took the photograph, the abbot and Viganò engage a moment in conversation and then, after some few minutes of conversation between the three of us, I steered things back to the interview.

Well . . . I go back to the first question. I might say I have twelve questions. Twelve topics.

Abbot: I understand.

So my first topic is, Jesus became angry when children were offended. And he said, for those who offend the child, better to have a millstone around their neck and be thrown in the depths of the sea than to offend one of these little ones. So I ask: Has the Church protected the innocent? And how can the Church be vigilant to always protect the children and the young people from abuse? Have we done enough?

Abbot: Well, I think obviously the answer is no. We have not done enough. And also because, after the Second Vatican Council, one of the first failures was the formation of priests. And also, the moral system in the

Church. Because in the United States there was that moral theologian, what is his name? Very famous.

**Fr. Charles Curran?**

Abbot: Curran. Then there was Bernard Häring and, I mean, Häring was good to a certain point. And then at the same time, there was this idea of situation ethics, and there was an "over-psychologization" of morality. The idea that the subject determines the goodness or the badness of moral choice.

And so you see that the Church became extremely vulnerable. And the bishops were no longer chosen for their sanctity but for their ability, for their talents, and most of all their ability to be good managers.

McCarrick was an extremely good manager. He was extremely shrewd. He was, as my abbot would say, he was as simple as a snake and as shrewd as a dove. You know, it's turning it upside down. But that's the paradox.

So with this type of bishops, they more or less mirror the type of priests, the type of formation, and the lack of formation also. Obviously these problems have always existed. They've always existed in the world. They were even given a philosophical foundation during the time of Plato and Socrates, *etc.*

But it became almost a structure in the mind of the Church after the Vatican Council. Because the question of homosexuality was in the forefront. Can homosexuals become priests?

Archbishop Viganò: I know the first document of Pope Benedict in 2005 was regarding the non-admittance of homosexuals to the priesthood.

Abbot: Exactly. But how did they get over that? You know. Because you always try to . . . You make the law and then you find the way to get over it, you know? And they made a . . . They distinguished between the . . .

Viganò: Inclination.

Abbot: Between the inclination and acting out. But that's a very fine line. It's a very, very fine line. And the inclination—he who has the inclination needs to find himself with a strong group of heterosexuals who can give him other reasons for sublimating his desire. Otherwise the acting out is . . . the inclination and the acting out are going hand in hand. So, often, unfortunately, an eye was closed, until both of them were closed.

Viganò: So when John Paul II summoned all the American cardinals regarding this scandal of homosexuality and the abuse of minors in 2002, I remember that at the press office, answering to one question, McCarrick said precisely, they excluded the "active" homosexual. So it was immediately . . .

Abbot: Thinking about his own situation.

Viganò: Yes. So I was really surprised about that. I remember that I noticed it at the time, thinking, "Look at this fellow."

Abbot: But you know . . . With regard to pedophilia, I think you have to make another distinction. Because not all homosexuals are pedophiles.

Viganò: Sure.

Abbot: And how many married people are pedophiles? So what's going on in the mind of the pedophile? Is it a sexual problem? Or is it another problem that's going on in the mind? Because, many . . . I had a monk here who died—he died at eighty-two years old—an American monk, who I kept closed in the monastery, and it was a drama. It was terrible. But I remember him telling me how he was abused when he was a child. So there is this element. You know?

**I believe . . . I say this all the time, hurt people hurt.**

Abbot: Yes.

**This is their way of . . .**

Abbot: Of getting back.

**Or, it's also their way of getting close to another human being, because that was how they were taught. It's the way they were taught to love.**

Abbot: Exactly.

**I mean, McCarrick, when I had lunch with him several years ago, he told me the story of when he grew up. His**

father wasn't there. His father died when he was three years old. His mother worked, was a single mother. He lived around a lot of family. He told me he was always sharing the beds with his cousins. And . . .

Abbot: Oh, yes. So we can only imagine. We repeat this.

**That's right.**

Abbot: Because the moment . . . Obviously, we have control of our *persona*. Because the ego is strong enough to have this control. But then when we find ourselves in the dark, in the shadow, all of this is coming out. All of this is being reacted, reenacted, reenacted.

**Yeah. This is why St. Paul, in one passage, says, "Be renewed by the transforming of your mind."**

Abbot: Exactly.

**"So that you become conformed to Christ." But this is the entire lifetime. And sometimes you can be too strict, and you can't make it, you become neurotic. Or sometimes you can be too lax, and you can't make it. You become dissolute.**

Abbot: Exactly.

**So this is formation. But formation is, I guess, more an art than a science.**

Abbot: Exactly. It is an art and it's a lifestyle. It's . . . The formation of a priest is something that enters into the very fibers of their being, of, really, who they are. It should be that. It should be that.

As a matter of fact, if you look at the lives of priests in the 1800s or the early 1900s, it was even a cultural experience. You would go to their libraries and would have certain types of books. And if you went to eat with them, there was nothing casual about them. It was all very formal. But it was all very good for the soul.

That's what I liked about certain traditional priests. Because it was like reading once again Bernanos. Because it was a lifestyle. You know? It wasn't you take off your clergyman and you become like one of the others; that didn't exist. It wasn't . . . And McCarrick . . . I didn't know . . . Now, this is very interesting. This is something to think about in writing a biography of this person. Because, you know, he will never have reciprocity. Because he's finished. Because this is a pontificate that cannot face reciprocity.

Viganò: What? Reciprocity?

Abbot: Reciprocity. It's the idea of . . . this pontificate cannot face those who need to defend themselves or to explain. Because the pope is strong. Because he . . . he's like Stalin. He cuts your head off. He does not allow for real dialogue or real . . . You know? Because perhaps he has such a shadow in himself. I have no idea. I never . . . Yes. A sense of omnipotence is a problem.

Viganò: Narcissism, able to confront any situation and winning despite every obstacle, because he was so strong. Francis is able to tell a lie and be sure that he's winning. You remember this bishop that was present . . .

Abbot: Right. I remember now.

Viganò: . . . at this conference also, at the Catholic University of Milan. So he told me—he was seated close to me . . .

Abbot: I remember now.

Viganò: So I asked him, "Did you know Bergoglio?" And he replied: "Sure. I lived in his house when he was provincial. He used people. He wanted to submit a person to himself, so the person would be under his own control, so that he would be able to do everything."

Abbot: They told me that many priests of his diocese, young priests, suffered from nervous exhaustion.

Viganò: I understand that many Jesuits left the province.

Abbot: He would pull them, pull them, pull them, pull them until they broke.

**That's interesting, because I had a couple one time who traveled with me in England, and they were from Argentina. She taught at the seminary and she never felt drawn to Bergoglio. Because, she said, every year she would attend the ordinations because she had to and wanted to, and as we see him in the Domus, you know, he has**

a long face where he doesn't smile. He's a different personality in the Piazza. And we see this all the time when we're there.

Abbot: That's typical of leaders who are dictators, you know, in private and in the piazza.

They come to life in front of the people.

Abbot: They come to life. They come to life.

On the one hand, he was always available to receive his priests, but they couldn't understand how, after becoming pope, he was a very outgoing and friendly person in general audiences; a man they had never seen before. The thing is that in Argentina he appeared as an introverted, gruff man, who did not seek visibility, who did not travel, very humble and modest, without any desire for power or career. Having become pope, he appeared very extroverted, always smiling, affable, close to the people; a man they'd never seen before. And they were at dinner with their mutual friend, the psychiatrist, and he said, in his mind it was because he realized, Bergoglio, what his whole life was about, that he was prepared for this moment and that this was a realization for his life.

Abbot: That's megalomania. There's nothing worse than to feel that you receive the unction, you receive the anointing.

But . . .

Abbot: And I'm sure that his agenda is . . .

Viganò: Was already prepared.

Abbot: Was already prepared.

Viganò: Since the '60s. I believe so.

Abbot: The Jesuits that are . . .

Viganò: I believe that. In the background of all that is happening is a strong deviation of the Jesuits. Of the Society of Jesus. This has been prepared by them.

**Well . . .**

Viganò: This is my theory. But, you know, when you read what happened during the General Congregations of the Jesuits starting from '65 . . . [there are] plenty of Jesuits, many from United States and other countries, [practicing] homosexuals, convinced Marxists, [even] for the violence and so on. They've already evangelized . . .

Abbot: And the universities in the United States, the most important ones, and even high schools are Jesuit.

Viganò: One of the first ones was the Land O'Lakes, in '67, regarding the colleges and university, free to teach what they want independently from the doctrine of the Church.

(We had lengthy conversations about the process of increasing secularization in the Jesuit order and priestly acceptance of worldly standards not in keeping with the traditional teaching of the Church. These discussions will be included in the second volume. The interview resumes with me eventually asking Viganò a question that elicited tears from him.)

# CHAPTER 35

# VIGANÒ IS AGAIN MOVED TO TEARS

*"Well, I mean it was my whole life."*
—Archbishop Viganò, on what the Church means to him

**CAN YOU tell me what the Catholic Church means to you?**

Archbishop Viganò: Well, I mean it was my whole life. I didn't answer hundreds of letters addressed to me because my work took all of my time. It was the Secretariat of State, the Holy See, the pope. So I also committed myself to Francis with all my heart when he became pope. Until I understood that he was himself the problem, that he himself was covering up what McCarrick had been doing, and that he was doing it consciously. He had no reaction when I said to him, "I don't know if you know who McCarrick is?" That was my naivete. I trusted him completely.

"If you ask in the Congregation for Bishops, there is a folder like this: the abuse of generations of seminarians and priests." No reaction. No conversation pertinent to the subject, only, "How do you know that?" He asked me: "How do you know that?" I knew it because I had received a letter addressed to the substitute and to the

Secretariat of State by this Sipe, a letter sent to Pope Benedict, it was in my hands.

**Sipe.**

Sipe. From California, I think. He was a former priest, former monk. And so I made the *appunto*, the note that the letter had arrived, and from whom, so I knew that. This was my professional duty, to document everything with care; this was my job, and I did it with very great care.

**When you presented McCarrick to an audience on different occasions, you said, "We all love you."**

Sure. Because I was invited by the Pontifical Mission Society by this Marian Father, I don't remember his name. He was a good man. There was a gathering to support missionaries, the Pontifical Mission Society. I was in Nigeria. I could not go because McCarrick was there? So when McCarrick was in the center, because he was the most important person, what did I say? "Your Eminence, we are here for the Missionary Society, to raise money, everybody loves you." What should I have said, "We know that you are a disgraceful person?"

I knew about him, but I treated him with charity all the time. (*Viganò, recalling McCarrick, begins to choke up and break into tears.*) I confronted him the first time in the nunciature after I was named to that post. I said, "You have done that!" And he, just speaking with very low voice, said, "I may have made a mistake. Sometimes

I slept in the same bed as a seminarian, as a priest, *etc.,
etc.*"

**He said that to you?**

Yes, he said it was a mistake. He admitted it. He admitted it for me to understand because I already knew what
he had done. But he didn't deny.

He didn't deny. But you know, for him there was
nothing wrong. It was not a real mistake. He has done
the same thing how many times? How many seminarians did he corrupt? Generations.

(In all of these hours of driving the car to the monastery
and the time spent in the monastery, Viganò had seemed
very calm, but I had also felt that beneath the calm was
a profound emotion which I respected. I wondered
whether I might ask a question which would enable him
to express that emotion and perhaps, in a kind of cathar-
sis, enable him to confront the entire trajectory from his
public denunciation of Pope Francis to his present status
as a hero to some and a traitor to others. And so I asked
. . .)

**Last question. Again. Your love of the Church?**

Well I mean it was all my life. (*He starts to weep.*) Well,
I mean I was living for that.

**Do you think you should write one more letter to Pope
Francis, an open letter?**

(*He shakes his head.*)

**No? So what will happen, do you think? To Pope Francis?**

Well, this is in the hands of God and Our Lady. They will do with him what they want.

# CHAPTER 36

# THE ABBOT'S VIEW—VIGANÒ WEEPS A THIRD TIME

*"I think that in yourself you're still seeking justice."*
—The abbot to a silent Archbishop Viganò, July 2019

Now Viganò sat in complete silence for an entire minute. Looking at him, it seemed to me at several moments that he was about to say something, but each time he remained silent. Finally, I broke the silence. "You're weighed down with many thoughts," I said. "You're tired." Viganò lifted his eyebrows to me but did not speak. Again, I said, "You're tired?" Still Viganò was silent. He seemed about to cry.

The abbot looked at me as if he recognized that Viganò was overwhelmed with emotion and with an arch of his eyebrow indicated that he wished to enter the conversation. I nodded. He began to speak on behalf of the archbishop, explaining what he sees in the man who is following his conscience and doing that which he believes God wants him to do. It is very intriguing as Viganò has almost shut down and the Abbot almost speaks for him. Abbot means "father," of course, and he seemed to take on an almost fatherly role with regards to the spiritual son who had come to seek refuge in his house when all the doors in the world were closed against him.

Abbot: Because you brought these papers out. And I think that in yourself you're still seeking justice, because you have received a lot of injustice. So therefore, when we are looking for justice, we're still attached to something that happened in the past. And you're asking him questions that also are looking towards the future. Because when you ask a person how he's feeling, one always feels for the moment, but also for the future, ahead. And, how is your heart, how is your spirit and that's always . . . One is feeling also how one feels towards his tomorrow. So I think now as an abbot, I would say to my monk, don't look anymore in the past, but look at what the Lord is doing in your life in the present and what he is preparing you for in the future and how your life is important for the life of the Church that you love and that you continue to work for really.

I think that bringing these aspects are interesting, but they will be interesting for the biography, but they're not interesting for his spirit. Because it's sort of weighing . . . It's sort of . . . holding him back. And obviously his dignity wants justice.

**Yes. We all do.**

Abbot: At a certain point in my life, we can go on saying, "Oh, I don't care and I'm not worried, I'm not afraid," but inside the dignity is still asking for justice. But I think that people . . . I think you could help the many people who are praying for you and who are waiting also to see you. I think that these encounters, because actually that's what's happening, you're having an encounter in this moment, not only a meeting, but it's an encounter, something much more profound. The people who read these profiles and these witnesses' testimony, I think they need . . . They can even begin to ask, "Well how in heaven's name is he still able to be so open to the Spirit?" And your witness would be a great help, because you know what is happening in many people's lives, especially priests. They're losing their hope.

And many are preparing, many are already living as though they're in schism. Many are already living as though the Church has already been divided, because there's no hope. There's so much confusion.

And if they could see the person, like Bishop Viganò, my God, he's been through hell and yet, despite going through hell, he isn't desperate.

**And he's still going to confession.**

Abbot: Yes, exactly. This is the way one remains faithful.

. . .

Abbot: "*Spes contra spem.*" That's what La Pira has on his tomb. "Hope against every hope."

**But this is what I see in you.**

Abbot: Hm? You see?

**I see this in you. I see hope in you. You give me hope. Do you still have faith? Where does your faith come from?**

Abbot: Nurtured by prayer. Before he came here, he went to confession. And he told me he went to confession. So, the Church is still nurturing him, the Church. It's incredible. You know, the very thing that many say he's trying to destroy or he's trying to criticize.

**He's still in . . .**

Abbot: He's being nurtured.

**By Holy Mother Church.**

Abbot: By Holy Mother Church. Because his object is not to destroy but to become an instrument of the purification. This is the great purification. This is the moment of purification.

**Should we say a prayer?**

Abbot: That's the best, bishop. It's the grace, it is.

(That evening, during evening prayer, Viganò seemed less weighed down by his thoughts, and with each hour that passed, he seemed to regain his balance and decisiveness.) Later, upon considering that quality of decisiveness which has so marked the man in his testimonies, and in light of what he had told me of his own father, I asked him for his views on fatherhood.

CHAPTER 37

# VIGANÒ ON FATHERHOOD

*"It is quite natural for a man to think to have children, as it is for a woman, to have children and to imagine what that would be."*
—Archbishop Viganò, reflecting on
the decision to become a priest

WELL, EARLIER you mentioned something that was beautiful about being a father.

Archbishop Viganò: About?

**About being a father.**

Yes.

And you were reflecting on your life and you said, "I am a priest, I'm not going to have children, but I will have spiritual children." Something like that. You had some reflection, but you didn't finish.

Sure. I was reflecting on how great the gift given to those who are married and who have children is. I was becoming more conscious of the meaning of the decision I had made, choosing to be a priest, which is, you know, it is

340

a different way to be a father. So that I mentioned the salvation of souls as a way of looking further, with the projection into eternity of fatherhood. . . . Also, a father has of course, he has to follow the children as much as possible, but when they grow up, they are going by themselves, like . . .

**So you said you realized that your desire to be fatherly, an innate desire, could be fulfilled by considering the eternity of the soul of the people you would take care of.**

Yes. I mean it is quite natural for a man to think to have children, as it is for a woman, to have children and to imagine what that would be. So I was thinking about that, and, of course, as something that is extremely beautiful.

**And did you write anything about it? Did you keep a journal or a diary?**

No, I didn't write anything. I am not a writer.

**Did this thought recur to you later?**

This was a reflection that was part of my experience, my spiritual experience, and I can go back and recall and reflect on it. It's there.

**So what you are doing now, with your various testimonies, do you feel it's being paternal? That you are being like a father to people in the Church?**

Well, I don't claim to be a father or somebody who would claim anything. I am not claiming anything. But you know, my conscience is telling me to protect the Church. I see that the devil has been entering into the Church, on the top of it, and so that I have to stand up.

**Recently, you have been commenting more and more on political affairs, something for which you have been criticized. But the Church has always had a voice in political matters. How are we to understand the importance of the Church in world affairs? How important is it for the Church to have relations with governments and public affairs? Why does the Church even get involved in this? Why doesn't it just stick with liturgy, catechism, convents, prayers? Is this maybe the problem of the Church? Too much involvement with the world?**

I mean, it's quite normal that you try to get a connection or relation with the top, with the government, in order that you may present, in a clear and steady way, a very convincing argument for your point of view, as a Catholic, as a Church, to help improve relations. This is a good thing. The Church should be present on every level.

**So there is a space for the Church to act in the world.**

Sure.

**And not just in the sacristy.**

There is no space where the Church should not be.

(Most dramatically, in the early summer of 2020, Viganò would make good on that statement when he issued an open letter to American President Donald Trump which circulated widely online at the time of its release.)

# PART VIII

# VIGANÒ ON FRANCIS

# CHAPTER 38

# STRONG WORDS

*"Of course I pray for him."*
—Archbishop Viganò on Pope Francis

JUST TELL me one thing: during these months, have you prayed for Pope Francis?

Archbishop Viganò: Well, Pope Francis is always in my intention. Of course I pray for him, and when I pray the Rosary, and also at the altar.

Do you think that Pope Francis understands you?

When you read the interviews he has given to Alazraki, this Mexican lady, and also when he went out two, three times, spontaneously calling me the "great accuser." I remain here. I am what he has sticking in his . . . What do you call it?

Throat?

In his throat. I am on the throat of Francis.

Meaning?

Meaning, you know, what he would most like to destroy. There is no doubt. These are facts.

**And . . . If you were pope, would you do the same thing?**

First of all, I would not be able to remain silent. No. I mean, I would be looking for the truth. Why does he not answer and say whether I told the truth or not? It's either true or it is not. I felt obliged to say what I said regarding McCarrick. *He* asked me about McCarrick. I had full trust in him as a new pope. I never met him before. I had full trust in him. So *he* asked me about McCarrick. Should I not have said the truth to the pope? I spoke to Francis, as I spoke to John Paul II, as I spoke to Benedict, with total transparency, all that I knew. I knew by having had the paper, the letter, in my hands. So I knew for sure the accusation coming through Sandri regarding McCarrick. How can that be in doubt? The appunto I transmitted to my superior never came back. So the Congregation for Bishops was informed.

**Do you believe your testimony is helpful to the Church? If so, in what ways?**

I mean, I'm continuing in declaring what I consider the truth and the good of the Church, following the perennial tradition of the doctrine and the moral teaching, which has been abandoned. Why has the pope never corrected the behavior of the homosexuals, corrected the sodomy? Is there a declaration of the pope saying that sodomy is a capital sin?

**No.**

There is not. This is one of the major sins that . . .

**The four great sins that cry out to God.**

Cry out to God. So, how is it possible that the pope never mentioned homosexuality and never mentioned or condemned the sin of sodomy?

**That's a legitimate question, but it seems that he takes all these criticisms or questions as politically motivated. Francis caused a stir when he said that he was happy to be attacked by American conservatives.**

It's an honor.

**It's an honor to be attacked. What type of psychology is this? How do you react to such a statement which seems to place you in a political category, in a global political battle?**

He said it . . . more to justify the fact, that he didn't, not only didn't answer me, but he lied in public about what I had testified, [thus] doing enormous damage to the faithful with his lies. I would like to ask this question.

In this behavior of the pope, what is he saying, what is the message of the pope? "I am the truth. The truth is what I'm saying over any other real truth, any other reality. If you are not with me" . . . this is the second. This is the second.

**Because he had made that . . .**

"I am the truth."

(The exchange below refers to a joke that Francis had made to the effect that Argentinians are so confident or prideful that it was actually an act of humility for him to take the name of Francis when he could have taken the name Jesus II.)

**He made reference to that joke in Argentina that he took the name, Francis. The joke was, "Well, at least I didn't take the name Jesus II."**

"I am the truth. All those who are not with me are liars, to be despised. I'm honored that the others, that they are criticizing me because I am the truth."

**Well . . .**

Are you Jesus II? Ask the question. Nobody can contest what you are saying, what you are doing, destroying the Church.

**Well, I hear what you are saying.**

Record that. I want to say that.

**Okay, but I still, I'm hoping that he was joking at that time. I'm hoping.**

No. No. There's nothing to hope anymore. This is his behavior, and he is destroying the Church.

PART IX

# AN IMPORTANT BOOK

## CHAPTER 39

# *IN SINU JESU*[35]

*"During this past year I have been reading a book which has moved me a great deal. It is the journal of an unnamed priest who is devoted to contemplative prayer and who recounts the words he feels Jesus has spoken to him in his heart. I have found the book consoling and interesting in light of our present situation in the Church. The book is entitled In Sinu Jesu, 'In the heart of Jesus.'"*
—Archbishop Carlo Maria Viganò, in a
recent conversation, speaking about the book
*In Sinu Jesu,* which he has been reading

"Do YOU know who the author is?" I asked Archbishop Carlo Maria Viganò after he told me he had been reading a book he appreciates very much.[36]

---

[35] This chapter features extracts from "Moynihan Letters" in which I wrote about my discussions with Viganò about the book.

[36] The archbishop was speaking about a little volume of reflections entitled *In Sinu Jesu: When Heart Speaks to Heart, The Journal of a Priest at Prayer,* which contains the words of Jesus that the author heard while in adoration from 2007 to 2016. The book has become in the past three years a sort of phenomenon in Catholic circles. It was published in English by Angelico Press in 2016 and has now appeared in eight different languages, including German, French, Italian, Spanish, and Czech.

"No," Archbishop Viganò replied. "The book is anonymous, and I have no indication of who the author is. But I read the book throughout the winter and spring, and it was a great consolation to me. If you can find out who the author is, let me know, so I may thank him.

"But the identity of the author is less important than what he tells us about his experience of prayer. And that is that the Lord is close to all who seek him and will never abandon us."

### The Archbishop and the Mystic

"Apparently, this book has been written by a priest who desired to find a way to participate in the healing of souls, and of our world, by recourse to Eucharistic Adoration," Archbishop Viganò says. "To me it seems providential that, precisely at a time when the holiness of priests is under such attack, a book like this should appear. I take it as a sign for our times."

At the very outset of the book, on the first day of the journal, the unknown author writes, "Our Lord, in instituting the Eucharist, foresaw outrages and sufferings—the sufferings, I mean, of a love that is wounded and spurned. He is seeking, today more than ever, priests who will console Him, priests who will adore and make reparation."

And the author adds:

> I opened the book by Dom Vandeur [Dom Eugene Vandeur, 1875-1967, a Benedictine monk of the community of Maredsous in Belgium] and I read: 'Make me entirely Thy priest, as was Saint John, Thy beloved

disciple, standing at the foot of Thy Cross, the Tree of Life.' The phrase describes perfectly the call that I received 30 years ago, a call to which I did not know how to respond, or to which I found myself unable to respond fully. There were too many obstacles in me, too many infected wounds, still waiting for the healing that had to come through the hands of Mary and by the precious Blood of Jesus. I want priests who will adore for priests who do not adore, priests who will make reparation for priests who do not make reparation for themselves or for others. I want priest adorers and reparators.

"Here is a passage which particularly moved me," Viganò says.

And he reads:

The spiritual redemption of priests in bondage to evil, the spiritual illumination of priests who live in darkness, the spiritual healing of wounded priests—and all of this by means of adoration of the Most Holy Sacrament. . . . I feel, perhaps for the first time in my life, that I am fully in the truth. My whole life has prepared me for this mission, for this call to adoration and to reparation—by a priest or priests. All the evil that I experienced, and suffered, and inflicted on others, will be thus redeemed, not by me, but by Him who is always working in the Eucharist to redeem back from sinners and those who have been wounded by sin.

The archbishop looks at me. "These words speak powerfully to me. But there is much more in this book."

"What I appreciate about this book," Archbishop Carlo Maria Viganò said, "is its great spiritual simplicity.

"Without complicated arguments, or psychological

jargon, it proposes a profound spiritual answer to the great spiritual crisis of our time.

"During the past year, I have been meditating a great deal on this question."

"What answer does the book give?" I asked.

"Well, the Church in our time has been passing through the long torment of the sexual abuse crisis, with all that that implies," the archbishop said.

"First, the abuse of innocent young people, sexually, psychologically, and spiritually. Many priests have tragically betrayed the trust of those who believed in them, doing terrible harm to them.

"Then, many bishops and religious superiors did not have as their major concern the protection of the victims. Instead, they tried to protect the institution of the Church by covering up what had happened. This made the wound to the Church deeper and more incurable, causing it to fester and putrify.

"They were wrong.

"All of this has blackened the image of Christ's Church before the world—including the image of those very many priests who have committed no wrong.

"So a general repentance is needed, and a universal commitment to make public the evil that has been done, and to do reparation for it, in order to begin to heal so many wounds.

"Some aspects of how to face this crisis have been explored by various bishops' conferences, and at various meetings like the one at the Vatican in February, but the deep spiritual roots seem not to have been touched.

"Something is still missing.

"And that is what I find in this book."

"And what is that?" I asked.

Viganò picks up the book to find a certain passage.

"The monk author," Viganò replied, "suggesting that the words he writes are the very words of Jesus to him during his time of prayer, says to us: 'The solution to the hardships and trials of priests, the answer to the problems that beset so many of them, causing them to fall into patterns of sin, is the friendship that I offer them. The Holy Spirit is poured out on every priest on the day of his ordination, and in that outpouring is given a marvelous capacity to live in My friendship and in the intimacy of My most Holy Mother.'"

"But then," Viganò continued, "the author adds: 'So few of My priests accept this gift and use this capacity for holiness that I bestow upon them.' And then the author writes, speaking now in the words of the Blessed Mother, Mary: 'I am for all my priest sons the Gate of Heaven. If any priest would ascend, even in this earthly life, into the glory of the heavenly liturgy ceaselessly celebrated by my Son before the Father's Face, he need only approach me. I will open the way into the mysteries of heaven for him. I will teach him the reverence, the silence, the profound adoration that befits one called to serve at the altars of my Son and in His place.'"

## THE ANSWER?

"But does this not seem too little?" I said, with a certain worry. "After so many years of such terrible abuses and cover-ups? That the Church, the priests of the Church, should return to prayer? That Eucharistic adoration is the answer to the sexual abuse crisis?"

The archbishop is silent.

"I am not saying this book offers 'the answer' to the crisis, or to any act of abuse that has taken place," he says. "No. Rather, I am saying that this book offers a diagnosis, the diagnosis of an absence of relationship to Christ, of an emptiness in the spiritual life of priests. And this leads to a prescription: that we must all return to prayer, to re-establish friendship with Christ. This is, after all, what it means to be a Christian. This is the only possible path for us to face the evil that has taken place, and to begin again.

"We must begin with ourselves, with the corruption and evil in each one of us. We must go to the Eucharist, the source and summit of our faith, to encounter Christ. To enter into a relationship with him, and to be healed by him. We cannot simply reform the Church. We must repent and reform our own lives, and that will help bring about the needed reform."

I am silent a moment.

"Well," I said, "since your 'Testimony' of August 2018, many have seen you as a type of 'Prophet Jonah' for our time, bringing some of this evil into the light, denouncing the sins and cover-ups of the Roman Catholic Church and its members as Jonah was called to denounce the sins of Nineveh. But what is your message really: that God is about to chastise the Church, as Niniveh was threatened with destruction, or do you believe there is still a chance to renew the Church through prayer and a renewal of priestly and lay spirituality?"

"The two possibilities you offer are not mutually exclusive," the archbishop said. "There may be both a chastisement, which will shake and diminish the Church, and also a reform and renewal of the Church, making her more resplendent in holiness. Both are possible. The Lord is not denying grace of conversion to anyone. Furthermore, it is really the deep desire of his heart, to ask for conversion and to have us accept his love for us."

# PART X

# FAREWELL

## CHAPTER 40

# FAREWELL

My TIME with Archbishop Viganò came to an end and we set out on the return journey. What would the world look like in the coming days, weeks, and months? What did the future hold for me, for him, and for the Church? We could not know, but we could pray.

**We do not have far to go now. I will be dropping you off soon and then heading for Rome.**

Archbishop Viganò: We should pray a Rosary for your safe return and in gratitude for our days together. The abbot was good to us. He allowed us space to reflect on many things.

(And so we prayed our Rosary and, after, continued our conversation.)

**Well, I am grateful. You took a risk by seeing me, and by agreeing to take that photograph! And to let it be published!** [Here I refer to the fact that he did, in fact, allow me to take a picture and we published it in one of my "Moynihan Letters."]

But not my face. You know, I heard that in Rome they saw that I have a beard, and they are starting to call me "il barbone" ("the homeless bum") (laughs).

**I think it was good we published it. Your position has changed now. No one has seen your face, but they have seen your back; they know you are alive and safe. You are no longer the "man on the run." You are now the man "imitating Pope Benedict"—hidden but holding up the Church and the world in your prayer, praying even for Francis, though you disagree with him on so many things.**

I do disagree with him. He has accepted the chair of Peter and he has not confirmed his brothers. He is breaking apart the Church.

But I feel I have to be careful. I do not want to tear down the office of the pope, or tear down the Jesuit order, but rather to raise them up, to be worthy of their callings.

**To create a hundred, a thousand, ten thouand Viganòs . . .**

Not ten thousand Viganòs (laughs). I realize my limitations. I pray every day that what I say will build up and not tear down.

**Then that is what we should pray for: to build up and not tear down.**

Although some things will have to be torn down in order for the rebuilding to begin.

**I'm curious. If you would advise someone else, someone like Cardinal Erdo, if Erdo was pope, what would you say would be the first, second, third things that need to be done?**

Well, there is the question certainly of dismissing many people of the Curia so that those who are corrupt would be removed. Then there is the question of the cardinals who have been appointed by Bergoglio; they should be examined one by one, carefully examined of course, and, if necessary, dismissed. And then, there would be the question of dissolving the Society of Jesus.

**Dissolving it?**

Dissolving it, straight away. And creating a new Society of Jesus, building it around those who are really Jesuits. A new start. Because there is no way that they can be reformed. They must start over. Be dissolved and rebuilt. But this is . . . This is just a dream. It is going to be a war.

(He lifts his hand to his forehead, his fingertips just touching his skin, then to his heart, then to each shoulder, in the sign of the cross, and he begins to intone the prayer.) "In the name of the Father, and the Son, and the Holy Spirit. Amen."

We ceased our conversation. We prayed in alternation, back and forth, as my father and I used to do, and the car moved forward and the trees and fields flashed by on either side and the sun descended in its swift arc toward the West. I left the archbishop, waved goodbye, turned, and took my way toward Rome.

## EPILOGUE

# VIGANÒ FOUND

### DON CAMILLO AND PRESERVING THE SEED

In the first days of September 2019, I made a second journey to see Viganò and again spent several days in conversation with him.

Since September, for the past seven months, we have been in regular contact by telephone and email. We have talked about the present crisis in the Church and the world, including the sexual abuse crisis in the Church, about the October "Pachamama" Synod, about the evident corruption of many Catholic religious orders, including the Jesuits, and about the possible ways these evils might be halted. We have also discussed the unprecedented resignation of Emeritus Pope Benedict XVI from the papacy in February 2013 and the election of Pope Francis to the papal throne on March 13, 2013.

(This first volume strives principally to truly "Find Viganò" and understand the man. A second volume will go deeper into many more controversial topics not covered in these pages.)

Already last September, months before the first case of coronavirus was publicly announced, the archbishop told me that a "worldwide crisis" prepared in part by the sins and lack of faith of individual Christians and by the apostasy of the Church was "imminent." It will begin, he told me, in July 2019, "before the end of the year."

His final prayer, he told me then, even in the face of every sort of terrible suffering, whether caused by something like the coronavirus or by evil leadership in the Church, is that we love, embrace, and defend our faith, and do everything possible in order to, in the words of Christ to Don Camillo,[37] "preserve the seed corn" of the faith so that the same faith of our forefathers may flourish again in generations to come.

The following is the transcription of Archbishop Viganò explaining the story to me. I believe it to be an apt metaphor in two ways: first, our struggle to understand

---

[37] Don Camillo and Peppone are the fictional protagonists of a series of works by the Italian writer and journalist Giovannino Guareschi set in what Guareschi refers to as the "small world" of rural Italy after World War II. . . . Don Camillo is a parish priest and is said to have been inspired by an actual Roman Catholic priest, World War II partisan and detainee at the concentration camps of Dachau and Mauthausen, named Don Camillo Valota (1912–1998). Guareschi was also inspired by Don Alessandro Parenti, a priest of Trepalle, near the Swiss border. Peppone is the communist town mayor. The tensions between the two characters and their respective factions form the basis of the works' satirical plots. . . . Don Camillo is constantly at odds with the communist mayor, Giuseppe Bottazzi, better known as Peppone (meaning, roughly, *Big Joe*) and is also on very close terms with the crucifix in his town church. Through the crucifix he hears the voice of Christ. The Christ in the crucifix often has far greater understanding than Don Camillo of the troubles of the people, and has to constantly but gently reprimand the priest for his impatience. (https://en.wikipedia.org/wiki/Don_Camillo_and_Peppone)

one another, our grasping for words, is analogous to Viganò, and all of us really, grasping for a way forward, a way to make it through this perilous time in the Church's history and emerge with a healthier, stronger faith, and secondly, to explain what Viganò feels he is doing by speaking out. Faced with the cataclysm of what he sees to be a "flood" of heterodoxy and confusion inspired by the devil, by speaking out, he seeks to preserve the seed corn of faith for future generations.

Archbishop Viganò: Valli,[38] he sent me also one dialogue of Don Camillo in one of his films, you know?

**Yes.**

The text he sent is in Italian. I will translate it for you as I read. "One day, the poor Don Camillo"—I translate it so—"he went to," you know, "to talk with Christ."

**So, Don Camillo went to speak his heart in front of Christ in the church.**

And he said: "What is this wind of craziness?" . . . This is Don Camillo to Christ. The crucifix answered, "Don Camillo, why are you so pessimistic? Then, my sacrifice, would it be useless? Would my mission have therefore failed because there's so much . . ."

---

[38]   Aldo Maria Valli is a very prominent Italian Catholic journalist who had a much-followed program on the Italian national television network. After it became known that he had helped Viganò prepare his testimony, he lost his job.

**Evil.**

Evil?

**Evildoers.**

"Evil men. They are stronger than the bounty of God?" Don Camillo answered, "No Lord. I had done it only to say that today the people believe only in what they can see and what they may touch. But the existing thing, essential thing that we cannot see, we cannot touch, like love, bounty, piety, honesty." How do you say?

**Modesty.**

"And modesty and hope and faith. Think that without them we cannot live." This is Don Camillo talking to Christ. "This is the self-destruction I was talking about. Man, it seems to me, is on the way to destroy everything. His patrimony, his spiritual patrimony, the unique rich- ness, true richness that in thousands of centuries he has been able to accumulate. . . . One day, not far away, we are going to find ourselves exactly like the *bruto*, or the caveman. The man in the cave. Now the man of the cave, the caves, there will be the sky scrape . . .sky . . ." *gratta- cieli . . .*

**Skyscraper.**

"Skyscraper, skyscraper, full of marvelous machines, but the spirit of man will be like the one of the caveman. Lord, people threatened . . ."

**Threatened.**

Threatened, the weapons is . . . *terrificante.*

**Terrifying.**

"Terrifying weapons that disintegrated man and everything. But I believe that only they, only they can give again to man his own richness, his own values, because they were going to destroy everything, and man, free from the slavery of the earthly goods, will look again for God. One would be destroyed completely all those, all those folks that speak of value, they're like . . . the man of the cave they are looking again for God. He will find and be constructing, building up and with planning we could start again the spiritual patrimony that today they are already [to] the point [of having] destroyed it completely. Lord, if that is not going to happen or if that, if it's what is going to happen, what are we able to do?" Christ smiled and said, "The thinking that is doing *il contadino . . .*

**The peasant.**

"The field worker. When the river is overboarding . . .

**Overflowing.**

"Overflowing the . . .

**The banks.**

"The banks, overflowing the bank and invading the fields, we have to save the seeds. When the river would come back to its bed, the fields would reemerge and the sunshine would dry up the land there. If the workers of the field, the *contadini*." What do you call it, *contadini*?

**Peasant. Field worker. Farmer.**

Yes, the farmer, "if the farmer had saved the seed, he may throw it out again so that [the land] would be more, would be made more fertile by what the deposit of the river . . ." the "*limo*", we say in Italian.

**The lime that . . .**

It's a kind of fertilizer that is from river.

**Silt?**

The seed would fortify and then the *spiga* . . . What do you mean *spiga*? The *spiga*.

**I'm not sure. The sprout, no?**

No, what is it, with the seed of the flour inside? We call them, "*la spiga di frumento*." The *spiga* of wheat. You know the seeds are inside the small plant.

**Either the sheaf of wheat or the ear of corn . . .**

The sheaf of wheat . . . It is an expression I do not know. It is what makes the flour for bread. The seed that makes the flour. *Spiga*, what we are making the bread, no?

**Sheaf. Ear.**

The ear, with inside many, many seeds.

**The bud?**

The bud? The bud is not only the last part of the plant or the seed.

**"*Spiga di grano*" is ear of corn, but bread is made from wheat, sheaves of wheat ground into flour.**

"The sheaves of wheat will blossom and swell. Swollen and golden, they will give to men bread, life, and hope.

"We need to save the seed, the faith. The seed is the faith. Don Camillo, we need to help those who are still in the possession of faith. Look at that. We need to help those who still have faith, to keep them intact. The spiritual desert is extended every day more. Every day new souls are drying up because they are abandoning the faith. But if we preserve the faith, we will preserve the seed for a new harvest, a new springtime of faith for the world."